THE WENDY AND EMERY REVES COLLECTION

Vlaminck, Bougival, *c.1905*

Wendy and Emery Reves at the Villa La Pausa in France.

THE WENDY AND EMERY REVES COLLECTION

Dallas Museum of Art

Published to commemorate the opening of a re-created Villa La Pausa
in the Dallas Museum of Art in 1985.

Editor and Publisher Robert V. Rozelle
Associate Editors Allen T. Rozelle and Gail Chancey
Editorial Assistants Melanie Bassett Wright, Vicki Vinson
and Annette Schlagenhauff

Designer Becky Wade
Photographer David Wharton
Composition Southwestern Typographics
Printed in England by Balding + Mansell Limited

Dallas Museum of Art
1717 North Harwood
Dallas, Texas 75201

COVER
Redon, *Flowers in a Black Vase,* c.1909-10

Daumier, Study of an Actor

Contents

Graham Sutherland Emery Reves   *Graham Sutherland* Mrs. Emery Reves

Donors

The responsibility of funding the re-creation of the Villa La Pausa was borne by a small number of the museum's closest benefactors, including:

Anonymous
The Effie and Wofford Cain Foundation
Mr. and Mrs. Vincent A. Carrozza
Mr. and Mrs. George V. Charlton
The Constantin Foundation
Mr. and Mrs. Leo F. Corrigan, Jr.
Edwin L. Cox
Mr. and Mrs. Richard W. Cree, Sr.
Trammell Crow Family Foundation
Mr. and Mrs. I.C. Deal
Diamond Shamrock Corporation
Mr. and Mrs. John F. Eulich
Dr. and Mrs. Sanford P. Fagadau
Leland Fikes Foundation, Inc.
The Glazer Family
Mr. and Mrs. Cecil H. Green
Mr. and Mrs. Albert G. Hill
Hoblitzelle Foundation
Hueppe Foundation, Inc.

Mr. and Mrs. Edmund J. Kahn
Mr. and Mrs. Rollin W. King
Mr. and Mrs. Lowell H. Lebermann, Jr.
Dr. and Mrs. Mark L. Lemmon
Mr. and Mrs. Irvin L. Levy
Mr. and Mrs. Tom F. Marsh
The Eugene McDermott Foundation
The Meadows Foundation
Mobil Foundation, Inc.
Mr. and Mrs. John G. Penson
The Pollock Foundation
Mr. and Mrs. George Poston
Wendy and Emery Reves
Mr. and Mrs. George A. Schrader
Ruth Collins Sharp
Mr. and Mrs. George A. Shutt
Mr. and Mrs. A. Starke Taylor, Jr.
Mrs. Max L. Thomas

The publication of this volume was made possible by Mr. and Mrs. Morton H. Meyerson.

Preface

Wendy and Emery Reves achieved extraordinary standards of connoisseurship and aesthetic presentation in the magical Villa La Pausa in Roquebrune-Cap Martin, France. Their home served as the setting of many treasured moments when the best in art, conversation and human experience were brought together in one place.

For the Dallas Museum of Art, the opportunity to re-create La Pausa could only be partially fulfilled. We lack the views of the Mediterranean, the perfumes of the Côte d'Azur and even the *vin de pays* to re-create totally a Riviera villa with a special history. We do offer, however, perpetual conservation of the cherished art so lovingly assembled by Wendy and Emery Reves and an eagerness to spread fine art appreciation to an audience who truly prizes the standards and quality which the Reves achieved.

Our Chief Curator, Steven Nash, has written eloquently and affectionately about the marvellous Impressionist paintings and drawings in the Reves Collection. Selected decorative arts objects have been described with authority and illuminating style by David Owsley, our consulting curator. In the future, the museum is committed to issuing scholarly publications which will focus in depth on certain aspects of the collection so as to insure their knowledge throughout the art world.

The story of the Dallas Museum's involvement with the Reves Collection is truthfully and interestingly told by Robert Rozelle in the last chapter of the donors' biography. George Charlton, Irvin Levy and I certainly enjoyed our roles in helping to bring the collection to Dallas. The participation of museum officers in such a personal and heartfelt way is to me the best example of inspired trusteeship and the type of citizen participation which so distinguishes Dallas. Our gratitude is boundless to that small group of generous donors who underwrote the museum's commitment to re-create the Villa La Pausa.

Wendy Reves is, of course, the heroine of this story. It is she who participated so completely with her husband, Emery, in collecting La Pausa's treasures. It is she who determined that the collection would come to Dallas and who, in spite of numerous obstacles, remained so dedicated to that purpose. The goal of re-creating the villa has been realized, and we are proud to open the Wendy and Emery Reves Collection for public viewing. Wendy Reves' mission has been to honor her husband; the biographical essay traces his illustrious career and her successful efforts to recognize his accomplishments. The devotion of his widow is a testimonial to the loyalty which he inspired.

Harry S. Parker III
Director

van Gogh, Cafe Terrace at Night, *1888*

Architect's Statement

8 Reproducing the Villa La Pausa in Dallas to house the beautiful Reves Collection – this was indeed a challenge. I vividly remember days in France at "La Pausa" with Harry Parker and Wendy Reves, looking out through ancient olive trees to the Mediterranean. We were wearing slippers so as not to damage the carpets, and we were sipping French wine. *And* we were checking every dimension of the house and measuring all of the important artifacts – to see if we could somehow reproduce the spirit of the place in Dallas. Now, on Harwood Street in Dallas, the views are of tall buildings, not the sea – and the rooms must serve as galleries – not as dining room, bedroom, and library. But I think in some way we have recaptured the spirit of the house. The little grass court with the surrounding classical cloister, the entrance hall with its grand stair to the balcony and, of course, the beautiful collection itself, all speak of happy days when Wendy and Emery Reves were together on the Côte d'Azur.

We have tried to combine the best display techniques: engineered lighting and hi-tech cases with period moldings, curtains, furniture, rugs, and even lamps from the house. The result is a decorative arts wing for the museum that is as different from other Dallas Museum displays, for example, as the gold room is from the Oldenburg. This diversity, this ambitious scope, is one of the things that makes the Dallas Museum of Art so interesting. The Reves Collection, housed in domestic surroundings and speaking to the personal taste of Wendy and Emery Reves, brings a new dimension. And there is room to grow. In addition to La Pausa's re-creation, there are three large new decorative art galleries.

Edward Larrabee Barnes
January, 1985

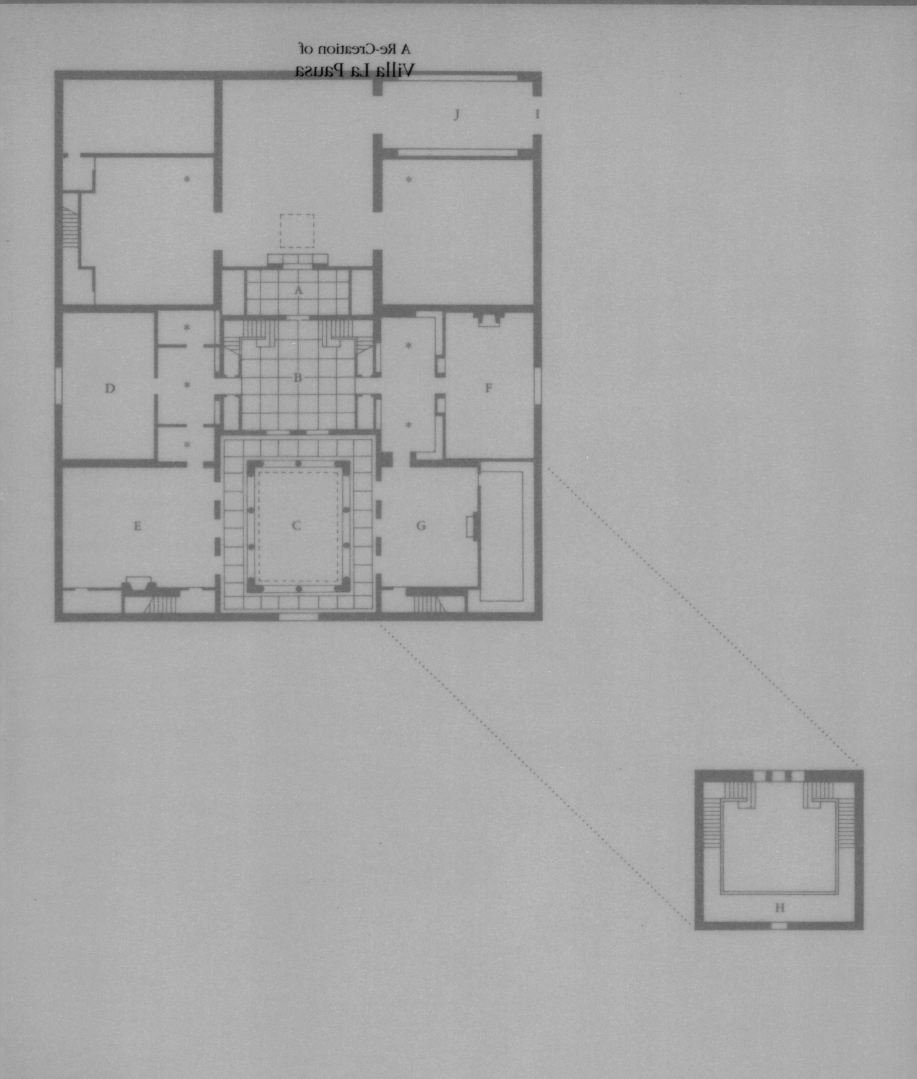

A Re-Creation of
Villa La Pausa

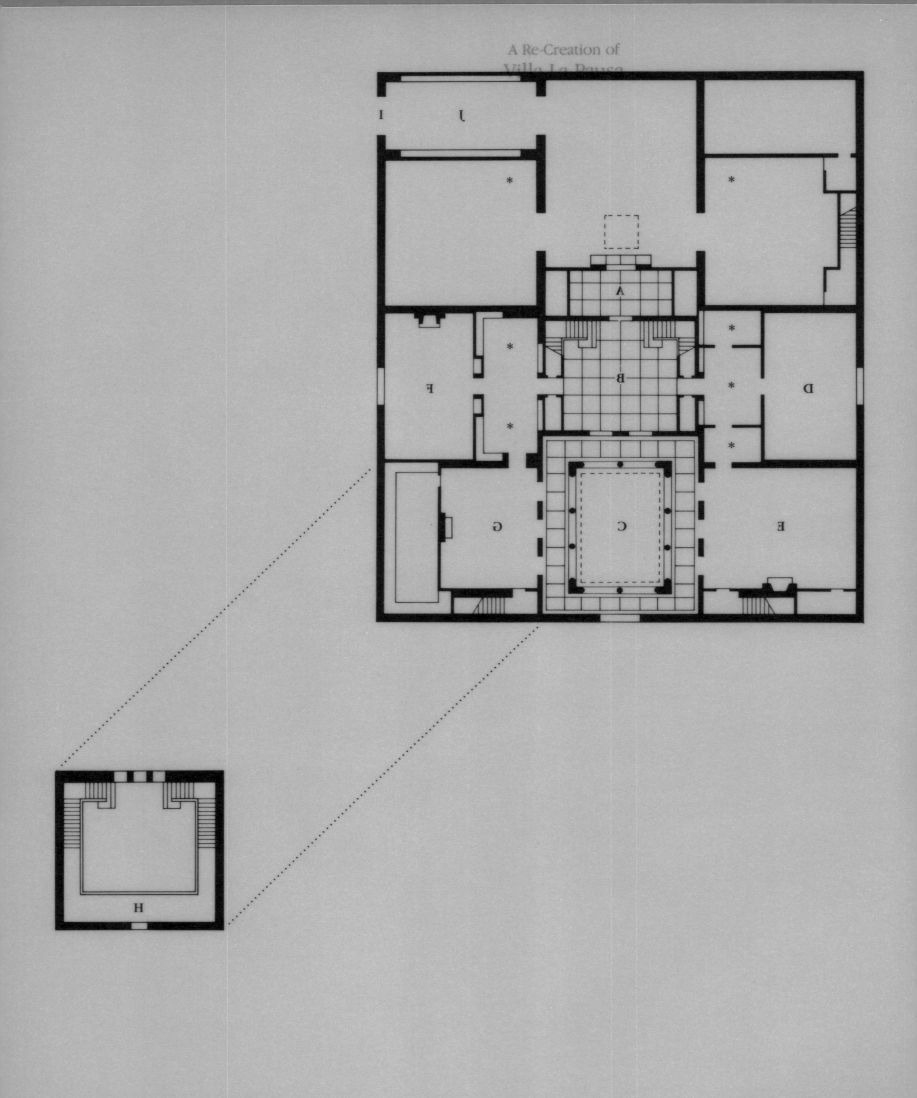

Total Area: 15,000 sq. ft.
Villa La Pausa: 11,086 sq. ft.

A Entry Hall
B Great Hall
C Courtyard
D Library
E Salon
F Master Bedroom
G Dining Room
H Gallery (above Great Hall)
* Additional Galleries

I Entrance to Decorative Arts Wing
J Hoblitzelle Collection of English Silver

ST. PAUL STREET

ROSS AVENUE

SCULPTURE GARDEN

CONTEMPORARY

EUROPEAN

PRE-COLUMBIAN

CLASSICAL

AFRICAN

ASIAN

ETHNIC

AMERICAN

14

15

10

13

10

11

11

11

8

9

7

12

12

1

6

5

4

3

2

HARWOOD STREET

Legend

1. Study Gallery for Prints, Drawings, Photography, Textiles
2. Parking Lot Entrance
3. Library
4. Museum Offices
5. Auditorium
6. Information Desk
7. Education Courtyard
8. Orientation Theater
9. Gateway Gallery
10. Flora Street Courtyard
11. Museum Shops
12. Handicapped Access
13. Temporary Exhibitions Galleries
14. Ross Avenue Entrance
15. Museum Plaza
16. Founders Room
17. Gallery Buffet Restaurant
18. Decorative Arts Wing, including Villa La Pausa

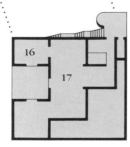

16

17

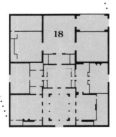

18

The Dallas Museum of Art.

The cost of housing and installing the Reves Collection, as well as the costs of shipping, insurance, taxes and planned publications, are all being paid by private donations. The Dallas Museum of Art was funded equally by private donations and a 1979 Dallas bond issue, and opened to the public on January 29, 1984.

Introduction

Together their lives spanned the richest history and the most turbulent events of the 20th century. Emery Reves was born in the early 1900s in a remote region of the Austro-Hungarian Empire. Wyn-Nelle Russell was born more than a decade later in rural east Texas where she grew up during the great depression.

He survived two world wars, introduced a revolutionary syndicated news service, befriended many of Europe's leading statesmen, and published and authored numerous works, including Winston Churchill's *War Memoirs* and his own political manifesto, *The Anatomy of Peace,* hailed by Albert Einstein as the answer to atomic energy control and eventually selling almost one million copies and reaching an estimated audience of fifty million people through *Readers' Digest.*

She escaped an impoverished childhood to become Wendy Russell, a top New York fashion model, a celebrated figure in Manhattan social life, and an independent businesswoman as a result of her distinguished modeling career, successful fashion rental business and outside investments.

After first meeting in America in the late 1940s, Emery and Wendy Reves traveled widely throughout Europe – living in London, Paris and Geneva – before buying Coco Chanel's historic Riviera villa in 1953. As a couple they assembled a varied and extensive art collection, and together they developed the Villa La Pausa as a showplace on the Côte d'Azur. Among the many international statesmen and famous personalities they entertained and hosted were Winston Churchill and his entourage, Konrad Adenauer, the Duke of Windsor, the Rothschilds, Onassis, Garbo, Somerset Maugham, Rose Kennedy and Graham Sutherland.

After Emery Reves' death in 1981, Wendy Reves decided to create a memorial to her husband by offering La Pausa's treasured art collection to a museum that would build a re-creation of their villa to house it.

Robert V. Rozelle
Dallas 1985

Renoir, The Stolen Kiss, *detail*

Emery Reves
The Early Years

At the turn of the 20th century, the Austro-Hungarian Empire of Franz Josef I extended into what is today northern Yugoslavia. It was here that Emery Reves[1] was born on September 16, 1904, in Bacsfoldvar, at that time southern Hungary. Prior to World War I and the subsequent partitioning of Slavonia, members of the Revesz family were middle-class property owners. Not long after Emery's birth, their only child, Simon Revesz, a wood supplier and grain merchant, and his wife, Gizella, moved to Ujvidek[2] where Emery attended grade school. When he distinguished himself as a student at a very early age, his parents moved yet again, this time to Budapest, so as to afford their precocious son the best possible opportunity for a superior education.

He was enrolled in Barcsay Utcai Gymnazium, a well known school whose reputation stemmed from its exacting academic standards and the ethnic diversity of its students. Exposed to multiple dialects and equally motivated students, Emery Reves demonstrated an uncanny facility for learning languages and a competitive desire to excel. He was blessed with an encyclopedic memory for detailed information and a maturity uncommon for someone so young, and he proved himself a formidable student. According to a relative, when he was asked by his father why he so frequently studied late into the night, the boy replied, "Above average results demand above average effort."

During his years in Budapest, Emery also demonstrated sufficient skills as a pianist to be regarded as a child prodigy. Consequently, he was groomed by his parents for concert appearances, from lengthy rehearsal sessions to his carefully coiffed hair. Although Emery dearly loved music, he disliked the absolute commitment practicing required of him to the expense of all other activities, and he resented the charade of pretending to be other than a rapidly maturing young man. As a result, he rebelled by cutting his curly locks and refusing to pursue music in a serious vein, even though he continued to attend operas and concerts when he could afford the few pennies it cost to stand in the upper balcony. Little else is known about Emery's youth, and nothing at all about the Revesz family during and after World War I, except that Simon's career as a commodities broker was gradually undermined by the inflationary post-war economy.

After graduating from the *gymnazium,* Emery left Budapest in the early 1920s to study at the University of Zurich in Switzerland. There in a boardinghouse dining room he met two fellow Hungarians whose intelligence he respected and whose friendship he grew to cherish. It was the beginning of a remarkable lifetime association, exceptional not so much because of its

Emery Revesz, ca.1916

Gizella Revesz with her only child at Christmas in 1914.

As a student at Barcsay Utcai Gymnazium in Budapest.

1 *Revesz was later anglicized when Emery Reves became a British subject in 1940.*
2 *Today known as Novi Sad in Yugoslavia.*

longevity but rather in view of the spectacular success each later achieved in his chosen profession. When Emery Reves met John von Neumann[3] and William Fellner[4], he discovered friends with whom he shared not only a national heritage, but also a youthful idealism borne out of the post-World War I climate of opportunity. They were young but mature, enthusiastic yet disciplined, and, above all, talented and ambitious. Each was a prodigy in his own right and would one day prove his potential by becoming highly successful in his respective career: von Neumann as one of the fathers of computer science; Fellner as a renowned theoretical economist; and Emery Reves as a publisher and author.

Although Fellner and von Neumann were from wealthy families and had grown up together in Budapest, they eagerly embraced the stocky, dark-eyed Reves, whose rural Jewish background was different from theirs, but whose straightforward manner, incisive mind and clever wit much endeared him to them. Together the three Hungarian students shared an intensely academic experience, periodically punctuated by recreational escapades. While each adhered to a rigorous discipline, it was not uncommon for them to indulge as a group in patronizing the city's thé-dansant parlors, where they sought female company, dark beer and hearty meals, and an opportunity to relax, briefly, from their demanding scholastic pursuits. Occasionally, they played the role of tourists, always absorbing whatever nuances distinguished their own cultural heritage from the sophisticated and intellectual environment of Zurich. While less affluent than his comrades, Emery developed a reputation for stylish dress; the few suits he owned he kept in impeccable condition, and his worn shoes were always well polished. As a fashion preference, he often wore tailor-made bow ties, a custom which eventually became a personal trademark. The outfit was invariably replete with hat, overcoat and umbrella, an ensemble befitting an earnest young man who would soon be recognized as an innovative entrepreneur and successful businessman. What most impressed his fellow students, however, and Fellner and von Neumann in particular, was not so much Emery's dress or even his innate intelligence upon which they relied for advice, but his shrewd application of a naturally pragmatic philosophy. Although he received his doctorate in political economy from the University of Zurich in 1926, Emery Reves was destined to practice his skills and employ his genius not as a professor in a classroom, but rather in the business world at large, and especially in the increasingly volatile field of political journalism spawned

Willy Fellner, Emery Reves and Johnny von Neumann (l. to r.) *were students together at the University of Zurich in the mid-1920s.*

by the creation of the League of Nations. A telling indication of Emery's gift for writing was the encouragement he received from a Zurich professor, who, after reading his doctoral dissertation on the economist Rathenau, recommended that Reves explore having it published. The combination of analytical and expressive qualities contained in the document and recognized by his professor, ideally suited Emery Reves for a role in journalism during the period of heightened nationalism which fueled European politics in the 1930s.

After graduating from the University of Zurich, the close-knit Hungarian trio left for Germany, where von Neumann accepted a faculty position at the University of Berlin, Fellner continued his studies, and Emery Reves managed to continue as a student only after a Berlin professor first assisted him in securing a job. It was not until years later that Emery learned his father had exhausted the family's financial resources so that he might profit from the best education available in Budapest and Zurich. With Berlin at that time paralyzed by an inflation crisis, Emery's job as a publicist ghost-

He earned his doctorate in political economy from the University of Zurich in 1926.

3 *John von Neumann (1903-1957) received his doctorate in mathematics from Budapest in 1926 and became a full professor at Princeton in 1931. His technical work led toward the development of the modern computer. In 1954 he was appointed to the U.S. Atomic Energy Commission, and he served a major role in the development of both the atomic and the hydrogen bombs. In 1956, von Neumann received the U.S.A.E./Enrico Fermi Award.*

4 *William Fellner (1905-1983) received his doctorate in economics from the University of Zurich in 1927. After immigrating to the United States in 1934, he taught first at the University of California at Berkeley, and later at Yale University where he became Sterling professor of economics. An author and editor as well as economist, Dr. Fellner served on Richard Nixon's Presidential Advisory Council on Economic Affairs; he also served as president of the American Economic Association and as resident scholar with the American Enterprise Institute for Public Policy Research in Washington, D.C.*

writing speeches and promotional articles for the owner of the large Odol corporation enabled him, temporarily at least, to prolong his student career and to pay for his room and board. Because his employer was politically ambitious, Emery was able to hone his writing skills while also absorbing firsthand the political ferment then beginning to shake the German government. However, the unstable economic and political conditions which so intrigued the journalistically-minded Reves produced a side affect which greatly saddened him. Foreigners, regardless of nationality or economic station, were no longer welcome in Berlin as they once were. As a result, both John von Neumann and Willy Fellner were forced to return to Budapest after learning from relatives that their family estates were threatened by new government measures designed to confiscate private holdings.[5] Since Emery's family had already suffered the loss of its properties and middle-class means, mostly as a result of his father's poor health and the effects of the depression, there was no urgency or reason for Emery to return to Hungary. Many years afterwards, he recounted having written a letter home on the blank backs of six 50-million Deutsch mark notes, "because it was cheaper than buying writing paper".[6]

The only known photograph of Simon Revesz (holding hat above the letter "o") *with his wife and son, ca.1922.*

Emery's parents had by this time moved back to Ujvidek and were living in a large house with his grandparents. When Simon Revesz died of a heart attack, his son sought to provide for his mother as best he could, and though he visited infrequently, it was always an occasion of great celebration. Preparations were made weeks in advance, and everyone in the family went to the train station to await the arrival of the well educated and increasingly sophisticated relative, who represented for them a window to worldly affairs beyond isolated Ujvidek.

The homecomings rarely lasted more than several days, but each occasion featured a festive dinner which included a large goose, Austrian pastries, platters of Hungarian salami, fresh baked loaves of dark bread, and, because of the circumstances, goose liver, which was considered a delicacy. Most of the conversations naturally centered on Emery's activities, as a student and later as a businessman: what he had seen, heard and learned, where he had traveled, and what his ambitious plans were. Uncharacteristically for him, he spent hours talking while seated in a large, glassed-in hall, the audience of family and friends enthralled by his stories of work and travel. From the eldest, his grandparents whom he called Opi and Omi, to his youngest relatives, he made each of them feel special by sharing with them his already astute observations of a world rapidly changing beyond the Hungarian countryside they knew as home, and had little reason to ever expect leaving. He inspired in them, especially the younger ones, a desire for opportunity and excellence, and when traveling he kept the family informed of his whereabouts and exciting adventures, often by sending postcards depicting famous cities and historic sites. The correspondence during such a depression era provided more spiritual than economic support, but it also served to reinforce the family's pride in having educated such a worldly man whose recent accomplishments seemed to promise an unlimited future of success.

In Berlin, as in Budapest and Zurich earlier, Emery was able to indulge in his enjoyment of music. By all accounts he was exceptionally musical, possessing perfect pitch and, amazingly, able to whistle from memory the entire score of a Beethoven symphony. Although he remained passionate about music, later attending concerts wherever his business travels took him, he chose not to pursue it as a career because of its narrow scope. It is interesting to note, however, that Sir Georg Solti[7] was Emery Reves' first cousin.

Despite Berlin's inflationary conditions, Emery enjoyed living and working there during the late twenties. He was energetic and ambitious, and the city offered an array of cultural opportunities, especially in music, and an urban vitality which greatly appealed to him. Because of the uncertain German economy, though, the capital was also the scene of turbulent political activity, a trend which as an outsider he was able to

5 *Both von Neumann and Fellner later immigrated to the United States in the early 1930s because of political and economic persecution suffered by their families in Budapest.*
6 The Times, *London, "The Idealist Who Sold Churchill to the World," September 7, 1981.*
7 *Georg Solti (b. 1912) immigrated from Budapest in 1939, and is the present conductor of the Chicago Symphony Orchestra. He has served as director of the Royal Opera, Covent Garden, in London, and earlier in 1961-62, as senior conductor of the Dallas Symphony Orchestra.*

observe initially with some objectivity, and later with growing alarm. While ghostwriting articles for his corporate employer, Emery had rediscovered his facility and interest in writing; his expression was direct and easily understood by the reader, and the compelling logic behind his observations was both provocative and persuasive. In fact, his success in writing promotional pieces, combined with an already keen interest in political affairs, soon led him to abandon the security of a company job and to try a new career as a free-lance journalist.

He began by seeking appointments with government officials, and it is illustrative of his character that without any prior journalistic experience or press authorization, he was granted private interviews, at first with city officials and later with such prominent German statesmen as Gustav Stresemann.[8] For several years and especially while studying in Zurich, Emery had followed the birth pangs of the League of Nations, and now that he had chosen to pursue a career in political journalism, he began to monitor more closely that international body of querulous members, spending as much time in Geneva as he did in Berlin. His free-lance articles were well received, and he even managed to sell a number of his exclusive interviews to more than one newspaper and in different cities, at that time an uncommon practice.

That initiative, as well as a remark by the French official, Aristide Briand, concerning the League's ineffectiveness, provided Emery with a brilliant idea which ultimately influenced his new profession in a fundamental way. Briand's remark, "We statesmen get along fine together, but when we get back home, we come up against a wall,"[9] impressed the young reporter with the need for improved international communications, in particular as a means of combating the rising tide of nationalism among European nations, and re-affiliating those countries overseas who were beginning to withdraw into isolationism. What was critically needed, Emery Reves decided, was a news agency that could get the views of one country published in another, thus undercutting the jingoistic viewpoint which most newspapers were then presenting to their readers. The concept was ingenious in its simplicity, and its potential value seemed undeniable.

When Emery described his idea to Lord Robert Cecil, who had helped to found the League of Nations and later won the Nobel Prize for his work in 1937, the Englishman enthusiastically endorsed the plan and recommended that he begin immediately approaching

prospective author-statesmen and organizations in order to implement the innovative system. Soon thereafter, Emery Reves created the Cooperation Press Service in Paris. The founder and president was only 26 years of age.

Reves founded the Cooperation Press Service in Paris in 1930 at age 26 after escaping arrest by the secret police in Berlin.

Emery had suspected for some time that virulent nationalism might lead to war, and his foreboding was based as much on personal experience as on his instincts as a journalist. The reason he had established his company in Paris rather than in Berlin was due to a frightening escape from the secret police in 1930. As a political writer who concentrated on developments in the League of Nations, Reves had developed an anti-Nazi reputation, and the fact that he was also Jewish made him a natural target for the National Socialist party then gaining control of the German government. His escape was made possible by a cleaning lady who telephoned him at work to ask that he pick up some laundry before returning home. He correctly interpreted her call as a message, since she never contacted him at the office and there was no laundry to collect. Instead, he left immediately for the rail station where the maid brought him a small suitcase and he boarded the first train departing Germany. When it crossed the border into Belgium, he embraced the conductor and

8 *Gustav Stresemann (1878-1929) founded the German People's party following his country's defeat in World War I. When the Ruhr occupation caused the total collapse of German finance and economy, he formed a new cabinet based on a party coalition. Stresemann's foreign policy led to Germany's admission into the League of Nations in 1926.*
9 The Times, *London, Sept. 7, 1981.*

wept, still a free man. Not long afterwards, he learned through a letter from a friend that his Berlin apartment had indeed been under surveillance that day, and that his arrest was being sought on a charge of seditious journalism. Reves also learned that his apartment had been sacked and all his possessions destroyed or confiscated, including his collection of German abstract expressionist paintings.[10]

From Belgium Reves made his way to Paris where he started his new company. He named it Cooperation Press because of its international application, meaning as it did the same in English, French and German. At first he worked alone out of his office apartment, a sparsely furnished bedroom with a balcony overlooking the Champs-Elysées. Drawing on contacts he had developed as a free-lance journalist in Berlin and Geneva and his overall knowledge of the European political scene, he wrote to numerous statesmen and various other public figures, inviting them to participate in the unique syndication service he was creating. Simultaneous to his efforts to recruit authors, he began negotiating the publishing rights with the network of newspapers whom he hoped would subscribe to the service offered by Cooperation Press. Not surprisingly, Robert Cecil wrote the first article which Reves succeeded in selling to a dozen newspapers in different countries. Within three years of the company's inception, the enterprising Reves had obtained exclusive contracts with 120 authors, most of them European officials, as well as service contracts with 400 newspapers in more than 70 countries throughout the world. In the United States alone, twenty independent newspapers, led by the *New York Herald Tribune*, printed articles translated and released by the Paris-based news syndicate.

Among the noted authors whose articles Reves controlled were British statesmen Austen Chamberlain, Clement R. Attlee, Lord Samuel, Alfred Duff Cooper, and Anthony Eden, who later became prime minister. His French clients included Paul Reynaud, who was elected premier in 1940, and Leon Blum, who served as provisional president of France in 1946. Cooperation Press also represented such diverse personalities as the Italian anti-fascist statesman, Count Carlo Sforza; the English mathematician, philosopher and pacifist, Bertrand Russell; and Eduard Benes, the popular president of Czechoslovakia who dominated the news for a while prior to the outbreak of World War II.

The syndicated press service of today is a familiar, practical and cost-efficient system, universally used because of the speed at which news can and must be reported. In the early 1930s, though, technology was only beginning to keep pace with global communication needs. The fact that Emery Reves introduced a system that not only fulfilled an increasingly urgent desire on the part of the public to be better informed, but one that also provided a technical solution in delivering topical news, was a development quickly imitated by other organizations such as Universal Service, to which the Hearst newspaper chain subscribed, and leading to the creation later of such industry giants as United Features and other modern syndicates.

Rapid acceptance of the system soon enabled Reves to expand his operations at 33 Champs-Elysées. A larger support staff was needed to help process the growing flow of correspondence, and to translate each of the syndicated articles into three languages. The company's effectiveness, after all, depended upon the speed and accuracy with which the articles were translated and distributed on a daily basis. Often working sixteen hours a day and rarely eating outside the office, Reves was prolific in his correspondence with authors and subscribers, both signed and potential, and because he was fluent in nine languages, he was indispensable in verifying the transcripts the company dispatched. A key figure in his operation and the company's success was the first person he employed, Rachel Gayman, a woman who worked for him for more than forty years and whose remarkable career also included a distinguished role in the French Resistance, a service for which she was later decorated.

Throughout the company's rapid growth, Emery Reves continued to act as the sole agent for Cooperation Press in contracting authors and placing the ensuing syndicated articles in a widening arc of international publications. As a result of his indefatigable efforts, often traveling 30,000 miles a year, the founder and president met most of Europe's leading statesmen during the 1930s.

In 1935 Reves acquired the syndication rights to articles by Winston Churchill, already a legendary figure and widely published author as a result of his exploits in the Boer War of 1899 and active involvement in the British government for two decades. The early thirties, however, represented Churchill's so-called 'wilderness years,' and it was Emery Reves who was largely responsible for re-introducing the eloquent spokesman to a public realm outside the British Empire. Because Churchill was then without a seat in Parliament, the fiery orator did not even have a forum at that time from which to address the critical issues confronting the English people and the European community at large.

10 *For a similar reference, see* 20th Century Journey, *Volume II,* The Nightmare Years, *by William L. Shirer, p. 193.*

It was Austen Chamberlain who made it possible for the two men to meet. As one of the Cooperation Press authors, Chamberlain had asked the publisher why Churchill was not represented in his syndication service. When Emery conceded that Churchill seemed to believe that he did not need Cooperation Press, Chamberlain replied, "A pity, he is our best man."[11] Chamberlain then promised to talk with Churchill about the advantages of Reves' service. The very next morning Emery received a call from Churchill's office and was summoned to his flat in Morpeth Mansions for an appointment. Years later Reves described to a reporter his first meeting with Churchill: "He was in the bathroom and started talking – then appeared at the doorway, completely nude, with a towel in his hand,"[12] never for a moment hesitating, and continuing to talk in an agitated manner. Churchill, it seems, was displeased that Reves wanted 40 per cent of all royalty fees to cover the heavy costs of the syndication service. Emery quickly explained that he was prepared to offer Churchill a fee more than double the amount he was presently receiving from Lord Beaverbrook, at that time Britain's best known newspaper publisher and one of Churchill's closest friends. Churchill was flattered that Reves would pay him such a handsome stipend (a guaranteed minimum of £25 for the foreign language rights of each article), and he was impressed even more by the amount of coverage he could expect to receive through the extensive range of newspaper outlets serviced by Cooperation Press. As a result of their negotiation, Winston Churchill signed a contract with Reves in 1936, and in less than six months Emery had placed Churchill's articles in 26 cities,[13] making him the highest paid author among the company's distinguished roster. The English statesman's political views rapidly became more widely known throughout European capitals, including cities such as Budapest and Warsaw, which already were beginning to experience the negative propaganda emanating from Berlin.

"It worked like this," Reves later explained in describing the syndication's method of operations. "Supposing Adolph Hitler made a speech. I would telephone Churchill [with the substance of Hitler's remarks] to answer it. By 8 p.m. his secretary would have telephoned his article to my office in Paris. I would have it translated in three languages, and by midnight it was sent off to subscribers [the newspapers with whom Reves had contracts]. So when people read Hitler's speech, they read Churchill's reply at the same time."[14]

The system was revolutionary because it eliminated lag time previously suffered by statesmen in responding to another national viewpoint. In a sense, Cooperation Press helped to bring the world closer together, because readers were now able to weigh the merits of one author's opinion while at the same time comparing it with the logic of an opposing argument. No longer did nationalistic denunciations go unchallenged, or Hitler's inflammatory tirades profit from an interlude before the public could read a balanced response. It must also be noted, however, that the innovative system also tended to heighten, rather than alleviate international tensions, since the simultaneously published and opposing viewpoints served to polarize existing factions and to underscore further the lack of understanding among European leaders. Although the press service succeeded in its objective of a better informed public, that goal alone did not prevent escalating nationalism or the war it would eventually trigger.

"I have tried to present all the conflicting views of Europe," Reves wrote in 1941, "and have often published also the articles of the Fascist spokesman, Virginio Gayda, inasmuch as it was possible for us [Cooperation Press Service] to print also from time to time foreign articles in Italian newspapers. But I have never published Nazi articles. In fact, as the crisis grew, the policy of my organization became more and more openly anti-Nazi until it was probably the only organization of this kind fighting Nazi influence and the Goebbels machine on the European continent."[15]

As international relations became increasingly strained, Reves' company expanded in size and the syndication grew both in its circulation and the diversity of its reading audience. The trend continued until late in the decade, when first the German and then the Italian governments began suppressing news by threatening managements with political pressure if those newspapers continued to print Cooperation Press Service articles. Consequently, there was a gradual, and irreversible, erosion in the number of subscribing papers, even among supposedly neutral countries bordering the Third Reich. Churchill, among others, was understandably alarmed and disappointed with the prevailing trend, representing as it did not only a denial of democratic principles, but also a loss of personal income. After learning from Reves that additional papers had prohibited the publication of his

11 The Times, *London, September 7, 1981.*

12 Ibid.

13 *Gilbert, Martin.* Winston S. Churchill, *Volume V, (London: Heinemann, 1978), p. 849.*

14 The Times, *London, September 7, 1981.*

15 *Reves, Emery.* "Publisher's Foreword"; *Thyssen, Fritz.* I Paid Hitler, *(New York: Cooperation Publishing Co., Inc. in association with Hodder and Stoughton, Ltd., London, 1941), p. 6.*

articles, Churchill wrote to Reves: "I am indeed sorry to hear that the net is closing round our activities, through fear of Germany. Luckily, you have already called in the New World to redress the balance of the Old."[16] Reves had made it possible for Churchill to reassert himself as a national spokesman, and the blatant suppression of his articles espousing a countering philosophy guaranteed deeper international misunderstanding and, in the case of Hitler's published speeches, fanatical, unchecked nationalism.

Reves with Winston Churchill in Paris at the height of the Munich crisis on September 21, 1938. Through Cooperation Press, Reves syndicated Churchill's warning articles to newspapers throughout Europe.

Reves most often met with Churchill on business in London or at Chartwell. However, when the Munich crisis reached its peak in 1938, Reves was at Churchill's side in Paris, and personally oversaw the worldwide distribution of Churchill's famous response attacking Neville Chamberlain's specious policy of appeasement: "It is not Czechoslovakia alone which is menaced, but also the freedom and democracy of all nations. The belief that security can be obtained by throwing a small State to the wolves is a fatal delusion. The war potential of Germany will increase in a short time more rapidly than it will be possible for France and Great Britain to complete the measures necessary for their defence."[17] In subsequent articles released by Cooperation Press, Churchill enumerated Hitler's repeated violation of similar accords and cited the Fuhrer's insatiable appetite for territorial expansion. Churchill knew that Neville Chamberlain's pact, extolled by the public and media alike as a solution for "peace in our time," could only lead to future confrontations[18] and, in all probability, the prime minister's

downfall. There exists no better example of the effectiveness of Cooperation Press than the critical role it performed during and after the Munich crisis, and the dramatic impact Reves' syndication service had on Churchill's political career, identifying him as a lone voice urging re-armament to combat Nazi militarism and expansion. In his first speech following the Munich Agreement, delivered at Saarbrucken, Adolph Hitler indirectly referred to Emery Reves when he shouted hysterically, "This propaganda by Churchill, Eden and Duff Cooper must stop!" Articles by all three men were exclusively syndicated by Emery Reves.

In the late thirties Reves broadened his role as a publisher by commissioning several books. In addition to his deeply ingrained conviction as a journalist that the public had a right to hear opposing arguments, it was also an opportunity for the Hungarian Reves to retaliate against the Nazi regime which had forced him to flee Germany in 1930. All three books were widely distributed, and the recognition they received, and the man who commissioned them, did not go unnoticed in Berlin. The commissioned works were: *Conversations with Hitler* (1939) by Hermann Rauschning, one of Hitler's ex-aides who, after being appointed by the Fuhrer as President of the Senate of the Free City of Danzig, later fled Germany and attempted to justify his conversion by revealing detailed information of both the schedule and means of Hitler's master plan for the conquest of Europe; *Between Hitler and Mussolini* by Prince Ernst von Starhemberg, an Austrian statesman whose anti-Nazi policies were all the more courageous in view of Austria's neighboring countries; and *I Paid Hitler* (1941), the memoirs of Baron Fritz Thyssen whose steel industry not only helped rebuild Germany's post-World War I economy, but whose financial contributions for more than fifteen years supported Adolph Hitler's ascendancy to power.

During the late 1930s, Reves expanded his role as publisher by commissioning several books, including Fritz Thyssen's attack on Adolph Hitler after the steel baron became a fugitive.

16 *Gilbert,* Churchill, *Volume V, p. 1068.*
17 Ibid., *p. 979.*
18 *"You were given the choice between war and dishonor,"* Churchill remarked to Prime Minister Chamberlain, *"You chose dishonor and you will have war."*

21

Reves first met Thyssen in Paris, six months after the fugitive steel baron escaped from Germany at the outbreak of the war in September, 1939. Despite Thyssen's conversion and absolute disillusionment with Hitler, he and Reves were natural political enemies: "I met him when he was a refugee," Reves later wrote in the Publisher's Foreword. "I made with him an agreement as between author and publisher."[19] Their ideological differences notwithstanding, Reves believed that information concerning Thyssen's role in the creation of the Wehrmacht was too critical to withhold from "the free peoples of the world (then) fighting a desperate war against Hitlerism."[20] As a result, he spent three weeks in the company of a collaborator and secretary on the French Riviera, working with Thyssen day and night, recording his recollections and preparing the memoirs for publication. Thyssen's repeated confession, though, of having misplaced his trust in Hitler as someone capable of leading German resistance to Bolshevism, was insufficient to exonerate him in Reves' mind of the disastrous consequences for which the Chairman of the German Steel Trust was now responsible. Such a confession, "Ein Dummkopf war ich...!" ("What a fool I have been...!")[21] deserved to be heard, however, and the astute president of Cooperation Publishing Company was determined to be the first to publish Thyssen's controversial memoirs.

As war approached Churchill urged Reves to leave France for London, but the publisher preferred to remain in his Paris office as long as possible because of its proximity to the network of European contacts he had so carefully developed. Long after the subjugation of Poland, Reves continued to operate from the nerve center of his communications empire. Not until May 10, 1940 did he realize that he might be forced to retreat once again. On that day the German army crossed the frontiers of Holland, Belgium and Luxembourg, and the war in the west began. France, alone, stood between Hitler and the English Channel and the Fuhrer's objective of a 'united' Europe. Reves was on the Riviera at that time, working with Thyssen on the latter's memoirs. Reves returned to Paris with the baron's incriminating manuscript in late May, only to learn that the Germans had already broken through at Sedan along the French border.

After France fell to Germany in June 1940, Reves fled from Paris to Bordeaux where he boarded a British vessel which transported him to England.

When rail service into Paris was commandeered by advance units of the German army, Reves desperately searched for some sort of vehicle in which to escape. From a friend he learned that a car was available, but because it was brand new and the owner was unable to collect it, the luxurious Hispano-Suiza would be expensive and difficult to acquire. Reves managed to contact the agent and went to the garage where the car was hidden. Without asking the sale price, he scattered a pocketful of currency on the hood of the car and indicated that it was all the money he had. Because the fall of Paris was imminent and he had little hope of selling the car to its intended owner, the agent accepted the cash, handed Reves the keys, and disappeared.

German storm troopers were already beginning to appear along the outskirts of the capital, and Paris, though having been declared an open city with no plans to defend itself, was gripped with panic. Reves returned to his office only long enough to collect a few personal belongings and to remove some critical documents, including Thyssen's manuscript, and to dismiss his loyal Cooperation Press staff.[22] He left Paris on the night of June 11th, driving slowly west on roads choked with refugee traffic, some of whom clung to the running boards of his car. The trip to Tours required fourteen hours, so congested was the highway with all manner of transport vehicles and frightened people of all ages and nationalities. Two days later, Reves resumed his flight, his destination Bordeaux, where he had made arrangements to rendez-vous with a Belgrade contact who was expert in providing false documents and in his ability to pass fugitives through enemy lines.

19 *Reves, "Publisher's Foreword"; Thyssen,* I Paid Hitler, *p. 15.*
20 Ibid., *p. 16.*
21 *Reves, "Publisher's Foreword"; Thyssen,* I Paid Hitler, *p. 11.*
22 *Reves later learned that when soldiers arrived at his Champs-Elysées office, they tortured the one secretary they found there, trying to discover his whereabouts. Like countless other victims, the woman was never seen again.*

The official French government had earlier relocated in Bordeaux and it, too, now faced inevitable defeat. Only days before France capitulated on June 22nd, Reves obtained permission to board an English destroyer, still lying at anchor in Bordeaux' harbor. He persuaded the captain to contact the War Office in London so as to confirm his identity. When Winston Churchill, recently elected as prime minister, returned the communique and personally authorized Reves' evacuation, the captain immediately ordered the ship's crew to get underway. Although Reves was forced to abandon his car and what few material possessions he had saved in Paris, he had with him Fritz Thyssen's coveted memoirs when the British cruiser escorted him out to sea where he was transferred to a British cargo ship. In a matter of hours, and in accordance with Churchill's instructions, Emery Reves was delivered safely on English soil, having once again barely escaped Hitler's reach.

Churchill did more than to enable his colleague to escape from almost certain German capture; he also recommended that the Hungarian-born publisher be made a British subject. The distinguished group who sponsored Reves' naturalization papers included: Anthony Eden, Clement R. Attlee, Maxwell Beaverbrook, Lord Samuels, and, of course, Winston Churchill.

Because of Reves' professional work fighting the spread of Nazism and his proven expertise in the field of communications, Churchill enlisted his friend to work briefly for the government. The prime minister wanted Reves to help reorganize the intelligence network and the Ministry of Information, both of crucial importance as England prepared to withstand a German assualt. After renting a small apartment near Whitehall, Reves went to work analyzing departmental shortcomings and the government's ability to secure reliable intelligence and how best to utilize that information. Considering his Hungarian background and the inevitable jealousies inherent in all bureaucratic agencies, it is not surprising that he received little cooperation and encountered considerable resistance in certain quarters in trying to fulfill the duties assigned to him by Churchill. He wanted more than anything to justify the prime minister's confidence in

On the back of this photograph Reves wrote: "The five men who, in 1940, made me a British subject (plus Lord Samuels)."
Pictured (l. to r.) *are: Maxwell Beaverbrook, Clement Attlee, King George VI, Winston Churchill and Anthony Eden.*

his ability. Of course, he also felt an understandable debt of gratitude for his recently acquired British citizenship, and therefore wished to contribute to England in some meaningful way during this time of uncertainty. Despite his efforts to befriend colleagues, however, and regardless of the value of his recommendations concerning departmental changes in policy, Reves was unable to accomplish anything substantive under the circumstances. Though anguished, he was not without a typically inventive recourse.

Reves knew that the war's outcome would be determined by the schedule and extent of American involvement, and he truly believed that he could better serve England's cause by conducting a propaganda campaign in the United States. He submitted a proposal to Churchill outlining the need for " 'one central organization' powerful enough to fight the German propaganda machine across the Atlantic."[23] The prime minister, in turn, forwarded the plan to the Ministry of Information, along with a note to Duff Cooper, "I hope you will not allow it to be weakened by official caution."[24] Soon thereafter, but not before he was seriously injured when his London flat was bombed in a Luftwaffe raid, Reves left for the United States via Portugal. Before departing, he and Churchill met one last time, with Reves reiterating the conviction that he would prove his usefulness to the prime minister by helping to sway American opinion from its present stance of neutrality towards more active support of the beleagured British.

Reves standing in the window of his London flat the morning after he was injured in a Luftwaffe bombing raid in the summer of 1940.

In Lisbon, Emery Reves, along with thousands of other refugees, waited several months before being able to board a ship bound for the United States. The German blockade had by this time severely restricted oceanic activity, and already the tactics of U-Boat wolf-packs were being reported with growing casualty figures. Reves finally left on one of the last passenger ships to leave Lisbon, arriving in New York in February, 1941. As he had done a decade before in Paris, he again converted a bedroom into an office, this time in the Plaza Hotel, until a short time later when he could rent work space in Rockefeller Center.

For the next several years, he concentrated on two activities, writing political articles for major newspapers and magazines, and reworking the proposal he had shown Churchill before leaving England in which he had advocated the creation of "one central organization" strong enough to overcome German propaganda. The latter was actually a treatise articulating his political philosophy, which he had begun to formulate years before in Zurich while studying the fluctuation of national economies and the corresponding impact they had on international politics. The document, *A Democratic Manifesto*, was published by Random House in 1942. As he had pledged to Churchill, the book helped "to propagate, not merely the policies, but also the ideals of the British cause,"[25] by stating categorically, "Only if we put force at the service of justice can we hope that it will not be used against justice."

As for articles written by Reves, they were published on a regular basis in such respected publications as *The New York Times* and *The American Mercury*. Frequently, they appeared in the "Letters to the Editor" column, where they received considerable attention because of their provocative subject matter, and stimulated widespread discussion of differing political systems through rebuttal letters often written by readers.

A Democratic Manifesto struck an equally responsive chord among its audience. Because the initial printing run was a small one, the book's success relied largely on favorable reviews by critics and word-of-mouth recommendation. In his review in *The New York Times* Simeon Strunsky wrote:

> By this test of creative novelty Mr. Reves has written as stimulating and heartening a primer on democracy in a new world order as one can recall. He has intelligence and he has, in exceptional degree, courage. We do not always find the two combined in programs of democracy ... A bold and honest and intelligent book, by a tough-minded idealist.

23 *Gilbert,* Churchill, *Volume VI, (Boston: Houghton Mifflin Company, 1983), p. 740.*
24 Ibid.
25 *Gilbert,* Churchill, *Volume VI, p. 744.*

Many reviewers, including Thomas Mann, cited the author's clarity of expression in discussing complicated issues and Reves' logical approach in readdressing problems which historically lead to war. "The book lays bare in a keen and pungent style," said *The Atlantic Monthly*, "many of the shams and hypocrisies of our time, because the author sees clearly some of the dilemmas of the present crisis [World War II] in the history of civilization." In *The Book-of-the-Month Club News*, William Allen White described Reves' 'manifesto' as "a blueprint for world freedom under international law." Louis M. Hacker wrote in the *New York Herald Tribune*: "It is sincerely to be hoped that this little book will get the widest audience possible, for it is one of those fascinating pieces of writing that at one and the same time can satisfy the requirements of both the most recondite and only the passably educated. Mr. Reves carries his learning effortlessly." In the April 1943 issue of *The New Yorker* in its "Talk of the Town" column, E.B. White referred to *A Democratic Manifesto* as "that indispensable little history book," and recommended that every U.S. Senator carry a copy for easy reference. Probably the most favorable review of the book, and a measure of its extensive reach and potential influence, was printed in the Brazilian newspaper *O Jornal* under the heading, "A Majestic Work." In it the author declared: "*Manifesto Democratico* is the best book published during this war. Let us go even further: we believe that it is the most important book published for a long time...It is bound to render an immense service. For Emery Reves, the first Nobel Peace Prize."

Although he never received such a recognition, Reves did not lessen his crusade for world peace or his efforts to inform the public as to the means of achieving it. In his article, "Wanted: A Declaration of Interdependence," published in *The American Mercury* in March 1943, Reves assailed the type of specious logic often applied to international politics which had resurfaced again in the Atlantic Charter, signed shortly after his book's publication. Co-signed by President Roosevelt and Prime Minister Churchill, the document's underlying idea, Reves thought, was a reiteration of the old doctrine of self-determination upon which Europe had been rebuilt after the First World War, and was at that very time under siege once more. Although hailed by most as "the hope of the world," the Atlantic

Charter represented to Reves a false promise of peace. In reviewing Reves' *A Democratic Manifesto*, Sterling North of the *Chicago Daily News* wrote: "Vital to the winning of this war is clearer thinking concerning democratic aims. Even the Atlantic Charter (has) fallen short of the mark. What is needed is a ringing, crystal-clear manifesto, based on the keenest logic, stirring as the finest poetry – at once a rallying call to the oppressed people of the world and a Magna Carta for the postwar world." North thought Reves' book might serve as such "a clarion call." To promote sales of its forthcoming issue in which Reves attacked the Atlantic Charter, *The American Mercury* paid for half-page ads in *The New York Times* which featured a ragged copy of the heralded document, unrolled to expose reference to the self-determination clause, and a headline of one-inch letters audaciously proclaiming, "THE FALLACY IN THE ATLANTIC CHARTER!"

Part of a half-page ad which appeared in The New York Times *in February 1943 promoting the March issue of* The American Mercury *and Reves' article criticizing the Atlantic Charter.*

Other wartime articles written by Reves at this time included: "Should the British Empire Be Broken Up?", also published in *The American Mercury*; "Sovereignty Expounded – It Would Appear Conceptions Should Be Revised," an argument first printed in *The New York Times*[26] and so compelling in its logic that Senator Joseph H. Ball of Minnesota requested that it be entered into the *Congressional Record*[27] as an extension of his remarks to the Senate on the same

25

26 The New York Times, *October 31, 1943.*
27 *U.S.,* Congressional Record, *Appendix, 1943, p. A5007.*

subject; a Letter to the Editor of *The New York Times*[28] concerning "the most appropriate ways and means of war financing," which reflected his academic background in political economy; and "How to Civilize Germany," published in *The American Mercury* not long before the war ended, and in which Reves proposed an unorthodox solution for converting "80 million Hitler-heilers into a nation of Nazi-haters."[29]

The critical plaudits *A Democratic Manifesto* received earlier in 1942 were restrained by comparison with the reviews accorded Reves' second and most enduring book, *The Anatomy of Peace*, first published by Harper & Brothers in June 1945 with an initial printing run of only 4,000 copies. As in his first work, Reves again attacked *nationalism* as the *one* cause for all wars. Unlike in the first book, though, Reves elaborated in *Anatomy* on what he believed was the *only* condition required for peaceful human relations, the creation of a World Federation governed by international laws instead of treaties.

Reves' proposal for world peace was introduced by an especially poignant dedication to his mother, whom he had learned only recently had been killed in the January 1942 'razzia' in Hungary:

This Book
is Dedicated to the
Memory of my Mother
who was atrociously and senselessly
assassinated, like countless other
innocent victims of the war whose
martyrdom can have meaning only
if we who survive learn
how to prevent the tragedy
of future wars.

In the book's opening chapter, "A Copernican World," Reves underscored what he perceived to be the fundamental flaw in the proposed charter of the United Nations,[30] and of its ineffective predecessor, the League of Nations: "Nothing can distort the true picture of conditions and events in the world more than to regard one's own country as the centre of the universe." With his premise attacking nationalism clearly stated at the outset, the author then proceeded in following chapters to cite the inevitable failures of such systems as capitalism, socialism, religion, and fascism in addressing human needs; to describe the evolution of feudalism into an international society of nation-states and the historical meaning of sovereignty; to distinguish between treaties, which lead to war, and law, which can ensure peace if enforced; to expose the

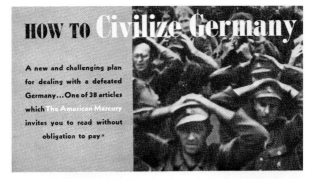

A 1943 article in The New York Times *by Reves on the subject of sovereignty was so compelling that it was printed again in the* Congressional Record.

The American Mercury *in 1944 placed this full-page ad featuring a provocative article by Reves in* The Chicago Sun, The New York Times, Washington Post, *and* New York Post.

Emery Reves was 41 years of age when The Anatomy of Peace *was first published.*

28 The New York Times, *September 19, 1943, p. 8E.*

29 The American Mercury, *"How to Civilize Germany," November 1944.*

30 The Anatomy of Peace *was originally scheduled for publication by Harpers on June 13, 1945. A decision to postpone the publication date was made in April when Cass Canfield, Chairman of Harpers, sent a telegram to Reves in late April expressing his fears about publishing the book before final adoption of the United Nations Charter. Reves, who at the time was in San Francisco observing the conference proceedings, immediately cabled the New York publishing office to assure Canfield that he would accept all responsibility for his sharp criticism of the creation of yet another organization erroneously based on the "sovereign equality of nations." As a result,* The Anatomy of Peace *was published only a few weeks before the Dumbarton Oaks agreement was signed and made public.*

fallacies of internationalism, national self-determination, and collective security in providing a universal, enduring peace; and to offer his own uniquely simple solution for an international society of lawful order and just government, "the true revolution of our age."[31]

Both Reves and Harpers eagerly awaited the critics' reviews. They were not disappointed. Orville Prescott of *The New York Times* wrote: "The logic of *The Anatomy of Peace* is simple and eloquent…It might be a good thing for the world if ten or twenty million persons read and discussed it." The Associated Press, through 1,600 papers, declared, "Few books about the dangers of war are as stirring as this one about the causes of peace." In *The Book-of-the-Month Club News*, Clifton Fadiman suggested, "Perhaps Mr. Reves' crucially important book will help to arrest our slow march to suicide."

Although the early reviews were unanimously enthusiastic, book sales did not increase accordingly. Nevertheless, another thousand copies were printed on the basis of the positive reviews, just in case.

Ironically, the ultimate success of *The Anatomy of Peace* was indirectly due to the explosion of the first atomic bomb at Hiroshima on August 6, 1945, an event which precipitated Japan's capitulation and the end of World War II, and introduced a new era in cataclysmic warfare. Within two weeks of President Truman's announcement, Pocket Books, Inc. published 273,000 copies of *The Atomic Age Opens*, a book which posed the crucial question: "How are men who are full of prejudice and fear and selfish national desires to live together in a world that has atomic bombs but has not generally accepted rule of law?" Those already familiar with Reves' book believed that *The Anatomy of Peace* was capable of answering the most critical question of the twentieth century. Then, in early September, the sixth anniversary of the outbreak of World War II, the respected American author and editor Carl Van Doren decided on his own to send copies of Reves' first chapter to 700 notable Americans, along with a cover letter in which he explained: "The most convincing account of the right road to a peaceful future that I have seen in print is Emery Reves' *Anatomy of Peace*…I can think of nothing more urgent for you to read."

Such an authoritative letter, combined with the provocative excerpt, resulted in influential discussions of the book in key circles, and increased sales enough to warrant a third printing of another 5,000 copies on September 14th. Soon afterwards, Supreme Court Justice Owen J. Roberts invited Reves to a luncheon in Philadelphia, where he showed the author a draft of An Open Letter to the American People which he had prepared and hoped to persuade prominent citizens to sign. The Open Letter was published on October 10, 1945 in more than 50 national newspapers, including *The New York Times*, *Washington Post*, *Philadelphia Inquirer*, *Chicago Sun*, *Kansas City Star*, *Des Moines Register*, and *Los Angeles Times*. Among those signing the Open Letter were: Owen J. Roberts; philanthropist Albert Lasker, Senator J. William Fulbright, author Thomas Mann, Carl and Mark Van Doren, Professor Albert Einstein, and other religious spokesmen, businessmen and leading intellectuals. The letter read, in part: "We urge American men and women to read this book, to think about its conclusions, and to discuss it with neighbors and friends privately and publicly." As a result of the ubiquitous ad, people began talking about the book in earnest, and another 5,000 copies were rushed off the press.

In an interview with Raymond Swing published in the November issue of *The Atlantic Monthly*, Professor Albert Einstein, whose famous formula was the basis of atomic research, was quoted as saying: "In a war fought with the atomic bomb, perhaps two-thirds of the people of the earth might be killed."[32] Such a devastating prediction was then followed later in the article by Einstein's recommendation that people everywhere read Emery Reves' book:

> "I myself do not have the gift of explanation by which to persuade large numbers of people of the urgencies of the problems the human race now faces. Hence I should like to commend someone who has this gift of explanation - Emery Reves, whose book, *The Anatomy of Peace*, is intelligent, brief, clear, and, if I may use the abused term, dynamic on the topic of war and the need for World Government.
>
> Since I do not foresee that atomic energy is to be a great boon for a long time, I have to say that for the present it is a menace. Perhaps it is well that it should be. It may intimidate the human race into bringing order into its international affairs, which, without the pressure of fear, it would not do."[33]

As a matter of fact, Einstein had read *The Anatomy of Peace* earlier in August when asked by Justice Roberts to sign the Open Letter. In a personal note to Reves, dated August 28, 1945, the physicist had expressed his admiration for "the clarity of (Reves') exposition of the most important problem of our time,"

31 *Reves, Emery.* The Anatomy of Peace, *(New York: Harper & Brothers, 1945).*
32 The Atlantic Monthly, *Volume 176, Number 5, November 1945, p. 43.*
33 Ibid.

Mr. Emery Reves
COOPERATION Publishing Co.
30 Rockefeller Plaza
New York 20, N.Y.

Dear Mr. Reves:

    I have read your book "The Anatomy of Peace" carefully and finished it in 24 hours. I agree with you wholeheartedly in every essential point and I admire sincerely the clarity of your exposition of the most important problem of our time. I appreciated it very much that you criticized all the wrong steps already taken (secrecy in armament under purely national viewpoints, especially about the production of the atomic bomb, occupation of strategic ports in the pacific under eclusive U.S.A. control).

    I believe that Justice Roberts' action is of the greatest value in the matter of enlightenment of public opinion in this country. I find the text of his Open Letter excellent and convincing and I am gladly willing to sign it.

    I shall be very glad indeed if you will give me the opportunity to talk with you about the whole problem, (I shall be back in Princeton by the middle of September) and I am gladly willing to help if you see any opportunity for me to do so.

            With kind regards,

            yours sincerely,

            Albert Einstein.

Albert Einstein wrote to Reves the day after reading his book and less than three weeks after the atomic bomb was dropped on Hiroshima.

and "wholeheartedly" agreed with Reves on "every essential point." At the close of his letter, Einstein suggested that he and Reves talk about "the whole problem" after his return from his summer residence in the Adirondacks in mid-September.

The two men later met in a series of meetings at Princeton. In addition to their general discussions of Reves' book, "Einstein was particularly worried about a statement issued by a group of prominent atomic scientists at the Oakridge atomic installation in Tennessee, recommending that a world security council be made the custodian of nuclear power in the world."[34] Believing that such an action would be "totally inadequate and naive," Einstein asked Reves to prepare a memorandum on the subject. In response to his colleagues, Einstein then stated:

> "The pathetic attempts made by governments to achieve what they consider to be international security has not the slightest effect on the present political conflicts due to the existence of competing sovereign nations. Neither governments nor people seem to have learned anything from the experiences of the past…The conditions existing in the world today force the individual states, out of fear for their own security, to commit acts which inevitably produce war…It is unthinkable that we can achieve peace without a genuine supranational organization to govern international relations."[35]

Einstein then recommended Reves' book to the other scientists, even offering to mail them copies.

In a subsequent note to Reves, Einstein authorized the publisher to reproduce a 'private letter', dated October 29th, on the jacket cover of forthcoming editions as a means by which to help promote book sales:

> I have read THE ANATOMY OF PEACE with the greatest admiration. Your book is, in my opinion, *the* answer to the present political problem of the world, so drastically precipitated by the release of atomic energy.
>
> It would be most desirable if every political and scientific leader in every country would take a little time to read this book. If this could be brought about, I feel it might avert the disaster of an atomic world war.
>
> Cordially,
> A. Einstein

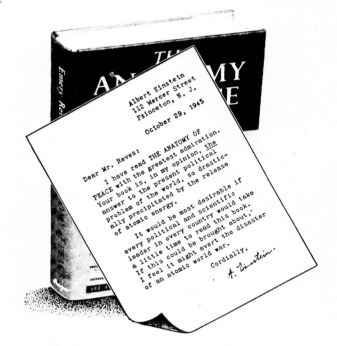

The book Albert Einstein calls <u>the</u> political answer to the atomic bomb

THE ANATOMY OF PEACE

By Emery Reves

At all bookstores   ☆   **$2.00**

HARPER

A second letter to Reves by Einstein was used with the author's permission to help promote sales of The Anatomy of Peace.

34 *Reves, Emery. "The Story of* The Anatomy of Peace", *DMA Collection, p. 3.*

35 *See* Einstein on Peace, *edited by Otto Nathan and Heinz Norden, (New York: Simon and Schuster, 1960), pp. 337-341.*

With Reves' permission, Harpers used Einstein's letter extensively as an advertising device, and book sales climbed at such a rate that the publisher was unable to keep pace with public demand, even after a fourth and fifth printing of 10,000 copies each.

So heightened now was interest in the book that beginning in its December 1945 issue, *Reader's Digest* printed an unprecedented three-issue condensation of *The Anatomy of Peace*, reaching an estimated fifty million readers, and predicting in an editorial comment that "it will be the most-discussed feature in recent years." Furthermore, the *Digest* editors arranged through its Program Service division to make the book available to more than 25,000 American clubs and discussion groups with three designated speakers at each meeting. When weekly sales began to indicate a 'runaway best seller,' two more editions were printed, of 10,000 and 20,000 copies, but still there were not enough copies to satisfy book orders. By March Reves' book had reached the top position in the best-seller lists in both *The New York Times* and *New York Herald Tribune*, where it remained for six months. No less a national spokesman than Walter Winchell wrote: "If you want to find out where you stand in this crisis and what wars are all about and why we have them and how we might avoid wars, then read a sensational new best-seller, *The Anatomy of Peace*, written in plain talk."

By this time public interest in the book was so great and its message so urgent that Harper's approached Pocket Books in March with a proposition to manufacture the book quickly, in quantity, and at such a low cost that it might be made available to *all* Americans. That evening Freeman Lewis, Vice President of Pocket Books, read the book so many were now discussing. The next day he announced, "This will either be the book of the century – or there may *be* no century," and authorized a printing of 100,000 copies in a new $1.00 edition to be mass-distributed at newsstands, in chain stores, and wherever books and magazines were sold throughout the nation.

At the same time Reves' book was being widely distributed, it was also being adopted as a textbook at Harvard, Yale, and Columbia, as well as the subject of sermons in churches of all denominations and the topic of lectures in countless civic organizations. Nor was the phenomenal swell of interest in *The Anatomy*

When Pocket Books, Inc. published a reprint of the Harper book in a massive and inexpensive edition, Reves' political treatise became a "runaway best seller."

of Peace confined only to its United States appearance. In the next several years it was published in 25 languages in more than 30 different editions in all west European countries, Canada, Scandanavia, the Balkans, several South American countries, India and China; it was also translated and printed in Arabic, Afrikaans, Urdu, Esperanto, and in Braille.

"This is a book for the young," editorialized the author of an article in *Penguins Progress*, announcing the joint publication of Reves' book in England by George Allen and Unwin and Penguin Books Ltd. "It is their world which is at stake, their world which will be saved or damned by what Governments and peoples are doing – or failing to do – now, to save the peace of the future. It may therefore be appropriate to print here 'An Appeal to the Students of England' which has been received from an American students' organization, Student Federalists Inc., of 299 Madison Avenue, New York City. It reads:

'We, Student Federalists, representing groups of students in 60 American universities and colleges, among them Yale, Smith, Vassar, Wellesley, Chicago, and Stanford, urge you, students of England, to read, study, and discuss Emery Reves' book *The Anatomy of Peace*.

'Most of us were soldiers in the last war and have just been demobilised. We are young enough to be soldiers of the next war. We feel certain you will agree with us that we must do everything in our power to prevent another world war, which this time with the atomic bomb may destroy our whole civilization.

'We have been studying this problem very carefully and have come to the conclusion that no treaty, no alliance, no league such as the United Nations, can protect us from another catastrophe. Only law can bring peace, only a world-wide federal government can bring world peace.

'We know of no book which deals with more clarity and conviction with the need for a world-wide legal order than *The Anatomy of Peace*. That is why we ask you to read it and to urge your friends to do so.'"[36]

* * *

In 1945 Emery Reves was by almost any standard enormously successful. He had also been exceptionally fortunate. Though only 41 years of age, he had survived two world wars and three times he had escaped almost certain capture by the Germans and possible death. He had helped to create a revolutionary form of journalism, established several lucrative businesses, met most of the leading statesmen of the World War II era, and had now authored two influential books, the most recent one eventually selling a staggering 800,000 copies.

Still a bachelor, he lived at the Plaza Hotel and officed nearby at Rockefeller Center. In the wake of his publishing success, he soon met the woman he would one day marry, Wendy Russell, at that time one of New York's most sought-after fashion models.

Eventually selling almost a million copies, The Anatomy of Peace *was adopted as a textbook at more than 60 American universities after first being reprinted in its entirety in* Readers' Digest, *reaching an estimated audience of fifty million people.*

36 Penguins Progress, (Middlesex, England; New York, U.S.A.: Penguin Books, Christmas 1946), p. 43.

Wendy Russell
From Marshall to Manhattan

To become one of Manhattan's premier fashion models, Wendy Russell had traveled far from her native roots and humble background. Born Wyn-Nelle Russell[1] in Marshall, Texas in 1916, she was the only child of Blanche Korean Murphy and David L. Russell. The couple was living at the time in nearby Hallsville where he owned and operated a barber shop, and she offered music lessons in order to supplement the family's income.

Dave Russell was an extravagant man. His uncommonly elegant dress attracted considerable attention in rural east Texas, especially among women who were drawn to him because of his colorful personality and charming wit. Though not particularly handsome, being slight of build and balding, he nevertheless presented a striking figure, dressed in handmade suits, expensive shirts and shoes, and always wearing a Stetson hat and sporting a diamond stickpin in his silk tie. His flamboyant dress was matched by an aggressive self-confidence and a debonair manner which belied his restless nature and earnest ambition to better himself. As owner of the barber shop, he supervised the business, personally cutting the hair of only a few preferred clients, while serving as raconteur in the town's liveliest gathering place. Because times were lean and his tastes expensive, Dave Russell was unable to save any money, or to provide adequately for a young wife and daughter.

At the time of Wendy's birth, Blanche Russell was both young and beautiful. She was also quite vulnerable. Her life had been a hard one, with her own mother dying when she was only six. Blanche had

Wyn-Nelle Russell at age 3.

Photograph, courtesy of Mrs. Alma Millstead

been raised by her aunt and uncle, Vesta and Elmo Murphy of Marshall, and it was Vesta who also helped raise Wendy and became such a dominant influence on the child during her impressionable youth.

In 1921 Dave Russell sold his barber shop and moved the family to Marshall where he opened a tailor and drycleaning business. Again, he offered personal service to certain clients, whose wardrobes he selected to show off the latest styles in men's fashion. Despite

1 *The actor Franchot Tone suggested that Wyn-Nelle change her name to Wendy after first meeting the model in New York during the early 1940s.*

being self-employed and apparently successful as a businessman, he squandered his money and the family continued to struggle. As a result of the financial strain on their relationship, he and Blanche first separated, and finally divorced when Wendy was six years old.

Wendy and her mother moved in with the Murphys who lived just outside Marshall. At the time Elmo Murphy and sometimes Vesta worked at the Perkins Dry Good Store in Marshall. Elmo was a small man, neither ambitious nor overly successful, who, after losing his job as clerk in the store, took up selling insurance. Although Blanche had been raised as an orphan in his house, Elmo resented her and it was due to Vesta's kind determination and not to any familial affection on Elmo's part that Blanche had managed to survive her own desolate childhood experience. Now, Elmo once again felt saddled with Blanche, who had a child of her own but no husband and no income. Elmo made certain that the mother and daughter earned their keep. Blanche was expected to help cook, and the young girl was given responsibility for most of the chores previously performed by Elmo: feeding the chickens, making buttermilk and gathering vegetables.

To support herself, Blanche secured a job in 1921 as an instructor in Piano Harmony at the College of Marshall from which she had graduated several years before. Professor Alfred H. Strick, the head of the music department, used his talented assistant as an accompanist for students taking voice lessons, but he also encouraged her to pursue a career in music. Soon Blanche found herself playing both organ and piano in regional concert programs and even singing occasional operettas in Austin. Because of her work load and the travel her job often demanded, Blanche was frequently required to be away from home, so Wendy spent much of her time with Nannie, whom she later credited for providing the strength and affection her mother and she herself needed during those difficult early years. Despite Nannie's affectionate care, it must have been a lonely experience for an only child, who with no toys of her own played with broken glass and stones under the large oak tree in front of the Murphy house. Much later, Wendy would recall sitting for hours on the front porch swing, shelling black-eyed peas, or churning butter and singing hymns.

Like many rural families, their lives revolved around the Baptist church, which they attended for weekly prayer meetings and service on Sundays. Wendy met other children through Sunday school and church picnics, and Blanche sang in the choir and helped organize the church music program. In a rural town, it was only natural that the church should serve as such a dominant focal point in their lives. Religion played an important role in their lives, but like the divided and segregated community in which they lived, it sometimes manifested itself in aberrant ways.

Racial violence erupted on a national scale in the 1920s, and the resurgence of the Ku Klux Klan was particularly active and virulent in Texas. Many of the same pious citizens who espoused Christian principles in church on Sundays were also engaged as self-appointed vigilantes with the Klan, an organization that had little to do with community protection but stemmed, instead, from barely concealed racism and spurious political ambition. The Murphy's home was located far enough outside Marshall to be fairly isolated, and an abandoned farm across the road offered the kind of secluded arena ideally suited for the Klan's nocturnal activities.

As a young child Wendy watched in fascinated horror from an upstairs window while Klan members gathered for their meetings, sometimes as often as once a week. Although the men arrived as individuals or in small groups, they became an awesome sight as anonymous, white-sheeted figures, wearing triangular masks and red crosses stained on their shapeless gowns and peaked miters. The swelling mass became even more sinister when wooden crosses were put to the torch and the mob rallied to march on yet another victim. The next day would reveal the victim's identity, but Wendy, like so many other innocent bystanders, rarely knew or recognized the daytime citizens responsible for wreaking the previous night's vengeance.

Not all of the local Klan's activity was confined to the remote property outside of Marshall. Wendy once witnessed two Negroes burned alive on the courthouse square in nearby Greenville, and such experiences made her all the more appreciative of the human values taught to her by Nannie. Her reputation for kindness attracted Negroes in search of a job to work on the Murphy homestead, even though the pay was little more than the food they received and the opportunity to live sheltered in the safety of one of the outbuildings on the property. These included Old Willy, a gardener, and young Cammie, who actually served as a governess for Wendy.

A more common, but no less shocking sign of the Klan's activity was the number of victims tarred and feathered for a variety of supposed misdeeds and crimes. Mr. Daniels, a close friend of the Murphy family and the manager of the Perkins Dry Goods Store, suffered just such treatment at the hands of the Klan. Though happily married, Daniels was much admired by his female employees because of his kindness. Whether due to his gentlemanly behavior, which the employees' husbands apparently resented, or to his

Blanche Russell as a piano instructor at the College of Marshall in 1923 and as pictured in the yearbook.

Photograph, courtesy of East Texas Baptist University Library

32

northern background which they distrusted, Daniels was seized one night and taken to the town baseball field to be tarred and feathered. Afterwards, he was returned to the courthouse square and abandoned. Because she was someone he could trust, he called Vesta Murphy for help, and Blanche and another relative drove into town and brought Daniels back to the Murphy home. The man's body was a pitiful sight, his clothes burned away and his skin scalded from the hot tar. Although the odor of chicken feathers and creosote made her nauseous, Wendy watched in silent admiration as Nannie and Blanche gently swabbed his wounds and restored Daniels' health, if not his pride, over the next two days. Though saddened by his departure, no one in the family was surprised when Daniels decided not to return to his job and left by train, instead, to return to the North.

Undoubtedly, Wendy's most frightening experience with the Klan occurred one night before her parents had divorced. From the porch where she and Blanche often slept together, she awakened to the sound of murmuring voices and discovered a group of sheeted men approaching the house through the garden in back. Terrified, the young girl woke her mother, who reacted calmly and told Wendy that she knew the Klan would one day come to punish her husband. When roused, Dave Russell begged his wife to plead with the men on his behalf. Returning to the back stoop and holding Wendy by the hand, she confronted the hostile group and stated that she and her daughter had no part in whatever wrongdoings her husband had committed. In a quiet but firm voice, she asked them to go, and slowly, and without a word spoken, the men left. It was the only time the Klan ever dared to invade Blanche's home, and it signalled the beginning of a final break in her marital relationship with Russell.

Although life at that time was not easy for Blanche and Baby-Nelle, as Wendy was sometimes called, neither was it altogether unhappy. Nannie maintained a cheerful household, baking Christmas fruitcakes in June and preparing the summer garden in late winter. From Nannie, Wendy learned to love gardening, especially flowers, and baking. She later recalled how Nannie flavored fruitcakes by adding a jigger of whiskey and an apple slice and then stored them under the staircase to let them age until December.

In this devout Christian household, and one dominated by women, Christmas was especially meaningful.

Nannie, as the family matriarch, organized the cooking and decoration. A Christmas tree, as tall as the parlor ceiling, was cut and trimmed with old-fashioned ornaments and candles. Because these were hard-scrabble times and there was rarely any money for individual gifts, the family thought of the tree itself as a gift, and inexpensive gestures of affection were stuffed inside stockings. On Christmas morning Wendy could expect to find precious supplies of raisins, almonds and walnuts, an apple and an orange. One year she discovered at the bottom of her stocking a tiny doll no larger than her finger. Her most memorable gift as a child, however, was presented to her by her Aunt Mabel, who, after learning that Blanche intended to give Wendy a doll for Christmas, spent weeks sewing an entire wardrobe of doll outfits – everything from bonnets and muffs to dresses and boots. Wendy never forgot the excitement of receiving such a gift or Aunt Mabel's kindness in making her feel so special.

These were but some of the family traditions and memories absorbed by the attentive, only child, who came to value her simple upbringing and distinctive cultural roots. One of Wendy's earliest childhood recollections was sitting at the kitchen table watching Nannie draw plans for a house she hoped to build some day. Vesta Murphy did build her house several years later, but the memory became even more significant when decades later Wendy realized a similar dream of her own.

Although she and her mother had little money or security at the time, Wendy was to remember much later, "We lived the most beautiful life in the most poor way you can imagine."[2] A similar observation was later expressed by one of Wyn-Nelle's teachers[3], who recalled:

> I never knew she was so poor. I suppose they were cheap, simple dresses that she wore to school, but the child had such elegance – oh, a flower in her hair, perhaps that she would seem stylishly dressed. Those were the depths of the Depression, and she and her family were deeper than most in a condition that everyone shared to some degree.[4]

After her divorce, Blanche was unable to earn enough money teaching music to support herself and Wendy, and she could not possibly consider, under the circumstances, the professional music career seriously recommended to her by Professor Strick. From a relative, she learned of an oil boom then underway in Louisiana, and thinking that job opportunities might be more plentiful there, she and Wendy moved to Haynesville in 1930. It was, of course, an unsettling experience for her teenage daughter, who was reluctant to leave church and school friends in Marshall and the warm home environment nurtured by Vesta Murphy.

2 *Interview with Wendy Russell Reves by author, 1985.*
3 *Mrs. Inez Hatley Hughes, Marshall, Texas.*
4 *Cramer, Rodger,* Marshall News Messenger, *March 31, 1985, p. 1C.*

Like Marshall, Haynesville was a small town. Oil money and several influential families dominated the local economy, but, as was the case almost everywhere in the early 1930s, the great depression was beginning to harden and the town was confronted with little foreseeable relief. After first renting a single room and kitchen in a small private home, Blanche began looking for work. Contrary to her expectations, she was not able to find a job teaching music, or enough students whose families could afford private lessons. Eventually, she did manage to get a job teaching kindergarten, but still, the income was such that there was often little to eat. Not uncommonly, Blanche was able to provide Wendy with only a 5¢ can of pork and beans, one-half for lunch and the balance for dinner. Despite such hardships, though, the mother's determination never wavered and, at least in her daughter's presence, Blanche remained hopeful, repeatedly reassuring Wendy that one day they would be comfortable and their future secure. The words of encouragement later proved to be more prophetic than either of them could possibly have imagined.

Wendy's adolescence in Haynesville was made all the more challenging when as a teenager from a single-parent family, she enrolled in a new school in a different town. Despite the awkward circumstances, though, she quickly succeeded in making friends and winning the respect of both her classmates and teachers. She may have worn cardboard in the soles of her shoes, but she had an ingratiating personality and she knew how to enhance her appearance with small touches and inexpensive accessories. Wendy was also an outstanding student, earning high marks in all of her subjects, and proficient enough in English, history, and algebra to represent the school in a statewide competition held in Baton Rouge where she won a silver medal in the algebra contest.

Not long after moving to Haynesville, Blanche decided to open a boarding house. She managed to lease a large, furnished house and rented the eight bedrooms to men working in the surrounding oil fields. Despite the occasional turnover, it was a happy household with the young, unmarried tenants treating Blanche like their mother and Wendy as a little sister. The house was always full and there was a waiting list of men eager to rent a clean, comfortable room in a home where the meals and company exceeded what was otherwise available during the lean depression years. Blanche and Wendy had come to Louisiana seeking a new start, and they succeeded in becoming an important part of the community. Though by no means prosperous, they were happily settled and their future appeared stable. The established pattern of life was soon disrupted, however, when Dave Russell reappeared.

He had learned of their whereabouts from the Murphys, and having himself started a new life and career as a used-car salesman in San Antonio, he was anxious to remarry Blanche and to move the family back to Texas. Perhaps the illusion of security and feeling the relationship could be mended led Blanche to accept his offer. Unfortunately, it soon became evident that he had not changed during the intervening years, and he and Blanche suffered from the same incompatibility which had resulted in their divorce almost ten years before.

Once again, Wendy found herself displaced in another new town, attending classes in yet another school. Though only sixteen, she was quite mature and appeared older than her age, circumstances which soon led to her becoming a model. Even then she was a born collector who enjoyed window-shopping and browsing through pawn shops where she spent her lunch money on inexpensive rings, a string of imitation pearls or a colorful scarf. One day she was asked by a store owner if she would be interested in modeling. Mr. Roache, an Englishman, operated the Canadian Fox Fur Company in San Antonio, and he intuitively found in Wendy someone he thought possessed the traits of a born model: classic facial features, trim physique and a natural grace. After seeing her wear several outfits, he immediately offered her a job as a model. When Wendy replied that she was still in high school, Roache suggested that she could work after school hours and on Saturdays, and that she should discuss his offer with her parents. Blanche, whose opinion Wendy trusted, encouraged her to accept the job offer and to try her hand at becoming a model.

The girl already carried herself with a certain natural style, but she learned the fundamentals of modeling from Roache: how to walk and turn dramatically so as to catch the viewer's eye, and, most importantly, how to emphasize through gesture and body movement the article for sale – dress, jewelry, shoes. Wendy admired Roache and sought his advice concerning a career, but her promising beginning as a model (one of her first clients was Joske Brothers) was curtailed within the year.

Shortly after she began working, she met a recent West Point graduate enrolled in flying school at nearby Randolph Field. Although Lieutenant Al Schroeder was engaged to a San Antonio girl at the time, he cancelled his wedding plans three days after meeting Wendy, and courted the young model instead. He proposed soon thereafter, and Blanche Russell, who had suffered herself from an impetuous marriage at an early age, was

Wyn-Nelle began modeling in San Antonio at the age of 16.

shattered by her daughter's request to marry the lieutenant. Wendy was barely sixteen years of age. Since Schroeder was soon to be reassigned to duty in Hawaii, Blanche persuaded Wendy to accept a compromise; if on her next birthday she still wished to marry Al Schroeder, then the mother would consent and she could join him in Honolulu.

The prospect of marriage represented an opportunity to escape from San Antonio, which Wendy did not like, and the unhappiness she felt as a result of her parents' incompatibility. As a young adult, she was increasingly curious about a world beyond rural east Texas, the Louisiana oil fields, and San Antonio. On her seventeenth birthday, Wendy Russell sailed to Hawaii where she and Lt. Al Schroeder were married in a military wedding at Wheeler Field.

Despite the birth of a son one year later, the relationship was not a happy one. Living on an army base seemed exciting to Wendy at first, but the novelty quickly disappeared when she discovered that most of the women on the post were twenty years her senior, and there was hardly anything for wives to do except attend a seemingly endless series of cocktail parties. The same people were always present, and there was little new or interesting to discuss. Being an officer's wife meant Wendy was also expected to host affairs for as many as sixty to eighty people, a laborious challenge for anyone, but especially to an eighteen-year-old bride who had recently become a mother. She managed the role with typical flair, but she found life on the base stifling and the marriage itself lasted only a few years. When her husband was ordered to report to Washington, D.C., the family moved back to the mainland and Wendy resumed her modeling career, posing for real estate and clothing ads. At that time her marriage finally collapsed and she and Al Schroeder were divorced. Wendy assumed her maiden name and returned to Texas.

In San Antonio she again worked for Roache, but only briefly. Despite her unhappy relationship with Schroeder, the several years away from Texas had made her all the more eager to see new places and to broaden her experience. Blanche Russell was understandably disappointed by her daughter's divorce, but she was wise enough to encourage Wendy to pursue her modeling aspirations, even suggesting that she consider moving to New York where more lucrative opportunities existed. Wendy agreed with her mother's logic, that if she wished to become a top model then she must first establish herself in New York. Anticipating how difficult such a transition might be, she reluctantly consented for her son to live with his paternal grandparents until she could support him in New York.

Like other American women of the thirties who daydreamed about movies and read a wide assortment of magazines, Wendy was familiar with the decade's prevailing fashions and the agency models who wore them. When at last she left for New York in 1939, she was determined to model for the influential John Robert Powers Agency, a career dream not unlike that of many others, but one which very few achieved. After first finding an apartment to rent for $10 a week, she called on the Powers Agency, hoping to receive an interview appointment. She waited for several days, seated among dozens of attractive and no less hopeful women also seeking to be hired as a Powers model. At six o'clock in the evening on the third day, she noticed that everyone, including the receptionist and secretaries, had left for the day and that only Mr. Powers was still in the building. The light was on in his office, and she could hear him answering the telephone. On impulse she entered his office, introduced herself as

After moving to New York, Wendy Russell became a top fashion model with the Powers Agency in the 1940s.

Wyn-Nelle Russell and asked whether Powers thought she could model for him. She later learned that he found it difficult to say "no" to anyone, but that he admired her audacity and persistence. At the time, however, he was very candid in his appraisal of her as a potential model. He did not think she suited the style of a Powers model; she was attractive, of course, but a model, or at least a Powers model, possessed a different kind of beauty. He then asked if he could assist her in any other way, even offering to help pay for her return trip to Texas if she was without funds. She thanked him for his honesty, the time he had spent with her and his offer of concern, but she believed she could find employment as a model elsewhere and she hoped one day to return to him for another interview.

The next day Wendy went to the wholesale district on Seventh Avenue and applied as a model in numerous showrooms. Getting a job took some time, however, since she had no connections in New York and only her work for Roache in San Antonio and a brief modeling experience in Washington to recommend her. Finally, she was hired for $30 a week as one of four models in a wholesaler's showroom. After she began working, she would rush over to Fifth Avenue during her lunch break to study the mannequins on display and try to analyze the image projected by quality fashion houses. She also studied the women who were window-shopping, but who were wearing, unlike herself, the expensive clothes so prominently featured in the store fronts. It did not take long for Wendy to appreciate what John Robert Powers had meant when he observed that she did not yet fit the mold of a top fashion model. She already knew, of course, that her inexpensive clothes were inappropriate for the role she sought, but she also came to recognize that she wore far too much make-up and that her platinum hair was no longer fashionable for a New York runway model. Her appearance was altogether too brash, her peroxide hair too bright, and her present image lacking in refinement.

The model from Texas learned quickly, though, and in less than eight months she succeeded in completely changing her image to that of a Fifth Avenue model. When at last she was satisfied with her new hair color, her skillful application and restrained use of make-up, and she had acquired a chic new outfit, Wendy returned to the Powers office as she had promised the famous agent she would. She did not reveal, however, that she had been interviewed before and

rejected. When Powers entered the lobby, he immediately noticed her among the other candidates, and invited her into his office to ask whether she had any modeling experience. Without describing in detail her Texas background or more recent work in the Seventh Avenue wholesale district, she responded simply that she was experienced and believed herself to be a capable model. "Good," Powers exclaimed, "then you will become my great runway model!"[5]

And so she did, with Powers perfecting the techniques she had first learned from Roache years before in San Antonio. While working in the garment district, Wendy had been lucky to make $30 to $50 a week, $15 of which she sent to her mother, the rest going to rent, food and what little clothes she could afford. After she was hired by the Powers Agency, her income increased almost tenfold, and Wendy was able to move Blanche to New York to live with her in a midtown apartment and later in a house on Long Island. No longer did she have to scrutinize her every expense, but a penniless childhood and the depression years had sharpened her attitude about money, and she wisely saved far more than she spent. Furthermore, she began to develop an interest in business, and learned from others how best to invest her money. Nevertheless, it was the prestige of being a Powers model which first launched her successful modeling career and made her other business ventures possible.

This picture was used in an advertising campaign promoting cosmetics.

5 *Interview with Wendy Russell Reves by author, 1985.*

Wendy Russell did more than simply become one of Manhattan's best known models; she is also credited with having influenced the profession, since her modeling technique represented a fresh approach.[6] Unlike most New York runway models, she was vivacious and her gaiety, as captured in still photographs, quickly promoted her popularity, among not only the clients who employed her, but also the photographers with whom she worked and the customers who purchased the merchandise she modeled with such effortless charm. During her trips down the runway or while posing for magazine ads, Wendy's face was invariably photographed wearing a radiant smile, and she was more likely to skip down the aisle than to present herself in a series of artificial poses. In effect, she embraced her audience rather than posing for it, always smiling and appearing excited about what she was doing and wearing. It was an innovative style and one which other models soon copied, establishing a trend. Wendy Russell relished her job, and her spirited enthusiasm was infectious, especially among buyers.

Her rapid ascent as a model did not go unnoticed by the press, either. She became a favorite target of the paparazzi, and pictures of her were printed on a regular basis in fashionable rotogravure sections. Wendy's name also began appearing in columns written by Dorothy Kilgallen, Cholly Knickerbocker, and even Walter Winchell, whose suggestive copy linked the effervescent model with such celebrities as Burgess Meredith, Pat de Cicco, and Nino Martini.[7] Despite the carefree image of her projected by the press, though, Wendy thought of herself as a serious, career-minded professional, and the success she achieved as a model intensified, rather than lessened her ambitious plans for the future.

When she realized that photographers and advertising agencies rarely provided the appropriate type and number of accessories needed to complete a particular image, Wendy started a business which filled a shortcoming in the fashion industry.[8] She hit upon the idea while posing for a fur ad. The photographer had no accessories for her to wear, so she volunteered some of her own. The ad was such a success and the props were so well received that the next time she was asked to furnish similar accessories, she charged a $15 supplier's fee. Her own personal wardrobe was extensive and eclectic, and word soon got out among photographers in need of additional props, and she began receiving requests ranging from shoes to fans, lounging garments to lorgnettes to walking canes. As a result,

Wendy introduced Wardrobe Service, a fashion rental business, with models, photographers, and ad agencies as her clients. She also began designing many of her own clothes and was able to charge an even higher rental fee on the basis of originality.

The business was a financial success, mostly because of Wendy's personal involvement in all aspects of its operation. She did everything from choosing and stocking the inventory to making deliveries in a small company car. Because they were not readily available, furs were her most popular as well as profitable rental item, and she was able to charge a $25-a-day fee. She and Blanche maintained some of the inventory, such as shoes, but most of the garments were sent out for cleaning and pressing afterwards, an expensive but necessary overhead cost. Wendy reinvested the profits in additional stock, and she wisely kept her modeling and fashion rental incomes separate. This practice enabled her to diversify her earnings, and would later pay future dividends in terms of financial security once her modeling career had ended.

Meanwhile, she was very much in the public eye. Fashion shows, such as those in the Oval Room at the Ritz-Carlton Hotel, brought her into contact with a growing circle of influential clients and customers. In 1940, Wendy met and married Paul Baron, one of New York's most popular orchestra leaders and the staff conductor for Columbia Broadcasting Company. He

Courtesy of Mrs. Raymond Ford

Pageant June, 1947

37

Wendy started Wardrobe Service, a fashion rental business, after discovering that photographers rarely provided accessories needed to complete a particular image.

This photograph of Wendy wearing a WAC uniform was chosen for the cover of The American Magazine, *a wartime publication.*

6 Lowry, Cynthia. Associated Press, "Modeling Is Specialized," 1942; quoted in Marshall News Messenger, March 31, 1985.

7 Lowry, "Modeling Is Specialized."

8 "Want To Rent A Wardrobe?", Pageant magazine (New York, June, 1947), pp. 75-81.

was charming and intelligent and a gifted pianist. In addition to conducting the Chesterfield Radio Show featuring Perry Como, Baron also performed with the popular program, "Luncheon at the Waldorf" with Ilka Chase.

The relationship with Baron carried Wendy into yet another sphere, that of big bands and hotel ballrooms, late nights and daytime radio shows. It was a new and altogether different world for the hardworking model, and she met many of the leading celebrities of the wartime era while attempting to juggle her career so as to accomodate her husband's professional schedule. Such a life was exhilarating but it was also exhausting, and she soon grew weary of the nighttime demands on her as the wife of an orchestra leader. The marriage lasted several years but came to an end when she and Baron were unable to synchronize their incompatible careers.

In 1945, shortly after the war in Europe ended, Wendy finally met a man whose strong personality matched hers and who succeeded in doing what no other man had accomplished – winning not only her respect and admiration but also her love. The relationship with Emery Reves, however, required several years to evolve.

The circumstances under which they first met were initially unpromising. While staying as a houseguest at the Hearst estate in New York, Wendy had agreed to a friend's persistent request to meet an acquaintance for cocktails. She was not looking forward to her appointment with a Brazilian businessman at the Plaza Hotel, but the coincidental presence of another man that evening eventually altered the course of her life. Emery Reves happened to stop by to discuss a business matter with the man and was introduced to her as the author of *The Anatomy of Peace*. Reves needed no explanation when she was introduced to him, since he recognized Wendy Russell from the many magazine covers and ads in which she had appeared for Macy's, Russeks, and I. J. Fox. Although she was flattered by the admiration he expressed for her work, she left shortly afterwards, explaining that she had an important modeling assignment scheduled early the next morning.

Two days later, while walking down Fifth Avenue with Blanche, Wendy encountered Reves again. She thought the older man might make a good companion for her mother, and when he called the following morning to invite her to dinner, Wendy suggested that he come by their apartment for a cocktail, instead, and

then he and Blanche could go out for dinner. "I am not interested in your mother," he said, "but in you."[9] Wendy declined the invitation and ended the conversation.

Wendy Russell and Emery Reves did not see one another again for more than two years. During the interval, she remained busy operating her fashion rental business, and her career as a model developed in a new direction when she was featured in a nightclub act, designed by Lester Gaba and produced by Eleanor Lambert. Reves, in the meantime, was also busy, pursuing publishing agreements on both sides of the Atlantic, working to secure the foreign language rights to Winston Churchill's *Memoirs*, and helping to promote a new organization, The Movement for World Federation Government, whose philosophical goals he had previously summarized in *The Anatomy of Peace*. A political economist by academic training, he was also investing in Europe's postwar recovery, buying substantial blocks of "penny stocks" in companies whose value would appreciate, he was certain, because of their overall importance to Germany's future.

When Wendy and Emery next saw one another, it was quite by accident. She had gone to the Pavillion Restaurant with two Hollywood producers and was surprised to discover her friend, Leonora Corbett,[10] having dinner with Reves. She later learned they had been discussing – ironically enough – the subject of marriage when she entered the room, prompting Leonora Corbett to remark, "Now there, Emery, is the girl for you."[11] He agreed with her, but recalled his unsatisfactory telephone conversation with Miss Russell two years earlier. Corbett, a prominent actress, was not one to accept "no" for an answer, and the next day she called Wendy and insisted that she come to her apartment at the Waldorf Tower for a small party. Wendy was unaware, of course, that Reves would also be present.

The dinner party was intimate and enjoyable, and Wendy's first real opportunity to get to know the seemingly shy Reves. To her surprise, he dominated the conversation that evening, leading the group in its discussion of a broad range of topics. He was intelligent and his opinions were obviously well informed. She found his wry sense of humor to be delightful. She listened attentively to his observations about world government, the postwar economy, and trends in art and current Broadway productions. Contrary to her expectations, Reves possessed a strong personality, and his way of speaking, though quiet, was forceful and authoritative. She knew nothing at that time about his Hungarian background, nor of his tragic wartime experiences, but she was attracted to his keen mind and

9 *Interview with Wendy Russell Reves by author, 1985.*
10 *At the time, Leonora Corbett was appearing in a Broadway production of* Blithe Spirit.
11 *Interview with Wendy Russell Reves by author, 1985.*

old-world European charm. Here was a man whose experiences far exceeded her own and whose knowledge of international affairs could teach her a great deal about life beyond the world of fashion. When Emery Reves escorted her home that evening, she accepted his invitation for dinner the following night.

Why, Wendy thought to herself, should she spend her time dating movie stars and agents when she could be in the company of someone so sophisticated and well educated. She had never before had time for school, but from Emery Reves she could learn almost anything, and at that point in her life, Wendy Russell's desire for enrichment was equal to her professional ambition.

She knew little about him except that he had written a book several years before. Thinking he was perhaps a professor with a small income, she suggested they go to dinner at Mario's, a popular but inexpensive restaurant. He did not like Mario's, he said, and wanted to go to El Borraccio, one of New York's more fashionable and costly restaurants. Much to her surprise, Reves knew the maitre d'hotel who seated them at one of the best tables, and she admired the skill with which he ordered the entire meal, including a selection of European wines.

Intent on learning as much as possible from Reves, Wendy initiated the dinner conversation by asking him to explain in understandable terms how the stock market functioned. She listened in quiet fascination as he described the principle of supply and demand and how it governed the market's activity. He talked about investors and how they increased their profits through business expansion and by diversifying their investments; how private individuals as well as governments influenced national politics and international economies through transactions on Wall Street. Reves never once mentioned his own investments, but it was apparent to Wendy that he was active in the field. His explanations were so lucid and his presentation so logical that she found the subject enthralling, and the dinner passed quickly. When they returned to her apartment, Reves asked if he might call her Wendy, instead of Miss Russell, and would she be interested in seeing him again. But of course, she replied.

That evening had been a marvelous beginning, but the relationship was soon interrupted by one of Reves' frequent business trips to Europe. Afterwards, whenever Emery was in New York, she would cancel whatever plans she had previously made. "The whole

universe was opening before me,"[12] she would later explain, and the chance to visit museums, attend concerts, or simply to have dinner was a precious opportunity to which she looked forward. Although she did not regard him as a father figure, she nevertheless felt somewhat childlike in Emery's presence since his experiences were so worldly by comparison with her provincial background. She absorbed all that he taught her, and he, in turn, enjoyed having such a charming companion with whom to share his interests. In many ways, their early relationship resembled the Pygmalion myth as each contributed to the other's personality.

Despite their cultural differences, they became kindred spirits. He loved music and shared with her his passion for classical music through Chopin, Bach and Beethoven. As a natural-born collector, she introduced him to the excitement of searching for antiques and decorative arts in little known boutiques she had discovered. At the time, he was staying at the Plaza Hotel, essentially living out of a suitcase, and the only luxuries he then collected were paintings he stored in his hotel closet.

At dinner one evening Emery announced unexpectedly that he was leaving New York for several months. He had business to look after, mainly in London, but also in Paris and Madrid. A secretive man by nature, he had told her little about his business activities, and nothing at all yet of his family background, but his plans to be away from New York for an indefinite period had an unsettling influence on her.

While he was away, Wendy was approached by Germaine LeConte concerning a possible modeling assignment. As part of the publicity campaign, the famous courturier wanted to use American models wearing French-designed fashions made from United States materials, in this case Haffner Fabrics. All of the photography was to be shot on location in Paris, the undisputed capital of haute couture. Since Wendy had never before been to Europe, she accepted the glamorous job offer. Prior to her departure, though, Emery

In addition to modeling and running her own business, Wendy also served as a styling advisor to several clothing manufacturers.

12 *Interview with Wendy Russell Reves by author, 1985.*

returned to New York, and when he learned of her forthcoming assignment overseas, he volunteered to meet her in England and to act as her personal tour guide. The *Queen Mary* docked at Southampton several weeks later, and Emery was there to greet Wendy, as he had promised, with a car and chauffeur. They had dinner at Claridge's that night, and spent the next week sightseeing London and the surrounding countryside. He escorted her to concerts and plays, and they toured a number of museums as well as historic sites. It was 1949, and Wendy Russell and Emery Reves were rarely apart ever again.

After the London visit, they left together in a new Jaguar convertible which Emery purchased for Wendy's first trip to France. He never spoke about his wealth, but such an extravagant gesture dispelled forever Wendy's initial misconception of him as a poor academician.

In elegance they drove through corridors of plane trees leading from Calais to Paris. The capital, itself, was still recovering from the effects of the war, so the sight of Reves arriving in Paris with a beautiful American model in such a luxurious car, must have made quite an impression on women still wearing wooden-soled shoes and working on reconstruction projects. The couple checked into the Royal Monceau Hotel where he had made arrangements for them to stay.

Despite Paris' legendary beauty, Wendy was unable to see much of it at first because of the heavy demands of her job on her time and energy. The hectic schedule included a press conference, followed by individual interviews and publicity stunts, time-consuming dress fittings, and the actual photography sessions themselves. She and Emery had dinner each night, but normally in the hotel, since she was expected to model again early the next morning. Only later when her work schedule became more relaxed did she begin to venture forth with Reves as her guide to sample the fabulous array of cultural opportunities Paris had to offer.

Once more, a new world of opportunities opened to her. His savoir faire and European acquaintances introduced her to a different life a and circle of friends unknown to her before. Wendy, in turn, became a participant in the trendy world of French fashion and a

In 1949 Wendy Russell went to Paris on a modeling assignment. She is pictured here with Maurice Chevalier.

celebrated guest in her own right. The combination of her professional and entertainment contacts and Reves' business interests and political acquaintances permitted her to experience Paris as few others could.

As a chic American model in Paris, Wendy became a favorite with the French press, who managed to link her romantically with a Russian prince, a French count and a Greek businessman. She was approached by artists who wished to paint her portrait. Advertising campaigns with Maurice Chevalier, among others, further increased her visibility in Paris and resulted in additional job offers. Despite Wendy's growing popularity, Reves never showed the least insecurity, and seemed content with her company when she was not otherwise engaged.

Emery Reves acted as Wendy's tour guide on her first trip to Europe.

After a while, she learned more about his business activities. She was impressed with his publishing office at 33 Champs-Elysées and was surprised to learn that he also maintained an office in London as well as the one at Rockefeller Center. She was even more surprised to discover that he rented an empty warehouse loft in which he stored a dozen paintings – a strange practice in itself, it seemed to her, but one made all the more remarkable when she recognized the artists whose works he was hoarding: Renoir, Manet, Gauguin, Pissarro, Degas and Sisley. When asked for his reasons, Emery explained by telling Wendy for the first time something of his background, how he had twice fled from the Nazis, first in Berlin in 1930 and a decade later in Paris. As a result, he had lost all of his possessions, either confiscated or destroyed, including a prized group of German Expressionist paintings and a rare collection of Louis XIV furniture. He had immigrated

to the United States in 1941 after his London flat had been bombed. Having lost great works before, he preferred to live in hotels, and the paintings which she admired were the only objects he valued. He hid them in such a manner, he said, not only for private viewing but also for safe-keeping. Wendy was moved by the account of events which had shaped Reves' life, but she remained puzzled by his behavior. The hidden paintings were a revealing insight into his personality, and Emery Reves was even more mysterious than she had imagined.

Nevertheless, she had grown ever more fond of his company, and after her Paris modeling assignments were completed, she and Emery began to travel extensively. They went first to Italy where she marveled at the art in Florence, the unique beauty of Venice, and the powerful ruins of both ancient and Fascist Rome. Wendy continued to return to New York once or twice a year to model and to visit Blanche, but her life soon established a pattern in which she and Reves alternated holiday excursions with his prolonged business stays in

London, Paris and Geneva, for the most part, but with occasional month-long visits to Berlin, Madrid, Lisbon and Vienna. Wherever they traveled and whether on business or for pleasure, he acted as her mentor, teaching her about art and music, European history and contemporary politics. She learned more about his publishing empire and came to appreciate the distinguished clients he represented, including Winston Churchill, at that time Britain's prime minister.

When she was alone in New York, Wendy missed Reves' company but not the constant European travel his business demanded of him. As a result, the couple began to discuss the idea of settling down, with Wendy expressing a desire for a home of her own, and Emery lamenting the fact that everything he had ever loved and owned had been destroyed by the Germans. She was weary of travel, and he was reluctant to establish roots. For five years, from 1949 until 1953, they continued to live and travel all over Europe.

At last an opportunity presented itself to own one of the foremost villas on the Côte d'Azur, and Wendy Russell seized the occasion as only someone pursuing a dream can do. Almost overnight she and Emery Reves decided to purchase the fabled property known as La Pausa.

Wendy and Emery in Switzerland where Reves, a British subject, soon established his residency.

41

The couple traveled extensively in the early 1950s, including this visit to Venice.

Among his talents, Emery Reves was an exceptional photographer and Wendy Russell was a natural subject during their holiday travels.

Villa La Pausa
A Brief History

42   The history of the Villa La Pausa, though relatively brief, is highlighted by an extraordinary number of famous people of the 20th century. The Duke of Westminster, cousin to King George V, built the villa for Coco Chanel in 1927.

Heir to one of the largest fortunes in England, Westminster, who was known to his friends as Bend-or,[1] enjoyed escaping his peer duties at Eton Hall and London's foul seasons by sailing his yacht in the Mediterranean. In 1927 the duke's "favorite cabin boy," as he called her among friends, was Coco Chanel, whom he had met four years earlier and who was now his mistress. Westminster loved France, especially the Côte d'Azur, and with Coco as his companion he embellished his reputation as a bon vivant by cruising the Riviera and hosting lavish parties aboard the luxurious *Flying Cloud*. Monaco was their favorite port of call, and the yacht's sleek silhouette, the uniformed crew wearing the duke's coat of arms, and the boat's illuminated rigging at night, became increasingly familiar sights to residents of Monaco, especially those who alternated between the casino at Monte Carlo and Bend-or's legendary cocktail parties.

Although the duke first met Coco Chanel at Christmas in 1923 at the Hotel de Paris in Monaco, it was not until three months later during rehearsals of *Train Bleu* at the Champs-Elysées Theater in Paris that the two became involved. She had designed the costumes for the ballet written by Jean Cocteau, while Henri

The Duke of Westminster onboard the Flying Cloud.

Sunday Telegraph

1 *The nick-name, Bend-or, derives from the famous horse owned by Westminster's grandfather, winner of the 1880 Derby.*

Laurens and Picasso had created the sets and Darius Milhaud composed the music. It was Coco who introduced the sophisticated Westminster to the world of avant-garde art, and during their frequent sojourns on the Riviera they were often joined by Chanel's numerous friends, including Picasso, Cocteau, and Diaghilev, in addition to public figures like Winston Churchill, a friend of Westminster's since the Boer War and an occasional guest at the duke's villa, Mimizan.

Because of Coco's desire for a home of her own, and because of her fondness for the Riviera and its proximity to her Parisian fashion house, she persuaded the duke to buy a five-acre piece of property on a height overlooking Monte Carlo and the sea. Westminster paid 1.8 million francs to the Mayen family of Roquebrune-Cap Martin for the property known as La Pausa, and the three buildings already on it.

According to Gallic legend, the property acquired the name, La Pausa, when Mary Magdalene fled Jerusalem after the crucifixion. While traveling through the region of Roquebrune – so the legend goes – she paused to rest in a peaceful garden setting filled with beautiful olive trees and there arose a chapel on the very site of her repose. Another chapel, built centuries later and dedicated to Our Lady of La Pausa, is still located next to the property.

The duke's purchase of La Pausa and the subsequent construction of the villa actually resulted from a meeting with Robert Streitz, a 26-year-old architect recommended to Mademoiselle Chanel by her friend, Count Jean de Segonzac, whose house in Roquebrune Streitz had restored. At the time, Westminster and Coco were attending the opening of a Picabia exposition in Cannes, and, as was their custom, they were staying aboard the *Flying Cloud*. Streitz's first meeting with the couple took place on the yacht during a cocktail party to which he had been invited by his friend Edouard

Gabrielle "Coco" Chanel, Paris fashion designer, in 1931.

Corniglion-Molinier[2], a young notary in nearby Menton, whom Chanel had approached earlier about real estate properties and through whose office the sale of La Pausa was later transacted.

Although Streitz came to the party expecting only to meet the Duke of Westminster and Coco Chanel, he was both surprised and elated when they asked him if he would be interested in designing a villa for them – on a property site not yet chosen. When he discovered that they had no specific design in mind, Streitz suggested that he draft a preliminary project proposal and submit it to them for discussion. This he did three days later, and Coco and the duke were equally enthusiastic about the majestic site he proposed and his initial drawings. It was Robert Streitz's first important commission[3], and 'the ideal Mediterranean villa' he envisioned – designed and built – would be situated along the grande corniche in a secluded olive grove high above the sea.

Intrigued by his proposal, Chanel informed Streitz that she wished to be actively involved in all phases of the project, from the villa's design to its actual construction. As for the duke, his only comment to the architect was, "I want everything built with the best materials and under the best working conditions."[4] The

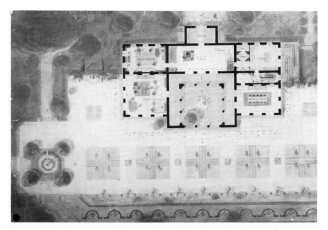

Robert Streitz's ground floor plan of La Pausa with garden.

2 *Edouard Corniglion-Molinier would later become a hero of the Free French forces during World War II and decorated a general.*
3 *Correspondence with Marc K. Streitz, son of Robert Streitz (1901-1984), July 1985.*
4 *Galante, Pierre,* Mademoiselle Chanel, *(Chicago: Henry Regnery Company, 1973), p. 117.*

solid rock and clay pockets and was precariously out of plumb. After his objections were overruled, Maggiore proceeded to lay a massive foundation with supporting beams whose cross-sections measured more than one yard.[6]

Although only new and expensive materials were used in the villa's construction, Chanel was determined that the house, when completed, radiate a patina of age. Her willful directive even applied to the roof, on which she insisted handmade, curved tiles be used – very difficult to find at that time. Because the villa's roof required more than 20,000 tiles, the contractor scoured nearby villages, buying up handmade tiles on older

44

plans were signed by Gabrielle Chanel, and according to Streitz, "This was the only signature between us. We never had a contract or any kind of correspondence. For me Mademoiselle's word was as good as gold. Nine months after the completion of Las Pausa every bill had been paid on the nail."[5]

Chanel's first design request was that Streitz re-create in the villa's entrance hall a large stone staircase which she remembered from the orphanage where she had spent her childhood. The architect traveled to Aubazine and photographed what Coco described as the "monks' staircase" with its worn tiles; he also visited with the mother superior, who still remembered Gabrielle Chanel, an illegitimate child born in the poorhouse and an orphan under her charge for fifteen years.

Coco personally discussed every detail of the project with Streitz and the contractor, Edgar Maggiore, either on the job site or in Paris. During the villa's construction she visited Roquebrune at least once a month to inspect the workers' progress, traveling on the Train Bleu to Monte Carlo where a taxi awaited her. Often, she returned to Paris the same day. On one occasion when she was unable to leave her design business, Maggiore dispatched a stucco worker to Paris so that Chanel could select the color of plaster to be applied to the villa's facade. On another occasion she sank to her knees in mud and laughter while examining the villa's foundation just after a rainfall.

Even from the beginning, Chanel proved to be a difficult client, demanding that the site she had chosen for the new villa be modified to accommodate the structure, despite the fact that the property consisted of

Architectural renderings of the villa.

5 *Galante, p. 117.*
6 *Galante, p. 119.*

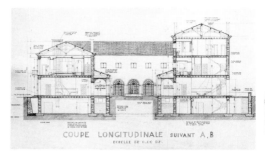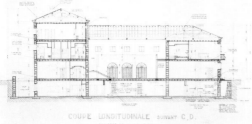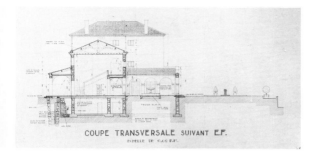

Architectural drawings of La Pausa in France.

structures, and then replacing them with newly manufactured ones. It was an exhorbitant procedure, but one authorized by Mademoiselle and paid for by the duke's unlimited budget.[7] Not surprisingly, the carpenter was instructed to age the new shutters he had so beautifully crafted – a disheartening process for the worker, but one that achieved Coco's desire for a weathered look.

When finished at last, the Villa La Pausa consisted of three wings, each facing inward toward a spacious patio enclosed by a wrought-iron grill and paved with one hundred thousand sand bricks. The openings onto the courtyard were graceful in their proportions, symmetrical in number, and vaulted in the Roman style. It was a classic Mediterranean villa, and its renowned beauty established Robert Streitz's reputation as an architect and lauched his distinguished career. So important was La Pausa in leading to numerous other commissions that Stretiz "always considered it as his 'good luck' building"[8] – a masterful early triumph by a young, then unknown architect.

Inside the villa, oak was used extensively for floor planks and paneling. The walls in several rooms were decorated from floor to ceiling with 18th century English rectangular oak panels of varying lengths. Chanel chose beige as the dominant color throughout the entrance hall and in her bedroom, which was furnished in beige taffeta, down to the curtains and bedspread. Large fireplaces were built into all the rooms while central heating was installed only in the grand hallway. As the focal point in the duke's bedroom, also exquisitely paneled, she used a 16th century, Elizabethan-style bed transported, as was much of the furniture, from one of Westminster's numerous English homes.

The villa while under construction in the late 1920s. In the photograph at bottom can be seen several large olive trees which Chanel had transported from Antibes to Roquebrune.

7 *As a result of Coco Chanel's usage of handmade tiles in La Pausa's construction, a speculative boom in old tiles was stimulated. Moreover, an ordinance dating from 1930 forbid the use of any roofing material in Roquebrune other than curved tiles, a policy enforced to this day.*

8 *Correspondence with Marc K. Streitz, July 1985.*

The salon.

The library.

The master bedroom.

Altogether, the Villa La Pausa cost 6 million francs to build — almost four times what the duke had originally paid for the property. In addition, the construction costs did not include what Chanel spent on interior fittings, decorations and exterior landscaping. Like everything else, the latter was both extravagant and expensive. Disappointed with the number of olive trees on the property, she directed Maggiore to locate additional trees appropriate in size and age. And she was not satisfied until he had transplanted, at great cost, twenty 100-year-old olive trees from Antibes to La Pausa.

Despite repeated offers, Coco Chanel never married the Duke of Westminster, preferring to remain his celebrated mistress rather than become one of several duchesses. At the height of their romantic idyll, from 1925 to 1930 and between his second and third marriages, Bend-or and Coco captured headlines with their travels, socializing, and miscellaneous activities, which included buying La Pausa and building the villa. As the chatelaine of her own villa, Chanel was now able to escape being reviewed by the duke's army of guards, footmen and old school chums, as was not always the case at his villa at Mimizan. When the duke stayed at La Pausa, he was her guest, and La Pausa's special environment, like the fashions Chanel designed, was her own creation.[9] Inspired either by her artist friends, Picasso and Cocteau, or by his friend Winston Churchill's practice at Mimizan, Westminster converted one of La Pausa's older buildings into a studio where he painted watercolors. A second, smaller home on the grounds, La Colline, was frequently used by Jean Cocteau as he struggled to overcome his addiction to opium and once while he was recovering from a serious case of typhus. Cocteau decorated La Colline with wall drawings (later destroyed during the German occupation) and also wrote *Sang d'un poete* while staying there.

Although Chanel and Westminster remained friends until his death, their affair ended in 1930 — not long after the Villa La Pausa was completed — when he married Loelia Mary Ponsonby, the third Duchess of Westminster. The separation may have disappointed Chanel, but she refused to allow it to depress her. Her house of design and haute couture continued to prosper, becoming even more lucrative after the introduction of a perfume, and Coco was able to enjoy her wealth and reputation until the threat of war began to affect both her business and personal life.

In the 1930s she was frequently seen in the company of Hans Gunther von Dincklage, a handsome German baron living in Paris. Spatz[10], as he was known to his friends, was wealthy, popular and married when he first met Chanel, but his interest in the famous couturier led him to divorce his wife in 1935, and he and Coco became a familiar couple in Parisian social circles prior to and during the war. When France surrendered in June 1940, Chanel, unlike other designers,

9 *An interesting reflection of Coco's design philosophy, whether collaborating with Robert Streitz on the villa or creating the fashions which carried her name, is the following observation attributed to Chanel: "Clothes, like architecture, are a matter of proportion."*

10 *A nick-name meaning "sparrow" in German.*

and for reasons of her own, closed her fashion house on Rue Cambon and spent most of the duration of the war at La Pausa.

Her wartime activities are not well known, but conflicting evidence suggests both collaboration and resistence. Contrary to most French citizens, she was able to travel freely in France during the German occupation, and she and Spatz were seen everywhere together, in Paris as well as in Roquebrune. Their relationship is puzzling in that it was later proven by counterespionage services that von Dincklage operated as an important Abwehr agent inside France as early as 1928. On the other hand, the BBC honored Chanel during the war by citing her help in the escape of Vera Bates Lombardi[11] from Italy in 1942. And though she and Spatz were living at La Pausa at the time, it is also known that at the request of Robert Streitz, Chanel interceded on behalf of a member of the Resistance whom the Gestapo had arrested. Her ambiguous behavior continued even after the war. When Spatz was deported from France by ministerial decree on July 9, 1947, Chanel left for Switzerland to join him.

July 1947 must have been doubly disheartening to her because the Duke of Westminster died of a coronary thrombosis on the 19th. Although he had married for a fourth time, Westminster and Chanel had remained in contact during their 17 years of separation, and his death undoubtedly marked the end of an elusive dream for the woman who had been born in a turn-of-the-century poorhouse. Sir Winston Churchill delivered the oration at Westminster's funeral, and the thoughts and feelings he expressed must have been shared by Coco: "He was happiest of all when he was giving pleasure to others… His numerous friends, young and old, will mourn and miss him, and I look back affectionately and thankfully over half a century of unbroken friendship."[12] Chanel had known Westminster only one-half that time, but she had benefitted no less than Churchill from her relationship with the Duke, and La Pausa was its offspring.

The postwar years were difficult ones for Chanel. Her couturier business had made her rich, but her fashions were now being copied on a massive scale by American manufacturers, and sales were beginning to decline. She owned several homes but had outlived almost all her friends. Disconsolate and bored when her relationship with Spatz ended in 1950, Chanel decided to revive her career. She remained interested in high fashion, but she was determined to complete directly with the ready-to-wear industry. She was more than a mere legend whose name lived on in a per-

fume, and she planned to introduce new fashion lines and still more fragrances to bolster her sagging reputation. In order to do so, however, she needed money so she sold most of her remaining properties including the Paris buildings on Rue Cambon[13] and the Villa La Pausa in Roquebrune, Cap Martin.

* * *

11 *It was Vera Bates, an Englishwoman, who first introduced Coco Chanel to the Duke of Westminster. She later married an Italian named Lombardi before the outbreak of World War II.*

12 *Galante, p. 114.*

13 *The single exception was 31 Rue Cambon, where Chanel had launched her career.*

* * *

For years Wendy and Emery Reves had lived in a series of hotels, mostly in Europe but also in the United States, wherever their respective careers had carried them and whenever their business schedules overlapped. In Paris they lived at the Royal Monceau, when in London, they stayed at Claridge's, and in New York they maintained a residence at the Plaza. These were cities where Emery conducted his publishing activities and pursued investments; they were also fashion capitals, and Wendy continued to model, especially in New York to which she returned at least twice a year. When they were not working, the couple traveled constantly, spending time each winter at the Palace Hotel in St. Moritz, and summers at the Chateau Madrid on the Côte d'Azur. Both business and holidays found them in Italy, Germany, Spain and Portugal, but after five years Wendy had wearied of travel and was determined to establish a permanent home.

At first they looked to buy outside of Paris, but the properties available, especially chateaux, had suffered both from German occupation and postwar squatters. While visiting Monaco on one of their frequent trips, Wendy decided that the Riviera was where she most wanted a home. When Emery noted that only older people lived there year-round, she replied that it was still the most beautiful place to live, and she did not intend to wait until she was old in order to enjoy it. Before they could explore the real estate prospects, however, Emery had to return to Paris on business.

Not long afterwards, they were having lunch at the Barclay Restaurant with Herve Mille, then editor of *Paris Match,* and his brother Gerard, a talented decorator. While Reves and the editor discussed business, Wendy and Gerard Mille conversed about properties for sale, in Paris and elsewhere. During the conversation, she learned from Mille, a Chanel acquaintance, that the Villa La Pausa was for sale. For years she had heard about Chanel's fabulous estate on the Côte d'Azur from Leonora Corbett, a mutual acquaintance. Without hesitating, Wendy interrupted Emery to announce that she was going to the south of France that night. When he asked why, she replied, "La Pausa. It's for sale and I'm taking the next train." After a brief pause, he responded, "Then we'll go together."[14]

The Train Bleu arrived in Monte Carlo early the next morning, and by 10 o'clock Wendy and Emery Reves were walking up the villa's sloping driveway. Even with the gardens in a state of disrepair, they felt excited as they approached the historic villa. Like the grounds, the house showed further, more serious signs

48

During the early 1950s, Wendy Russell commuted between Europe and the United States, returning to New York at least twice a year on business.

Before buying the Villa La Pausa in 1953, Wendy and Emery spent part of each winter in St. Moritz and stayed at the Chateau de Madrid on the Riviera during the summer.

14 *Interview with Wendy Russell Reves by author, 1985.*

of absentee ownership: the stuccoed walls were crumbling in spots, and the shutters and trim desperately needed painting. Inside, the villa was in no better condition. What presumably had been beige walls were gray from age, and cobwebs in the ceiling corners and around the vaulted openings revealed how long the house had remained unoccupied and its care had been forgotten. The patio was overgrown from neglect, and the glassed-in atrium erected by Coco Chanel had produced an indoor jungle.

Despite the villa's deplorable condition, Wendy was able to appreciate La Pausa's attributes: its perfect proportions, the elegant simplicity of the architecture, the classic progression of the floorplan, and the materials and quality of the construction. It was an archetypal Mediterranean villa, and worthy of whatever effort and expense were needed to restore it. As someone whose homes and possessions had been destroyed in Berlin, Paris and London, Emery Reves was less enthusiasic, but he was willing to defer to Wendy's wishes. He had never denied her anything, and he was not going to allow his appraisal of the villa to interfere with Wendy's dream of restoring it. As they strolled back down the driveway, they stopped to admire the ancient olive trees and she whispered, "Pucy, this is it, the only home I want to own."[15]

They spent only two hours at La Pausa on that first occasion, but during lunch afterwards at the Hotel de Paris they agreed to buy the villa. Wendy knew that she could rebuild it as the most beautiful home on the Riviera, and Emery never doubted that she would. The couple returned to Paris that night, and Emery contacted Chanel through Gerard Mille. The transaction required months to complete, however, and Reves would later observe that negotiating Churchill's *Memoirs* had been an easier task than buying La Pausa from Coco Chanel. At one point during the negotiations, Chanel invited Emery and Wendy for dinner in her Paris home to better acquaint herself with La Pausa's future guardians. Although the conversation was pleasant and covered a wide range of topics, it did not include a discussion of the villa. "It's a page I have turned," Chanel remarked, "and I do not wish to look back. You will discover its magic for yourself. I am happy that you will live there," she said to Wendy and Emery, "It deserves someone like you."[16]

When the couple first saw La Pausa, the historic villa was in disrepair and the grounds were overgrown.

15 *The couple often addressed one another using* Pucy, *an Hungarian term of endearment.*
16 *Interview with Wendy Russell Reves by author, 1985.*

"Pausaland"
The Golden Era

50   Emery and Wendy bought La Pausa in 1953, but because of its deteriorated condition they did not actually stay in the villa for several months. Instead, two servants were sent from Paris to prepare the house for their arrival. Emery also decided that if he and Wendy were to live in the south of France, they would need a car so he purchased a 1948 Rolls Royce which the couple then drove to the Riviera, arriving at the Villa La Pausa on New Year's Eve. Despite the servants' efforts, the house was still uninhabitable, making Wendy all the more determined to restore the villa to its former beauty.

While restoring the Villa La Pausa, Emery and Wendy lived at the Hotel de Paris in Monte Carlo.

  During the renovation, which required more than a year to complete and began immediately after their arrival in Roquebrune, they lived nearby at the Hotel de Paris in Monte Carlo. While Emery continued his usual business activities, working out of a hotel room once again, Wendy supervised the reconstruction project, often spending 14 hours a day at the villa. She even

converted the garage into a workshop, where experts worked to conserve some of the valuable pieces of furniture included in the sale. For Wendy, the project represented the challenge of realizing a dream she had long coveted – the creation of her own home, and it extended beyond the villa itself, since the grounds were also in a sad condition and several of the buildings on it, including the gatehouse, had been virtually destroyed during the German occupation.

  During the remodeling, Wendy was surprised one morning while she was working in the patio when a middle-aged man approached and introduced himself as Robert Streitz, the architect of La Pausa. Obviously overcome with emotion, he was generous in his praise of the changes being made, and said to Wendy, "You cannot imagine the joy you are giving to me by restoring my villa to the way I originally designed it."[1] Among other modifications, he was referring to her removal of a glass wall which Chanel had erected to enclose the cloister and to Wendy's decision to glaze the three vaulted openings so that the patio would no longer be a part of the great hall.

  After the villa's renovation, Mary Lasker was the first prominent guest to stay at La Pausa. In fact, it was she who suggested that Wendy cover the guest bedroom walls in shades of blue satin, and who interested Wendy, initially, in collecting fine porcelain by presenting her with a gift of Lowestoft platter. Emery Reves knew Albert Lasker through their mutual involvement in postwar humanitarian projects on behalf of displaced Jewish refugees, and the two couples often saw one another in New York, as well as during holidays together in Europe and elsewhere. With Mary Lasker's visit, Wendy began using a guest book for distinguished guests to La Pausa. The "Golden Book," as she referred to it, served many times during the next two decades, and the list of historic personalities recorded in its pages outshone even the famous figures known to have visited the villa during Coco Chanel's time.

Wendy with one of the workers in the library and organizing Emery Reves' vast book collection in the salon.

1 *Interview with Wendy Russell Reves by author, 1985.*

Altogether the villa's restoration required fifteen months, but when completed, Wendy had succeeded in reviving La Pausa's legendary "magic" and Emery was enchanted with what she had created. For them a golden era was born, and the legend of La Pausa grew.

* * *

Workmen removing vines in La Pausa's courtyard.

Wendy supervised the work crews during the villa's reconstruction and converted the garage into a workshop for conservation of furniture included in the sale.

A fireplace was installed in the dining room and a terrace was built outside the salon.

During his second term as British prime minister (1951-1955), Winston Churchill frequently came to the Riviera to escape the London winter and occasionally unfavorable political currents. For years he stayed with the Duke of Westminster at Mimizan, but after Bend-or's death he stayed as a guest at Lord Beaverbrook's Villa Capponcina. Churchill often asked Beaverbrook to include Emery Reves as a dinner guest so that the three men might discuss their numerous publishing ventures. After the end of World War II, Reves and Churchill had once again allied as businessmen, much as they had been at the height of Cooperation Press in the mid-thirties. In 1946 Reves successfully negotiated the publishing rights to Churchill's *War Memoirs* in the United States, and not long afterwards the Hungarian publisher purchased for himself all the foreign language rights to the series, a business transaction which made both men wealthy. As a measure of their respect and admiration for one another, and also as an insight into their respective personalities, it is interesting to note that Reves paid Churchill an unprecedented sum of money for the foreign language rights to the *Memoirs* without a signed agreement and before the author had begun to write.

According to Martin Gilbert, Churchill's official biographer, Reves did far more than simply act as publisher for his colleague's work. "A very gifted person," Reves also served as a "first-class critic"[2] in helping Churchill arrange his material and in determining the *Memoirs'* overall style and presentation. Moreover, Gilbert credits Emery Reves with titling several of the books, a series that would eventually consist of six volumes, from *The Gathering Storm* to *Triumph and Tragedy*. Both Churchill and his publisher were understandably honored when the English statesman received the Nobel Prize for Literature in 1953.

After one of his business dinners with Churchill at Capponcina in 1955, Emery casually informed Wendy at breakfast the following morning that he had invited Churchill to La Pausa for lunch that day. Prior to that, Emery and Wendy had entertained very little, having focused all their efforts until then on the villa's restoration. Emery's pride in "Wendy's project" would soon change that, however, and his luncheon invitation to Churchill marked a true turning point in their lives.

Reves, who syndicated articles by Winston Churchill through Cooperation Press during the 1930s, negotiated the publishing rights to the foreign language editions of Churchill's War Memoirs *after 1947. Also pictured is Sarah Churchill.*

Without a chef or even servants, and with the villa only partly furnished, Wendy quickly marshalled her talents to make the necessary preparations in the four hours remaining before Churchill's scheduled arrival. She created floral displays, arranged the large banquet table, and cooked most of the food. Emery tried to calm her by suggesting that Churchill was disdainful of fanfare, but the thought of Sir Winston as a guest in her home was an opportunity to show off La Pausa, however informal the occasion.

The Churchill party soon arrived in chauffered cars. Despite a stroke the previous June, Churchill approached the house unassisted except for his customary walking cane. Emery warmly welcomed his friend, and Churchill enthusiastically greeted Wendy by expressing admiration for the restored villa. In view of his numerous later visits, he must have felt at home in La Pausa from the very beginning. Not surprisingly, he took an immediate liking to the library, where he settled comfortably in a 17th century chair and proceeded to entertain all those in his presence. It did not escape his notice that among the library's bulging shelves were the many books published by Reves, and the volumes most prominently displayed were those Churchill had authored. Being an avid amateur artist as well, Churchill also recognized and praised the quality of the paintings throughout the villa. It was not often that one could enjoy such company surrounded by

2 *Interview with Martin Gilbert by author, June 1985.*

great art and by one's own literary accomplishments. The Villa La Pausa was indeed a special place for Winston Churchill.

The luncheon was memorable. From the cellar Emery produced wines to complement Wendy's meal. The table decorations, like the house itself, were casually elegant and conversation was relaxed and enjoyable – enlivened by Emery's dry wit, Wendy's *joie de vivre*, and Churchill's always amusing anecdotes. After glasses of brandy, the group went onto the terrace to enjoy the cool Mediterranean air and stroll the grounds amidst the fragrance of lavender. It was not until six o'clock that Churchill left, and he returned his hosts' hospitality by inviting them to lunch the following afternoon at La Capponcina.

The next day Wendy and Emery were understandably pleased that their luncheon had been such a success and they were looking forward to visiting Beaverbrook's villa and seeing Churchill again. It was a beautiful day, and they enjoyed driving the Rolls along the scenic coastal route. When they arrived at Capponcina, Churchill welcomed them from the verandah and escorted them into the salon. The first thing Wendy noticed was a row of paintings leaning against the wall. When she commented how lovely she found them, Churchill asked which painting she liked the best. Wendy pointed to a particular landscape, and he said that he wanted her to have it. Without knowing it, Wendy had been reviewing Churchill's artistic output during his holiday, and he was now offering her one of his paintings, a very rare act since he only parted with half a dozen of the hundreds of paintings he completed.[3] He also insisted that the canvas be sent to London for framing before returning it to Wendy at La Pausa.[4]

As had been the case the previous day, everyone enjoyed lunch and one another's company. The table conversation focused on the attributes of living in the south of France, and Churchill even expressed an interest in acquiring his own villa. As a result, he and Emery met with real estate agents the following day, but the appointments failed to produce a suitable investment prospect. At dinner that evening Churchill again commented how much he loved the region and asked Wendy if she would have him as a guest at La Pausa.

Flattered, she responded, of course, by saying they would be honored to have the prime minister as a houseguest. It was the beginning of an enduring friendship, and according to Mary Churchill Soames, "It was due to their hospitable blandishments and to the fact that he was then, and on successive visits (to La Pausa), so comfortable and happy in their house, that he abandoned the search for a villa of his own."[5]

53

Churchill enjoyed painting while on vacation in the south of France. Pictured is a painting he gave to Wendy Russell in 1955, entitled The Custody of the Child *and depicting the Riviera coastline below Lord Beaverbrook's Villa Capponcina.*

3 *Graebner, Walter,* My Dear Mister Churchill, *(London: Michael Joseph, Ltd., 1965), p. 90.*

4 *Like three other Churchill paintings, signed WSC,* The Custody of the Child *now belongs to the Dallas Museum of Art, as part of the Wendy and Emery Reves Collection. It depicts two larger cypress trees overhanging a smaller one with the Côte d'Azur in the background, and was painted by Churchill from below Beaverbrook's villa at Cap d'Aix.*

5 *Soames, Mary,* Clementine Churchill, *(Boston: Houghton Mifflin Company, 1979), p. 608.*

Wendy Russell dining with Clementine and Winston Churchill at the Chateau de Madrid.

Churchill's desire to stay at La Pausa required substantial alterations in the villa and the normally reserved life preferred by Emery and Wendy. He, especially, was reluctant to have their world of privacy invaded by journalists. Furthermore, he was accustomed to controlling reporters, as he had done when he directed Cooperation Press during the 1930s, and he suspected that the press would be difficult to manage during the visit of so celebrated a figure. He expected the villa's gatehouse to be besieged by writers and photographers eager to interview or glimpse one of the world's most recognized statesmen.

For her part, Wendy began rearranging La Pausa's living quarters in anticipation of Churchill's stay and devising a feasible schedule of daily operations appropriate for such a guest's visit. Because Churchill would be accompanied by members of his immediate family as well as staff personnel and security guards, the villa itself and other buildings on the estate had to be renovated to accommodate the large party. Churchill, it was decided, would use Emery's bedroom for this first visit, since it opened onto a sitting room and represented a self-contained suite. Later, however, an entire top floor was redecorated for his personal use during visits. The gatehouse was designated for use by the French police, who were expected to provide round-the-clock security during Churchill's stay, and several rooms were created above the three-car garage to provide additional living quarters for clerical personnel. Lastly, a butler's pantry off the dining room was converted into a hallway, a major design modification resulting in its being christened "Churchill's Alley." Incredibly enough, all the changes were completed in less than six weeks and in time for Churchill's arrival.

La Pausa's physical changes, though functional and outwardly dramatic, were less critical, however, than internal developments initiated by Wendy, who knew that the importance of an efficient staff of servants could not be overestimated when entertaining such a distinguished guest and his large entourage of family, staff and expected company.

Resourceful as always, Wendy approached Roquebrune's mayor, Monsieur Gioan, to solicit his advice in securing the services of a staff suitable for such an occasion: a maitre d'hotel, butler, chambermaids, gardeners and the like. The mayor promised to find the finest help available, and Wendy soon had a full household staff to train and supervise. She decided to dress the chambermaids in uniform, and so colorful were their outfits that Churchill affectionately referred to them as "Wendy's Pink Brigade."

Just as important were the arrangements Wendy made in order to feed the number of guests and their anticipated support staffs. She contacted Papa Sarti at the Chateau Madrid, where she and Emery had spent so many holidays, and asked him to recommend a chef capable of preparing meals for such a gathering. The avuncular hotelier surprised her by offering the services of his own chef, saying that he would prepare one gourmet meal a day if Wendy could hire another cook responsible for the day's secondary setting.

When Churchill finally arrived at La Pausa, his wife Clementine was not with him. She had been hospitalized unexpectedly in London and planned to convalesce afterwards in Ceylon. Included in the Churchill party on his first stay at the villa in January, 1956 were Diana Churchill, his daughter; Anthony Montague Brown, Churchill's private secretary; Miss Pugh, another secretary; Sergeant Murray of the Scotland Yard; a personal chauffeur; and an escort of French police.

Given the numerous constraints, it is a measure of their combined talents that Wendy and Emery managed to make Churchill's first visit a success. During his stay, Emery saw to the menu, and Wendy took care of everything else, a responsibility not unlike that of the manager of a small but exclusive hotel. No facet of the overall organization was too minor for their attention, nor any logistical problem too great for them to handle. Thinking of Churchill's health, they even made arrangements for a local physician, Dr. Roberts of Monte Carlo, to make daily calls at the villa.

Reves enjoyed his role as host. He relished selecting the gourmet menu and seeing to the proper temperature and decanting of rare wines chosen to complement the meals. Wendy, in turn, met early each morning with her staff to chart that day's planned activities and to make whatever adjustments the schedule demanded, such as additional guests for lunch or those who were expected to spend the evening. Most of all, the hostess delighted in providing a personal

From 1955 until the early 1960s, Churchill was a frequent houseguest at La Pausa. Not surprisingly, he preferred to relax and work in the library where he could admire the art on the walls and the various books he had authored and Emery Reves had published.

Public interest in Churchill's frequent visits to La Pausa stimulated the local economy to such an exent that Britain's former prime minister was made an honorary citizen of the town of Roquebrune in 1959.

touch, however small, which enhanced a guest's visit and earned Emery's admiration – a lovely floral arrangement in the villa's entrance; specially made dinner ware to commemorate an occasion; a splendidly dressed household staff; and impeccable service and sumptuous meals which earned La Pausa a reputation as one of the great tables of France. Churchill, his family and friends, and the many other guests who came were charmed by La Pausa and their hosts' hospitality. During that first visit, Churchill's letters to Clementine in Ceylon were "full of the beauties and comforts of the house, and of the care, kindness, and thoughtfulness of his hosts."[6] When his brief stay was over, Churchill, who once remarked, "My tastes are simple, I like only the best,"[7] knew that he would return again to what he now called "Pausaland." In fact, he visited La Pausa many times, and the widespread public interest generated by his stays in Roquebrune-Cap Martin stimulated the region's economy to such an extent that Churchill was made an honorary citizen of Roquebrune.

6 *Soames, p. 608.*
7 *Graebner, p. 57.*

During Churchill's first visit, a pattern of life began to emerge at the villa. The soon established routine featured two large meals per day, plus an informal tea at 5 p.m. In general, Churchill remained in his suite until late morning, working on correspondence, writing articles, or editing galleys of *The History of the English Speaking Peoples*, which he had first begun to write in 1929. After a midday luncheon, to which as many as five to eight guests would be invited, Churchill often enjoyed setting up his easel and painting, either on the villa grounds or in the dining room. In the late afternoon, he preferred sitting on the terrace, nursing a whiskey and cigar. If Churchill was not up to getting out, he and Emery would spend hours playing bézique in the library or salon. The elder statesman so enjoyed his visits at La Pausa that his secretary once reported to Charles Moran, Churchill's private physician in London: "For the last three weeks he seemed twenty years younger."[8] Moran knew that the signs were somewhat misleading, since the prime minister always experienced an "uplift in spirits" when visiting the Reves in the south of France, and the stroke which Churchill had suffered in 1955 still left him susceptible to periods of intense depression once he returned to England[9]. But he was a different man at the villa, young in spirit despite his physical infirmities, and alive with interest both in his work and the guests he received while staying there. Churchill visited Pausaland many times between 1955 and 1961, often staying for weeks at a time; Mrs. Churchill came on four of those occasions and was relieved to discover that, in the words of her daughter, "Winston wanted for nothing at La Pausa, and was surrounded by care for his every need."[10]

Not surprisingly, many heads of state and world dignitaries came to La Pausa to honor Winston Churchill, and the villa came to serve as a gathering place for wartime heroes and statesmen, eager to renew friendships and understandably inclined to relive the glorious roles they had once performed. This was particularly true of the many cabinet ministers who had served under Churchill during the wartime era.

Wendy with Mary Churchill Soames standing beside Rodin's The Poet and the Contemplative Life *in La Pausa's courtyard.*

Among them were: Field Marshal Bernard Montgomery, the hero of El Alamein and Britain's most decorated officer; Anthony Eden who together with Churchill had sponsored Reves as a British subject and who visited the Reves with his wife over the next two decades; and Lord Cherwell, Churchill's scientific advisor and the man most instrumental in England's development of the atomic bomb. Because of Emery's association with Albert Einstein, as a result of *The Anatomy of Peace*, conversations among Cherwell, Churchill and Reves were animated, for all of them had personally contributed in a significant way to world peace.

Perhaps the most difficult guest to receive at La Pausa – at least for Wendy who did not believe in pomp – was the Duke of Windsor. Although Edward VIII had abdicated the throne in 1936, the duke's friendship and previous stature were such that Churchill even persuaded Wendy to curtsy, saying, "After all, dear, he was my king."[11] The duke's visit, though brief, was made all the more enjoyable because of his keen interest in gardening, and there were few estates anywhere more beautifully landscaped than La Pausa.

8 *Moran, Charles,* Churchill – Taken from the Diaries of Lord Morgan. *(Boston: Houghton Mifflin Company, 1966), p. 737.*
9 *Moran, p. 737.*
10 *Soames, p.609.*
11 *Interview with Wendy Russell Reves by author, 1985.*

Eugene and Jeanne Rothschild, in whose castle in Vienna the Windsors had stayed prior to visiting La Pausa, soon became regular guests themselves at the Reves' villa. A beautiful actress, she came alone on several occasions to act as a companion for Churchill and to play card games like chemin-de-fer and bézique which Churchill and Emery so often did in the afternoon and evenings.

R.A. Butler, Britain's new prime minister, came to Pausaland to see Churchill. The purpose of his visit was to brief his predecessor on the status of government business and to enlist his advice on Parliamentary matters, but Rab Butler most enjoyed admiring the Reves' collection of paintings, since he collected Impressionist works as well. As was customary, the dinner lasted several hours with guests served coffee and brandy at the table rather than in a smoking room so as not to interrupt the conversation or to disturb the intimate atmosphere. Another reason for Butler's stopover in Roquebrune was to determine for himself whether Churchill's health was being looked after in a proper manner. And it was all too apparent to Butler that Churchill's happiness was due as much to his hosts' kindness as to La Pausa's beautiful environment, both of which seemed to revive Churchill's sometimes sagging spirits.

President René Coty of France (1954-1959) visited La Pausa during Churchill's first stay at the villa. Since Churchill had only recently stepped down as prime minister (April 1955), there was heightened interest on the part of the media and public alike when it was learned that the two statesmen were meeting at the Reves' villa. In an attempt to satisfy the press, Reves opened La Pausa's gates for a one-hour photo opportunity. Overzealous journalists abused the occasion, however, and it was the last time they were allowed access to guests visiting the villa. The luncheon for Coty went very smoothly, though, in part because of Wendy's insistence on informality. Several days later, Coty acknowledged the Reves' hospitality by inviting them to his summer estate near Grenoble. The invitation was delivered in a box wrapped in French tri-color ribbons and embossed with Coty's seal of office.

Jeanne Rothschild and Wendy in the villa's great hall. Above them is Degas' The Bathers *and beside the doorway is a Rodin bronze,* I Am Beautiful.

Inside were exotic feathers from game birds bagged during a recent presidential hunt, which Coty knew Wendy would appreciate and somehow incorporate into her chic wardrobe.

Another European statesman anxious to meet Churchill was Konrad Adenauer. The West German chancellor (1949-1963) came to La Pausa so that Churchill, who was not well, would not have to travel. Once again, the customary absence of protocol at the villa enabled everyone to be more relaxed, even in the presence of strangers. Because Adenauer spoke only halting English and Churchill no German, Emery served as interpreter during the luncheon between the former wartime foes, easily employing his language skills to stress points or to recount anecdotes in English, German and French. So delightful was the luncheon and so comfortable were the guests that at 7 o'clock Wendy instructed her staff to set additional places for dinner. When several days later Adenauer extended an invitation to the group to visit his home in nearby Grasse, Emery accepted so as to continue the discussion of post-war politics and business, but Wendy declined because of the fatigue she always experienced after a Churchill visit.

As Churchill's private physician, Charles Moran was a frequent guest at the villa, and he and Wendy became close friends when Sir Winston developed pleurisy during his stay in February 1958. Naturally, Churchill's illness attracted considerable public concern and led to dozens of journalists camping at the villa's gatehouse for any news that might be released. Lady Clementine, Sarah and Randolph Churchill and the Christopher Soames family all stayed at the villa during the lengthy illness. With the press outside La Pausa's walls, there was no privacy whatsoever, and the melancholy atmosphere inside was deepened by the uncertainty of Churchill's recovery. When a despondent Churchill refused to follow Moran's advice, Wendy aided the doctor in cajoling the stubborn patient to take the medicine he needed. Ultimately, of course, Churchill did regain his health, and the care he received at the villa and the spectacular view from his bedroom window, looking east towards the Maritime Alps and the sunny Mediterranean, most certainly contributed to his recovery. Wendy saw to it that his room was provided with daily arrangements of flowers picked on the villa grounds — a gesture which eventually inspired in Churchill a renewed interest in painting and hastened his convalescence. When cautioned not to exceed himself, Churchill replied, "You'll see. I'll be out with the brushes before any of you think I will."[12]

During one of Churchill's stays, Noel Coward came to La Pausa with designer Edward Molyneaux as an unexpected mystery guest. Song and laughter resounded throughout the villa as guests and hosts alike joined in repeated refrains of "Mad Dogs and Englishmen" until late in the afternoon. The party ended with Coward wearing a magnolia blossom as a hat, dancing to the amusement of a revived Churchill.

Another celebrity who signed Wendy's Golden Book was Aristotle Onassis, who arrived with Randolph Churchill, then staying as a guest on the Greek shipowner's yacht the *Christina*. The dinner conversation that evening was awkward, since Onassis was not yet known to Churchill, but the millionaire's flamboyant reputation was such that everyone was curious about the man and, with some coaxing by Wendy, the group accepted Onassis' invitation for lunch. Driving down to Monte Carlo the next day, they easily spotted the *Christina*, sporting more yachting flags and decorations than any other vessel in the harbor. They also discovered members of the press lying in wait, eager to photograph the meeting between Churchill and the powerful shipping magnate as they walked down the gangway. The Onassis luncheon featured large servings of caviar, expensive wines, and a small uniformed orchestra playing beneath the festooned rigging. Afterwards, the Churchill party was again encircled by journalists who pursued them as far as the sanctuary of La Pausa. Onassis returned as a guest to the villa on later occasions, but the Greek's appetite for extravagance and publicity prevented him from becoming a close friend of Reves.

There were so many guests to La Pausa during that period that Emery and Wendy entertained constantly, and the Villa La Pausa developed a reputation as one of the premier showplaces on the Côte d'Azur. Somerset

Photograph, courtesy of Martin Gilbert

A renewed interest in painting hastened Churchill's convalescence from pleurisy in 1958.

Emery and Wendy seated beneath a Fauve Vlaminck at La Pausa during the villa's golden era.

12 *Fishman, Jack,* My Darling Clementine. *(New York: David McKay Company, Inc.), p. 163.*

Maugham and his companion Alan Searle became close friends and often came to La Pausa to sample the Viennese food Emery then specialized in serving. Wendy once seated Maugham next to Mrs. Rose Kennedy at what proved to be one of La Pausa's most memorable parties. Being a great hostess is not an easy task, and entertaining public figures required all of Wendy's skill and gracious charm. Although Mrs. Kennedy came during her son's presidency, Wendy had known Joseph Kennedy much earlier in the 1940s, at the height of her modeling career in New York. Mary Lasker and Gerald van der Kemp[13] were also present at the Kennedy dinner.

Another celebrated guest at La Pausa during its golden era was Greta Garbo, who appreciated the Reves' hospitality and the privacy of the villa which she found so difficult to find elsewhere. Hubert Humphrey – at that time a U.S. senator and someone Wendy had met years before in New York – arrived unexpectedly at the villa one morning wearing a yachting cap. Humphrey was staying as a guest with Mary Lasker at La Fiorentina, but he was determined to see La Pausa, having promised Wendy earlier that he would one day visit her villa.

Anna Rosenberg, Eisenhower's Undersecretary of War, was a close friend of Wendy's and another frequent guest at La Pausa. Her husband, Paul Hoffman, and Emery knew one another through their respective involvement in the United Nations. Hoffman, as head of the UN's Special Fund, was a natural candidate for Reves to lobby in his efforts to redirect that organization towards a World Federal Government based on international law instead of treaties.[14]

Christiane and Paul Reynaud, were another couple who often stayed with the Reves. Wendy had first met Reynaud at a cocktail party in 1948, shortly after arriving in Paris for a modeling assignment. So taken was she with his intelligence and charm that she surprised a reporter by replying, "Paul Reynaud," when asked with whom she would most like to have dinner. It was not the answer expected of an attractive and vivacious American model on assignment in the world's capital of fashion. Emery, of course, had known Reynaud for an even longer period of time, since the thirties when he had syndicated articles by the French statesman through Cooperation Press.

Although Reynaud later served as premier of the Vichy government (1940), he survived the German occupation and he and Reves renewed their friendship after World War II. The close relationship would last another two decades. In fact, the Reves and Reynauds were dining together and planning a joint trip to Japan only three days before Paul Reynaud died. Furthermore, a photograph taken by Emery of Reynaud with Churchill at La Pausa was widely published in newspapers throughout the world in 1966 when news of Reynaud's death was announced. Not long afterwards, Christiane Reynaud offered Emery her late husband's lovely Paris office at 5 Place de Palais Bourbon. For years, both before and after the war, Reves had officed at 33 Champs-Elysées, but in honor of his former colleague, he accepted the offer and relocated his publishing and business affairs. Reves kept Reynaud's former apartment office for another fifteen years.

Among the many artists to stay at La Pausa during its golden era was the violinist Nathan Milstein, who spent ten days at the villa with his family while he performed nearby at the Menton Festival. Others included sculptor Oscar Nemon, author John Gunther and industrial designer Raymond Loewy. Hubert de Givenchy, the French couturier, also came to visit and was particularly impressed with the Reves' splendid collection of rugs.

Because of his extensive publishing affairs, it is not surprising that many of Reves' business acquaintances came to La Pausa to stay as houseguests. Michael Berry, owner of London's *Daily Telegraph* which published Emery's articles on a regular basis, frequently visited the villa with his wife Pamela. So also did Lord Beaverbrook and Henry and Becky Laughlin of the Houghton-Mifflin Company in Boston, who offered Reves the highest price to publish the North American edition of Churchill's *War Memoirs*, and at whose palace in Ireland Emery and Wendy occasionally visited.

Lord Beaverbrook, a prominent British publisher and close friend to Churchill and Reves, came often to visit at the villa.

59

13 *Gerald van der Kemp was at that time director of the museum at Versailles and a longtime Reves acquaintance.*

14 *Emery's interest in the creation of such a global body was a logical outgrowth of the central theme he had first postulated in* The Anatomy of Peace *(1945). The Movement for World Federal Government, in fact, maintained offices in New York, Geneva and London, all of which Reves visited often between 1945 and the mid-1950s in order to lecture and attend seminars. The organization's rallying call: "Those who want Peace no longer prepare for War. They prepare for Federal Government," * was an understandable attitude adopted by a generation who had suffered from a second world war, and who believed that the United Nations represented an ominous echo of Santayana's warning: "Those who fail to learn from history are condemned to repeat it." Emery Reves acted as a popular spokesman on behalf of the World Federal Government Movement until internal dissension within the organization led him to abandon his active affiliation, but not its cause. So respected is Reves' name as a principal advocate of World Federal Government that a recent conference in London (July 1984) was held as "a memorial to Emery Reves."*

* *World Federalists Conference (Montreux, August 1947) program, published by The British Branch of the World Movement for World Federal Government, London 1947, p. 15.*

Among the Reves' many friends, though, none were closer than artist Graham Sutherland and his wife Kathy. Emery commissioned Sutherland to paint portraits of him and Wendy, and the artist's study of Reves, as well as the finished portrait, are both distinguished by Sutherland's fluent draftsmanship and his unusual palette of colors. In each, Sutherland successfully captured Reves' urbane expression and personal determination that had enabled the publisher to succeed in a life so disrupted by personal tragedies. The portrait of Wendy Russell Reves, on the other hand, was painted many years after that of her husband's, and is unusual because of its size and the formality with which the subject – a woman known for her vivacious personality – is depicted. Wendy was so overwhelmed when she first saw the portrait, that she questioned Sutherland about the painting's large scale. "But Wendy," the artist replied, "you really are bigger than life!"[15]

A unique work in the Wendy and Emery Reves Collection is the *Ely Cross*, created jointly by Graham Sutherland and Louis Osman as a commissioned work for Ely Cathedral. The Reves first saw the *Cross* in an art gallery where it was being shown as part of an exhibition tour prior to its intended installation on the cathedral's nave altar. The sculpture's emotional appeal transfixed them, and they sent a telegram to Sutherland expressing their admiration for what they truly believed was one of the great works of modern art. Not long afterwards, Wendy was startled to read in the London *Times* that the committee responsible for the commission had declined the *Cross* on the grounds that it was too modern and therefore inappropriate for its planned setting in a Norman church. Several days later, Wendy saw Graham Sutherland at a party and approached the artist to say how dismayed she was with the committee's decision. She then boldly announced that she wished to buy the *Cross*. He was delighted, of course, and promised to contact the Worshipful Company of Goldsmiths in London, which was acting as a broker for the sculpture. In two days Sutherland secured the guild's sale price and indicated to Wendy that it was a reasonable one. When the *Cross* was delivered to La Pausa in 1964, Graham and Kathy Sutherland were present for the occasion. Together the artist and Wendy placed the sculpture on a stone socle in a prominent corner of the great hall, where all who entered the villa could admire it.

60

The Reves with artist Graham and Kathy Sutherland watching the annual procession of La Pausa.

The Our Lady of La Pausa chapel as decorated by Wendy in 1967.

Behind Wendy Reves in this photograph is the Ely Cross *by Graham Sutherland and Louis Osman, which she acquired in 1964.*

15 *Interview with Wendy Russell Reves by author, 1985.*

Several years later, the Sutherlands came early to an Easter luncheon the Reves were hosting. Graham Sutherland was carrying something bulky in padded cotton, and when he unwrapped the parcel, they stood in awe as the artist produced a wax model of the crucifixion, and announced, "Wendy, this is my Easter present for you."[16] The "Little Christ," was all the more meaningful to the Reves because it, unlike the other cast elements in the *Ely Cross,* had actually been created by Sutherland's own hands.

In looking to the future, Emery and Wendy Reves began considering in the late 1960s how best to preserve La Pausa's art collections. In view of Emery's troublesome heart condition, and without any immediate relatives, it was important to both of them that the collection remain intact and, if possible, in the villa itself.

Consequently, Reves initiated contact with André Malraux, the Minister of Culture. The distinguished French author and the British publisher shared a natural affinity for literary works, of course, but Malraux was also a great admirer of Reves' collection of Impressionist paintings, and he hoped that the couple would donate their villa to France as a private museum. To that end, Malraux agreed to recognize the Reves' legitimate ownership of the art, especially the paintings and works on paper, which Emery had purchased over the years in New York and elsewhere before bringing them into France to install in the villa. The agreement was of critical importance, for without official French government sanction, customs officials could refuse a later attempt to export the art. Malraux believed, at the time, that his agreement with Reves would ensure that the private collection would remain in France.

As a matter of fact, Reves' original intent was to donate the villa to the town of Roquebrune, an option he explored seriously with the mayor, believing that the official would gladly receive the gift in exchange for maintaining La Pausa as a private museum. However, when the mayor began his discussion with Reves not by admiring the art, but rather by asking pointedly the monetary value of the estate, Reves was so offended that he immediately changed his mind about the donation. The gift was far too valuable to bestow on a town whose mercenary mayor was apparently insensitive to the art itself. A person interested only in the value of the gift, Reves concluded, was neither capable nor trustworthy of serving as the recipient and custodian of La Pausa and its collections.[17]

As a result of this disheartening experience, Emery and Wendy were compelled to consider other alternatives. The earlier understanding with Malraux had been reached in good faith but finally to no avail, since Reves decided that neither the French government nor the town of Roquebrune would be able to meet the stipulations of the gift—which were that the Villa La Pausa be maintained in its existing state, and that no individual work could be separated from the Reves Collection for any reason, including the sale of works thought perhaps necessary to create an endowment for maintenance of the estate.

Their mutual concern for La Pausa's future led Emery and Wendy to make two vitally important decisions. After years of living happily and traveling together, they decided to marry in Thonex, Switzerland in 1964. In view of his chronic heart condition, Reves and his lawyers persuaded Wendy that the only legitimate way to protect the villa and its art, and therefore to guarantee Emery's avowed wishes, was for her to become his legal heir through marriage.

61

When his heart condition worsened in the late 1960s, Emery Reves and his wife began considering the future of the villa and La Pausa's art collections.

16 *Interview with Wendy Russell Reves by author, 1985.*
17 *Another important, contributing factor in the Reves' decision to reject the town of Roquebrune as the beneficiary of La Pausa was the persistent, and ultimately successful, effort by a real estate developer to construct a multi-story apartment building in front of the villa. Although Reves was able to delay the building's construction for almost ten years through his involvement in the preservationist organization,* Association pour la Sauvegarde des Sites et de la Nature *the Chateau de la Mer was built in the mid-1970s. The siting of the apartment complex now blocks, in part, the villa's previously unobstructed view overlooking Monte Carlo.*

In the obituary it published in September, 1981, the
London Times *described Emery Reves as "a man who*
seemed to represent a larger slice of the history of
our times than many more famous figures."

62

Their other important decision was to seek an alternative beneficiary for La Pausa's art collection – the gift originally intended for Roquebrune. They discussed numerous prospects, museums in America as well as Europe, but always with the idea in mind that the villa itself somehow be re-created and the art collection maintained intact. "Every government was after it," Wendy Reves would later be quoted as saying. "We were offered a great palace in England, a wine chateau in Switzerland. Seven American cities were considered, but one or two wouldn't build a wing, and the others didn't have the money."[18] The Reves continued searching for a host for the next fifteen years, but for various reasons a choice was not made and the decision was postponed.

In the 1970s Emery Reves' heart condition worsened. He was no longer able to travel as he once had, indeed as he had done most all of his life since first leaving Budapest for Zurich in the early 1920s. The little the couple did travel was restricted mainly to moving between their two homes, the villa in Roquebrune where they spent the winter months, and the classic chalet they had built in Glion, Switzerland, where they stayed during the summer. Reves continued his correspondence as a publisher, but he could no longer withstand the strain of constant travel, which at one point in his life had averaged 30,000 miles a year. Instead, he conducted his business and investment transactions by telephone, and he contented himself at home by listening to his immense collection of classical records, comfortably seated in the villa's library where he could admire his Impressionist paintings. Each morning he drove his Rolls into town to purchase

five daily newspapers at the local tabac.[19] He kept abreast of contemporary politics by reading, among other publications, the London *Times*, *Daily Telegraph*, and *New York Herald Tribune* in English, and *Le Monde* and *Le Figaro* in French. He still loved beautiful clothes and dressed elegantly in English suits made by Kilgore & French and in monogrammed silk shirts, made either in Geneva or by Lanvin of Paris. In later life he abandoned bow ties in favor of chic scarves knotted above custom-made waistcoats.

Emery Reves was sophisticated and successful. He had traveled far from his modest Hungarian background during a life of adventure and accomplishment. Through Cooperation Press, he had helped resurrect Churchill as a world spokesman during the Englishman's "wilderness years," and the prime minister, in turn, had personally sponsored Reves as a British subject. As a publisher, Reves had met Joseph Stalin and knew David Ben-Gurion. As an author he had written a book regarded as the bible of the Movement for World Federal Government. In his later years, Emery Reves had much to look back upon, and though he still projected a quiet dignity and authoritative presence, he no longer possessed the dynamic energy which had driven him to a lifetime of achievement the likes of which few others have known. He was confined increasingly to bed, and when his condition deteriorated still further, he and Wendy lived only in Switzerland so as to be nearer a hospital and his personal physician.

When at last he knew he was about to die, Emery consoled Wendy and provided guidance for the disposition of their estate. Despite lapsing into a coma, there were periods of his lengthy illness during which he was lucid and painfully reminiscent of the brilliant personality who had befriended an impressive circle of the 20th century's greatest men and women. On the day of his death, he recovered long enough to whisper to Wendy, "You have always spoiled me."[20] The remark was his last, and in her mind her husband could not have summarized more graciously and meaningfully their life together, than by that simple declaration of appreciation and affection.

With his death on September 5, 1981, the golden era of La Pausa ended. In an editorial obituary, the London *Times*, [21] described Emery Reves as "a man who seemed to represent a larger slice of the history of our times than many more famous figures." After summarizing Reves' long and impressive career, the writer concluded, "As so often, illness and death came not early but too soon."

18 *Owens, Mitch, "Why the Dallas Museum of Art?",* Dallas Observer, *May 16-29, 1985, p. 16.*

19 *Mr. and Mrs. Josef Marinovich own the restaurant "Le Roquebrune" and operate the town's only tabac.*

20 *Interview with Wendy Russell Reves by author, 1985.*

21 *Berthoud, Roger, "The Idealist Who Sold Churchill to the World",* Times, *(London), September 7, 1981.*

The Arts Limited Collection
From the Côte d'Azur to Dallas

As they flew to France in late January 1982 to meet Mrs. Emery Reves, representatives of the Dallas Museum of Art were uncertain of what to expect. George V. Charlton and Irvin L. Levy, Chairman and President of the museum's Board of Trustees, and Director Harry S. Parker III discussed together the little they knew about Mrs. Reves and the purpose of their trip, all of it based on several telephone conversations with Gerald van der Kemp, curator of the Musee le Chateau Versailles. Van der Kemp, a longtime friend of Mrs. Reves, had acted as a self-appointed emissary on her behalf in contacting Irvin Levy about a possible gift of a large private art collection. Levy had known van der Kemp for years because of his interest in the internationally known curator's efforts to restore Versailles and also as a result of several trips the Frenchman had made to Dallas. Irvin Levy communicated the nature of van der Kemp's unofficial inquiry to Harry Parker, who subsequently called the French curator for additional information about Mrs. Reves' art collection and what restrictions, if any, the donor might impose on a bequest.

Van der Kemp revealed to Parker that in addition to a remarkable group of Impressionist paintings, the Reves Collection also included an extensive series of decorative arts – Spanish rugs, Chinese export porcelain, Venetian glass, European silver and ironwork, and an eclectic assortment of furniture. In short, the prospective gift consisted of virtually an entire Mediterranean villa in the south of France. Van der Kemp's description of Madame Reves' estate and his impressive reputation as an aesthete and museum professional, were more than sufficient to interest the three Dallas Museum officials in contacting Mrs. Emery Reves and making arrangements to visit her at the Villa La Pausa.[1]

After her husband's death in 1981, Wendy decided to seek a museum re-creation of La Pausa as a means by which to honor the memory of Emery Reves.

Wendy was not surprised that Director Parker wanted to see her private collection, but she was pleased that he wished to come almost immediately and, moreover, in the company of the two top leaders of the museum's Board of Trustees. After agreeing upon a date, plans were made for Charlton, Levy and Parker to travel to France and to stay at the Hotel de Paris in Monte Carlo, only five kilometers from the villa.

1 *It is interesting to note that almost six years earlier, in 1977, Emery and Wendy Reves had accepted a Dallas Museum request for members of its Associates program to visit in their home as part of a DMA trip to France to see private collections. Equally interesting is the fact that Irvin Levy's wife, Meryl, was chairman of that particular Associates' trip, and many of the arrangements were made with Gerald van der Kemp's assistance. The visit to the Reves' home was cancelled, however, when Emery Reves became ill. When Harry Parker telephoned Wendy Reves in 1982 to make arrangements to meet, both recalled the previously scheduled visit and noted the irony of the situation as it had developed. She even remembered having purchased several dozen blue silk slippers for the expected Dallas guests to wear inside the villa.*

By the time they arrived in Monaco (the day preceding their appointment with Madame Reves), the Dallas group had become increasingly curious about both the woman they were going to meet and the art works in her possession. So curious were the three men that they rented a car to drive to Roquebrune, hoping to be able to see the villa from the road and to gain some insight into the size of the estate. With some difficulty they found their way along the corniche and located the Avenue de la Torracca address, but they were unable to see anything of La Pausa because of the steep terrain which rose from the gatehouse and the massive wrought iron fence which enclosed the property. They could tell, however, that the house was situated on a majestic bluff and that from inside the grounds there were probably commanding views in all directions overlooking the Mediterranean. Somewhat disappointed with the results of their scouting expedition, they returned to the hotel to review the little information they had.

It did not consist of much. Madame Reves had grown up as Wendy Russell in Marshall, Texas, had later become a successful New York model, and eventually married Emery Reves, a man who had published many of Winston Churchill's books. Apparently, Reves had written a popular book himself, entitled *The Anatomy of Peace*. As a couple, the Reves had accumulated what was reputed to be one of Europe's great private art collections and they had purchased a villa on the Riviera originally owned by Coco Chanel. Such was the broad outline of their information, and though there were many unanswered questions, the story's basic details were fascinating enough to have warranted a trip to France.

The next day, Madame Reves' personal assistant, Flavio Berio, picked up Charlton, Levy and Parker at their hotel and drove them to La Pausa. The gates were opened at the appointed hour, and as the Mercedes proceeded up the winding driveway, the Dallasites admired the ancient olive trees, the fields of lavender, and the views overlooking the Italian border and the Maritime Alps. In the near distance, they saw for the first time the villa whose owner and contents they had traveled so far to see. It was exactly five o'clock and she was expecting them for cocktails. Not knowing Madame Reves' age, they were surprised to be greeted at the villa's front door by a young-looking woman glamorously attired in a sweeping gold caftan, wearing a colorful headband and a disarming smile. She informally introduced herself as Wendy Reves and welcomed them to La Pausa.

When they entered the villa, the men were amused by the custom of removing their shoes in favor of slippers, a longstanding practice, their hostess explained, designed to protect the valuable rug collection. The foyer achieved its intended effect on the guests. Displayed about the room were a magnificent Redon pastel, a grand Baroque mirror, an unusual assortment of medieval ironwork, and table arrangements of rare porcelain vases and platters, exquisite silver objects and peacock fans. An enormous chandelier hung overhead. The guests knew at once that they were in a grand home and eagerly anticipated seeing more art inside.

The entry hall, or porch, at the Villa La Pausa in Roquebrune (1982).

Wendy, as she insisted they call her, ushered the group into the great hall where they sat down together. After several minutes of pleasantries, she informed them that this was a business meeting and that before touring the rest of the house, she wished them to understand the conditions upon which she would consider making a gift of her collection. While she outlined the terms, it was somewhat difficult for the men to concentrate, busy as they were scanning the art on the walls, draped over the balcony, and decorating the tables – in fact, everywhere they looked. Beneath the banister was a large van Gogh from his Haystack series painted in St. Rémy, on the opposite wall above the couch was a vivid and explosively colorful Fauve Vlaminck. The Dallas Museum did not own a single Vlaminck, and its one van Gogh, though beautiful, was from an earlier, less classic period in the artist's career. On an easel beside them was a Manet, on the table a Rodin, and all around were handsome antiques and an impressive assortment of objets d'art. In the hall's far corner was Graham Sutherland's famous gold and silver *Cross,* originally intended for Ely Cathedral.

Wendy Reves was not unaware of her distracted audience but felt nevertheless that it was important that the museum representatives understand clearly and fully the terms of her proposed gift. There were a

Two views of the great hall (Roquebrune, 1982)

representatives felt that the funds needed to build a re-creation could be raised, even though the museum was still in the midst of a $25 million campaign to finish construction of a new 210,000 square foot building scheduled to open in late 1983 or early 1984. Almost all of the $25 million had been raised in the private sector to complement the $24.8 million in city bonds authorized by Dallas voters in an historic election in November 1979. Dallasites were exceedingly generous, they explained to Wendy Reves, and the city was increasingly aware of the importance of committing more support for the arts. Since Charlton and Levy had been personally responsible for leading the successful fundraising drive, they, more than anyone else, were well aware of how realistic the chances were of raising the additional funds needed to secure the Reves' gift and to construct a re-creation of the villa.

The library (Roquebrune, 1982)

number of conditions. First and foremost, the Villa La Pausa had to be re-created in an entirely new facility, or at least enough of its rooms to suggest accurately the home's stately presence, classic architecture and refined appointments. Individual art works could not be separated from the Reves Collection, nor installed in another part of the museum. None of the works could be sold for whatever reason without her permission. Works could be loaned for important touring exhibitions, again with her approval, but not for more than three months, and afterwards must be returned to their customary place in the re-creation. Lastly, a re-created La Pausa would be installed with her guidance and in similar fashion to its French setting inasmuch as possible.

Without yet committing themselves, the director and trustees were openly enthusiastic about the possibility of such a gift and expressed confidence that the museum's Executive Committee and Board would seriously consider her conditions. There were some issues troublesome to Parker, but the Dallas

After Wendy finished enumerating her conditions, she invited them to tour the house, and with her as their guide, they began to appreciate the extent and quality of La Pausa's art collections, made all the more meaningful by the anecdotes she related concerning their acquisition or background. She explained what they had meant to the two most important men in her life, her late husband, Emery, and Winston Churchill, who over the years had been a frequent houseguest in what he called "Pausaland." Walking from the great hall into the library, the men learned about the working relationship between Reves and Churchill, publisher and author, as well as about Reves' other career interests as the author of a best-selling book and the director of a syndicated press service he had created in Paris in 1930. She told them of her husband's crusade against Nazism and his narrow escapes from the Gestapo before the outbreak of World War II.

While listening to these intriguing stories, the three men gazed at the art. In the library were a classic Cézanne Provence painting and one of his finest watercolors, a very unusual early Monet, a small Manet, a beautiful Gauguin from his Breton period, a ceramic head of Gauguin's mistress and a vintage Sisley landscape, plus a small Bonnard, a Vuillard and several outstanding Courbet drawings. There was also a stunning collection of art books, and a complete set of Winston Churchill's works in first and multiple language editions published by Emery Reves, many of them rare and signed by the author, as well as several photographs taken by Emery of Churchill at the villa.

From the library the group moved into the salon, whose spacious dimensions gave it an entirely different character. It was no less remarkable, however, for the art it contained. The visitors' attention was first drawn to two splendid marquetry cabinets, which Emery had presented to Wendy on her fiftieth birthday. Above the

Two views of the salon (Roquebrune, 1982).

elaborately carved ceiling mantle was a clock encircled by sun rays. There were several different seating areas, easily capable of accommodating the Churchill entourage and other celebrated parties Wendy described as having taken place in the salon during La Pausa's "golden era." Again, the Dallasites found it difficult to take everything in, so numerous were the objets d'art and paintings of every imaginable subject and size. Two large Renoirs flanked the fireplace, a Manet still life

hung on a far wall next to a portrait by Corot and a Pisarro *Self-Portrait*. The accumulated effect of so many great works of art by masters convinced them that this was, indeed, a collection of museum quality, and though the Dallas Museum of Art did not at that time have a decorative arts collection, a gift such as the Reves' villa would create such a department in one sweeping windfall. The painting collection, alone, was worth instigating another fundraising campaign. For the time being, though, the men kept their thoughts to themselves, eager as they were to continue their tour of the house.

From the salon they looked across a lovely courtyard and a towering marble sculpture by Rodin. Wendy began telling them the story of the villa's creation, of how Coco Chanel, at that time the Duke of Westminster's mistress, had worked with a local architect by the name of Streitz to design "the ideal Mediterranean villa." She also recounted the legend of La Pausa, in which Mary Magdalene rested, reputedly, on the site of the present villa while traveling through Roquebrune.

As they strolled into the dining room, Wendy described the many dinner parties she and Emery had hosted for European statesmen, famous personalities, politicians, businessmen and representatives from the world of publishing and investments. The three Dallasites admired the antique banquet table, Chinese porcelain, silver candelabra and platters, and a magnificent and rare Holbein rug on the floor. Nor was the room without its share of paintings. A beautiful *Vase of Flowers* by Bonnard hung at one end of the room, and there were still lifes by Courbet and Cézanne. Resting on an easel in a corner of the room was a Manet depicting a brioche and pears. Again, the total effect was one of loveliness and hospitality. Small wonder, the men thought, that La Pausa's dinner parties had been so successful and that visitors like Churchill, Garbo, Adenauer, and Lady Bird Johnson had so enjoyed coming to the villa. It was not too difficult to imagine Noel Coward entertaining Churchill and the Reves by singing "Mad Dogs and Englishmen" while wearing a magnolia blossom on his head.

Upstairs, Wendy led the men through the guest rooms, one of which contained a very large and beautiful Degas pastel. She pointed out the suite where Churchill had spent so much time editing *The History of the English Speaking Peoples*. The list of names she recited of guests to La Pausa was most impressive:

The dining room (Roquebrune, 1982).

The master bedroom (Roquebrune, 1982).

Montgomery of Alamein, President Coty of France, Lord and Lady Avon, Albert and Mary Lasker, *et al.* In the exotic master bedroom, the men marveled at the profusion of objets d'art, a 19th century papier-mâché headboard and Napoleon III furniture, a massive, gilt-framed mirror, scarlet silk drapes woven in Lyon, and the room's overall dramatic appearance. Displayed in book shelves and scattered throughout were Wendy's exceptional collection of fans, a fitting expression of her colorful background as a model and hostess.

The tour completed, the group returned to the great hall to resume their discussion of a possible gift to the Dallas Museum of Art. Having earlier stated her requirements, and now that they had seen all that La Pausa had to offer, Wendy asked again if the men were interested in the gift and whether they felt Dallas could satisfy the conditions she had set. Together the men expressed how impressed they were both with the quality and scope of the collections, but they wondered aloud whether the Dallas museum could actually re-create the magical environment of La Pausa. When one of the men suggested how wonderful it was that Wendy, as a native Texan, wanted to give her art to a museum in Texas, she made it clear that she was not offering the gift because of her Texas background, but rather because she believed that Dallas was destined to become a great city in the future. "You have the money to build what I want," she stated candidly, "a museum dedicated to Emery's memory, and the life we shared together in this beautiful house on the Côte d'Azur."[2]

Irvin Levy reminded her that accepting such a gift and its conditions required that they present the proposal to the museum's Executive Committee, as well as overall Board of Trustees, for approval. George Charlton repeated that he and Irvin would be willing to lead another fundraising campaign, and, based upon what they had now seen and admired, he believed they could solicit the private funds needed to build a re-creation. Harry Parker stated that a decorative arts collection had long been an ambition of the museum, and he was of the opinion that a Villa La Pausa in Dallas would be of tremendous interest and educational value not only to the Dallas community, but to the entire Southwest.

The first of what proved to be a series of negotiations with the benefactress ended after six hours with the trio of Dallasites toasting Wendy Reves' prospective gift offer in the candlelit dining room over glasses of white wine. It was 11 p.m. when the group left to return to Monte Carlo. While driving back, they excitedly shared mental notes of all they had seen and the dramatic stories they had heard. It would not be easy to raise the funds necessary to secure the gift, but the villa's fabulous art collection was a dazzling goal worth extraordinary measures. The men were resolute in their determination to make it happen.

Shortly after their return to Dallas, a special meeting of the trustees' Executive Committee was convened. The three men explained the purpose of their recent trip to France and their meeting with Wendy Reves, and they described in considerable detail the nature of the collection and what they believed to be the quality of the works, especially the paintings.[3]

In a memorandum prepared by Parker for the February 1982 meeting, the director characterized the potential of such a gift:

"Mme. Reves offers The Arts Limited Collection (the art holding entity established by her late husband) as a gift to the Dallas Museum of Art together with, at her death, her own fortune, the Villa La Pausa, a chalet near Geneva, and the copyright to certain Churchill publications.

"As The Arts Limited is based in the Bahamas and the art objects were purchased by British citizens largely outside of France, it is anticipated that the French Government will grant export. We must obtain representation that the objects can be exported and any agreement would be conditional upon their safe arrival in Dallas. The value of the proposed gift is the largest gift ever offered to the Dallas Museum of Art. It is certainly tantalizing both for the quality of the art objects and the diversity of the collection which would considerably expand the range of the Museum's collection. The decorative arts collections especially would have enormous appeal to a broader museum audience...

"Several of the conditions, however, represent real problems to the Museum's professional standards and must be carefully explored to see if negotiation is possible."[4]

The director then outlined what he perceived to be potentially troublesome factors in accepting such a gift: the need to raise additional funds from the private sector so soon after the successful fundraising campaign for the new museum; the challenge of re-creating a Mediterranean villa inside a modern museum; the problematic, museological issue of not being able to install Reves' works, in particular the Impressionist paintings, alongside similar works in the museum's existing collection.

After Parker's report, George Charlton and Irvin Levy stressed the importance of the art collections, especially from the point of view of strengthening existing areas of the museum's own collections. They also described their altogether favorable impressions of Wendy Reves. Both had been struck by her candor and the sincerity of her wish to create a living memorial to honor her late husband, Emery Reves. They recounted some of the more fascinating anecdotes Wendy had told them and reiterated their belief that such a re-creation would be a very popular attraction in Dallas not only because of the art, but also because of the history of La Pausa itself. Everyone agreed that

2 Interview with Wendy Russell Reves by author, 1985.
3 The Reves' collecting activities were well known to André Malraux, the French Minister of Cultural Affairs, and the meticulous records which Emery Reves kept, on the paintings in particular, served as the legal basis later for export of the Reves Collection.
4 Parker, Harry. Memo to: Members of the Executive Committee, DMA, February 1982.

such a bounteous collection, representing as it did, an entire household of paintings, furniture, silver, porcelain, glass, almost *ad infinitum,* would be a truly remarkable way to launch the Dallas Museum of Art in a new direction, that of decorative arts. Moreover, the educational value of creating a new department could not be overestimated in further stimulating the community's interest in the arts in general, and in the art museum in particular. They predicted that it would increase the number of visitors to the new museum, then under construction.

The response by the trustees was predictable: they were intrigued by the donors' history and overwhelmed by the description and photographs of the villa and its art collections. The consensus was that the director should not hesitate to proceed with the museum's efforts to secure the gift, and that DMA architect Ed Barnes should be contacted immediately to consider the feasibility of adding to the museum's existing design a wing that could accommodate a re-creation of the Villa La Pausa.

The trustees were also unanimous in their belief that no one was better qualified or more likely to succeed in raising the estimated $5 million needed to build such a decorative arts wing than the proven team of George Charlton and Irvin Levy, whose term of office as Chairman and President of the Board of Trustees had already witnessed the greatest growth in the museum's history. Not only had more art been acquired during their stewardship, but the museum's membership programs had also expanded dramatically. Most significantly, the two men had been largely responsible, along with Harry Parker, trustee Richard Haynes and staff member Philip Seib, for the successful bond election which resulted in the city's purchase of nine acres of prime downtown real estate upon which a major art facility was now in the process of being constructed. Immediately following the board meeting, Charlton and Levy met to chart their strategy for one more fundraising campaign.

For his part, Harry Parker immediately contacted architect Ed Barnes in his New York office and explained the opportunity which had presented itself and the challenge he thought it represented from an architectural standpoint. Several years earlier when Barnes had submitted his final design for the new Dallas Museum of Art, the drawings had anticipated future museum expansion. Both men now agreed that the most logical area to accommodate a decorative arts wing was atop the 15,000 square-foot education wing, called the Gateway Gallery, the columns of which had been designed strong enough to support another level. Although the wing did not include an elevator bank, one was located in the building's main corridor and, therefore, a decorative arts wing could be easily reached from an elevator on the third floor. Furthermore, a viewing platform off the non-western art galleries could be attractively designed to serve as the entrance to a decorative arts wing without altering the museum's existing circulation pattern. Barnes expressed excitement about the gift offered by Mrs. Reves and indicated that he was very eager to travel to Roquebrune to see the villa and determine how best to re-create it in the contemporary museum he had designed for Dallas.

Together, the architect and director left for France in late March. Accompanying them was Dr. Steven Nash, the museum's deputy director and chief curator, whom Parker had asked to examine The Arts Limited Collection from a scholarly perspective. Their first morning meeting with Wendy Reves consisted of walking through the beautiful villa, with frequent pauses for Ed Barnes to admire the home's classical architecture and for Steve Nash to scrutinize the numerous art works displayed within. Both men were elated to be in so grand a home in the presence of so many great paintings and such a splendid array of decorative arts. Barnes had brought with them architectural concept drawings, which he used in their afternoon session to describe where and how the Villa La Pausa could be incorporated into the museum's existing structural design. Wendy Reves provided Barnes with the villa's original architectural plans, and she found his proposed adaptation to be plausible and satisfactory. Although the project would undergo still further changes and considerable discussion in the next few years, the group agreed upon the important rooms to be re-created in Dallas: the entry hall, the great hall, the library, salon, dining room, master bedroom, and, if possible, the patio courtyard. Perhaps the most significant result of the session, according to a memorandum later written by Parker, was the "apparent agreement that the rooms need not be treated as replicas of the La Pausa originals but could be changed and adapted as museum spaces which evoke the originals."[5]

5 *Parker, Harry. Memo to: Members of the Executive Committee, DMA, April 8, 1982.*

After the visit, Ed Barnes expressed confidence that he could design an architectural solution, and that he would begin work on the drawings immediately. Steve Nash summarized his impressions and emphasized that the art collections were without question of the highest quality, that the paintings in particular were uniformly superb, and that the opportunity of introducing decorative arts into the museum on the basis of so rich and varied a collection was an unprecedented occasion and would be a remarkable boon to the city's art museum.

Relieved that their findings confirmed his professional instincts, Harry Parker communicated their respective evaluations to Charlton and Levy. He also made arrangements to return to Roquebrune a month later to resume negotiations with Wendy Reves. Traveling with the director on this trip were Meryl and Irvin Levy and Walter Coakley, a lawyer with Sullivan & Cromwell who agreed to represent the Dallas Museum's interests in the negotiations. Also present for the discussions were Wendy Reves' lawyers, Hans Frank of New York and Jerry Smith of London, and her Geneva banker, Pierre Darrier.

The session was both pleasant and productive, and the spirit of progress achieved was later summarized in the report Parker prepared for an April 30th meeting of the museum's Executive Committee. Concerning the issue of an "endowment" to ensure the gift's future protection, the director wrote: "Wendy is insistent, even against her lawyers' urging, that her intent is to ultimately bequeath to the Museum her chalet in Switzerland, its contents, the 'Swiss Fortune' left by Emery Reves, and, most likely, the Villa La Pausa. She is prepared to write a will making the Museum her residual legatee."[6]

But could the Dallas Museum, she had asked at the meeting in France, satisfy the conditions of her bequest? It could, Levy and Parker reassured her, but time was needed in order to raise the funds. Nevertheless, architect Barnes had been authorized to begin at once on the drawings, and the quarry in Indiana, which would ultimately supply more than nine million pounds of limestone for the new museum, had been notified of a pending order for additional limestone slabs for the facade of a decorative arts wing. Moreover, the fundraising campaign only recently launched

Wendy Reves in La Pausa's library in France.

by the Charlton/Levy team was well underway, they told her, and it had already elicited a favorable response among prospective donors excited about the villa's description and La Pausa's wonderful art collection.

In his April memorandum, Parker also cited the still worrisome issue of "Art Export" as "the least resolved element of the proposed agreement."[7] Despite the export permits secured by Emery Reves and signed by French government officials in 1968, there was no assurance that the French would allow the art to be exported. Only by actually attempting to export could the adequacy of the permits be tested. And although Wendy's advisors recommended an attempt as soon as possible, she herself was "reluctant to export until the facility (Dallas re-creation of La Pausa) is prepared and insistent that the objects not be shown until arranged in their final setting."[8] In Roquebrune at the time of the meeting, everyone present had felt that seeking informal discussions with French museum officials in advance of application for export would inevitably involve a compromise gift of major works to the Louvre.

6 *Parker, Harry. Memo to: Members of the Executive Committee, DMA, April 30, 1982.*
7 *Parker, Harry. Memo to: Members of the Executive Committee, DMA, April 30, 1982.*
8 *Ibid.*

Two and one-half weeks later, Parker returned to France again, this time to be present for the photography of the villa's six principal rooms. Bernard duPont of Paris had been recommended by Gerald van der Kemp on the basis of his interior photographs of Versailles. During his stay, Parker was also able to review with Wendy the specific content of her intended gift. In a subsequent memorandum detailing his fourth visit to La Pausa in less than five months, Parker summarized the extent and flexibility of the tendered gift: "Essentially, what is proposed is the entire contents of the six rooms including such 'non museum items' as the books in the bookcases if these are valuable to the ambience...In addition, those paintings, drawings, and prints (carpets and ceramics) from other areas of the house are also to be included."[9]

In the ensuing year and a half Parker, Levy and Charlton were to make five trips together to meet with Wendy Reves in Europe to inform her of progress being made on the villa's re-creation. On one of those occasions (September 1982), at the Hotel Victoria in Glion, Switzerland, they presented her with the first model she had seen of the new museum already under construction. The series of meetings were of critical importance also in ironing out the endless number of details involved in such a bequest, which included real estate holdings as well as The Arts Limited Collection itself. The transaction represented by far the largest gift and the most complex legal issues the Dallas Museum had ever faced. Charlton and Levy reported on the status of their ongoing efforts to raise funds needed not only to construct the facility, but also to cover the anticipated costs required to crate, insure and transport La Pausa's art collections. Throughout the lengthy negotiations, the museum's strong point was its willingness to proceed with a reconstruction of the villa, while the art collection itself remained in France and before a legal commitment had been secured. A contract with J. W. Bateson Company, the general contractor, was signed in early December 1982, and actual construction on the shell of the facility began the first of February.

A Donation Agreement was reached with Wendy Reves in Geneva on May 31, 1983. As signed by both parties it included an escape clause based on her final

Photo by Nan Coulter 1984

Photo by Daniel Barsotti 1985

Throughout the negotiations with Wendy Reves, the Dallas Museum's strong point was its willingness to proceed with construction of a La Pausa re-creation, while The Arts Limited Collection remained in France and before the gift had been completed. The two photographs depict the great hall at different stages under construction.

and complete approval of the "re-creation." The confidence of museum officials that the gift would ultimately belong to Dallas was due in large part to a personal judgement of the donor's character. Much to her credit, Charlton, Levy and Parker agree, Wendy Reves never once wavered from her original stipulations by making additional demands during the project's evolution. She remained absolutely consistent in her conditions and expectations, which were that "the essential character and atmosphere"[10] of La Pausa be re-created in the Dallas Museum.

9 *Parker, Harry. Memo to: Members of the Executive Committee, DMA, May 10, 1982.*

10 *Parker, Harry. Memo to: Executive Committee, DMA, July 20, 1983.*

In September 1983, Parker flew to France with the museum's registrar, Deb Richards, to help supervise the packing of the more than one thousand art objects included in the Reves gift. On his arrival in Roquebrune he presented Wendy with a general's cap, a gesture intended to recognize her important role in directing the move and to help ease the trauma of such an emotionally as well as physically disruptive experience. For several weeks the two of them supervised the packers[11] in the careful preparation and labeling of the crates which would someday travel, they hoped, to Dallas. Though time consuming, the packing went smoothly and the art was placed in storage after first being appraised by two Paris firms. The appraisals were important as a necessary step in order to apply for export, and represented a growing belief on the part of museum officials that a legally binding donation agreement could be achieved and that the art could be successfully exported later. Everyone involved in the negotiations was pleased with the appraisal of the collection's worth based on current values in the world art market.

However, a snag in the Reves project developed in early November. The problem concerned obtaining export permits from France for so large a collection of art, in particular the paintings by French artists. In his report to the museum's Executive Committee, Parker summarized his Paris meeting with French officials:

> "At the request of our shipper, Pierre Chenue, I flew to Paris to meet M. Hubert Landais, Director of the Museums of France, on Tuesday, November 8. M. Landais had earlier summoned M. Chenue to inform him that he would recommend denial of the export applications for the Reves paintings and had expressed his dismay with the Dallas Museum's failure to approach the Museums of France in advance.
>
> "My meeting included M. Didier Quentin, Consul General of France in Houston, who happened to be in Paris and who had visited the Dallas Museum and had seen the new wing just two days before at our invitation. M. Quentin had some six months before, advised the Government of the pending export based on information he had learned in Texas.
>
> "M. Landais explained that such an export posed a difficult problem for France. The French newspapers would be bound to describe the loss of French patrimony. I noted that we were sensitive to the public relations problem and would try to be helpful, even allowing the French Government to participate in the announcement. M. Landais noted that the best way to offset the loss of the collection would be to negotiate an off-setting gift to France. This would require a full review by the French curators of the total collection."[12]

The new Dallas Museum of Art opened to the public on Jaunary 29, 1984. Though not yet ready, a new Decorative Arts Wing featuring a re-creation of the Villa La Pausa was well underway.

Photo by Daniel Barsotti

All of these events unfolded during the most dynamic period in the museum's history. While the staff and operations continued in the old building in Fair Park, the new facility including the shell of the Reves addition was under construction in downtown Dallas. The museum hosted several major traveling exhibitions, including *Master Paintings from The Phillips Collection*, the internationally acclaimed *El Greco of Toledo*, *The Shogun Age* from the Tokugawa family collection in Japan, and *Pierre Bonnard: The Late Paintings*, which, along with the *El Greco* show, the Dallas Museum had helped organize. When not directing the museum's daily operations in Fair Park, Harry Parker could be found on the construction site downtown, giving one of countless tours he conducted day

11 *André Chenue & Fils Transports Internationaux was paid to transport and pack the Reves Collection.*
12 *Parker, Harry. Memo to: Members of the Executive Committee, DMA, November 10, 1983.*

and night for interested parties, potential patrons and various other special interest groups whose political, financial and community influence could be meaningful in advancing the museum's cause and ensuring its continued growth.

Likewise, Irvin Levy and George Charlton had never been busier in their lives. As trustee officers, they also were involved in the museum's exhibition schedule. Now they were actively canvassing the Dallas private sector once again for donations to the Reves project. The success of the fundraising campaign was of paramount importance since Wendy Reves would not release her art collection until she approved the museum's re-creation of La Pausa. And the villa could not be reconstructed in Dallas unless enough pledges were obtained and the collection of funds begun. The stakes were high, especially the challenge of securing a satisfactory exportation agreement, but the prospect of delivering the Reves gift to Dallas was incentive enough for the three museum officials to pursue the gamble.

On January 29, 1984, the new Dallas Museum of Art opened to the public. It immediately received favorable reviews, not only from architectural and art critics, but more importantly from the people of Dallas. Approval within the community was easy to measure since the museum's attendance more than tripled during its first year of operation in the new downtown facility. Dallasites were proud of their new building and its art collections, and excited about the museum's expanded programming and future exhibition schedule.

In mid-February, and just after the opening of the new building, Dallas Museum officials learned that Hubert Landais had met in Paris with Durant des Aulnois, a notaire engaged by Wendy Reves, to discuss a compromise solution to the impasse over the export of the Reves Collection. In exchange for a donation by Mme. Reves of three works by Renoir, Redon and Degas, the French government would be willing to authorize the collection's release. Disheartened by such a proposal, Dallas officials countered by offering to donate a fund to the museums of France for the purpose of acquiring works of art of their choice outside the Reves Collection. The Dallas offer was rejected by French officials, but they requested another meeting.

In late February, George Charlton, Irvin Levy and Harry Parker traveled to Paris to attend the opening at the Centre Georges Pompidou of a Bonnard exhibition, which had been co-organized by Musée Nationale d'Art Moderne, The Phillips Collection in Washington, D.C., and the Dallas Museum of Art. At the Bonnard reception, Parker noted a postcard appeal by the French museums soliciting public support for the acquisition of a Bonnard painting, *Nu à la Baignoire* (1931), then offered for sale by the Beyeler Gallery of Switzerland. Parker, who planned to meet with French officials concerning the Reves Collection, thought perhaps a donation in honor of Emery Reves toward the purchase of this painting could serve as an alternative solution to the French request for a contribution in kind. At the meeting the next day, director Hubert Landais, and Michel Laclotte, chief curator of the Louvre, accepted the Dallas proposal as a most appropriate way to celebrate Franco-American collaboration on the historic Bonnard exhibition.

At lunch the following day, Charlton, Levy and Parker met with notaire Durant des Aulnois, director Landais, and M. Maheu, president of the Pompidou Centre, to conclude the arrangements. It was agreed that a memorandum detailing the discussions would be prepared and that the signing of export permits for the Reves Collection would be tentatively scheduled for April 2nd.

One month later Harry Parker returned to Paris with Irvin Levy who personally delivered the Bonnard donation to the French museums on behalf of the Dallas Museum at a meeting held with all senior French officials present. By coincidence, a group of Dallas trustees, including Vince Carrozza and Lawrence Pollock, Jr., were also in Paris and joined Parker and Levy in celebrating the exportation agreement at a luncheon hosted by des Aulnois at his club, and later that evening at a dinner party given by Irvin Levy. Everything seemed in order, at last.

Such, however, did not prove to be the case at Charles de Gaulle Airport on April 3rd. Despite prior notification through proper government agencies, reassurances from French officials and Parker's presentation of the recently signed export permits, almost all of the crates containing the Reves Collection were reopened and their contents closely examined. Unable to reach anyone in authority, Parker called Levy at his hotel, who also tried to contact appropriate French officials. He and his wife cancelled their business and personal plans, and joined the beleaguered director at the airport. The delay amounted to eight hours of frustration and anxiety before customs officials finally confirmed that the ownership papers and permits

were, in fact, legitimate and that the art works could therefore be legally exported. With considerable relief and gradual satisfaction, Harry Parker relaxed once the flight was airborne and the valuable cargo finally on its way to Dallas.

On April 3, 1984 Director Harry Parker returned to Dallas from Paris on a chartered DC-8 whose entire cargo was the promised gift of the Wendy and Emery Reves Collection.

The privately chartered Flying Tigers DC-8[13], whose sole cargo was the treasured art collection from the Villa La Pausa, did not arrive in Dallas at the freight terminal at D/FW Airport until well past midnight. A number of museum staff members and officials, including Ellen Parker and George Charlton, had been awaiting the plane's touchdown for several hours. Also present were the museum's chief of security along with five plainclothes Dallas police officers in unmarked vehicles, two U.S. Customs agents, and three North American Van Lines trucks ready to be loaded with the Reves Collection. Apart from the pilot and crew, the plane carried only two passengers, Parker and museum registrar, Deb Richards, who were seated just behind the cockpit. The rest of the DC-8 was loaded with palettes containing the Arts Limited Collection, mounted on rails for easy removal. When Parker emerged from the plane, his beaming smile noticeably offset by lines of fatigue, it was apparent that the experience of the past 24 hours had been both a challenge and an ordeal. After embracing his wife and shaking hands, he joined the small group in sharing a bottle of champagne. At 3 a.m. the all-night process of unloading the plane began, and by morning the Reves Collection had cleared U.S. Customs and found a new home in Dallas, Texas.

Despite the fact that museum officials and Wendy Reves had been negotiating the gift for several years, information about the impending gift and its shipment

had been successfully concealed so as not to jeopardize the transaction.[14] With the arrival of the cargo-laden jet, the museum, with permission from Wendy, was now ready to release the information. No one, however, expected the explosion of interest caused by the announcement. On April 4th both Dallas papers carried front-page stories, banner headlines, and color reproductions of individual paintings to illustrate the caliber of art included in the gift. "The DMA Takes a Giant Step" trumpeted *The Dallas Morning News*, while the headline in the *Dallas Times Herald* proclaimed "The Art of Success: Museum's Diligence Led to Landmark Acquisition."

Moreover, news of the Reves' gift so prominently extolled in the Dallas media created an instant ripple effect, with a story shortly appearing in *The New York Times* and carried by AP and UPI. Articles appeared in newspapers everywhere, from Nashua, New Hampshire to Chattanooga, Tennessee, from Richmond to Beaumont to Mankato, as well as in Philadelphia, Chicago and Los Angeles. Magazines began contacting the museum's publicity office, requesting photos and additional information, and a number of editors expressed interest in dispatching writers and photographers to Roquebrune to interview Wendy Reves and to photograph her villa. However, after the ardous and psychological ordeal of packing-up her household for shipment to Dallas, Wendy had suffered a physical relapse and was neither eager nor willing to grant interviews at that time. Her inaccessibility and relatively mysterious background along with that of her late husband, made the Dallas announcement all the more intriguing, not only to the general public, but to the art world at large. Who was this woman, they asked. What was Emery Reves' professional relationship with Winston Churchill? Where and how did she and her late husband acquire such a fantastic collection of art?

The answers to these and other questions began to surface one year later in April 1985, when Wendy Reves returned to the United States for the first time in years to see the facility built by the Dallas Museum of Art to house the Villa La Pausa. The purpose of her visit was to approve completion of the villa's reconstruction.

Also included on her agenda was a sentimental visit to Marshall, Texas, where she had grown up during the 1920s, and whose citizens were eagerly awaiting the return of one of their most celebrated natives. In addition to her gift to Dallas, Wendy planned to donate

13 *Use of the DC-8 had been provided by William H. Bricker, Chairman and Chief Executive Officer of the Diamond Shamrock Corporation, a DMA Corporate Council member.*
14 *Parker, Harry. Memo to: Executive Committee, DMA, July 30, 1983: "Prior to the opening of the facilities no party to the agreement shall voluntarily initiate any advertisement, press release, public announcement or other publicity with respect to the collection."*

underwriting funds to the Michelson-Reves Museum of Art in Marshall, as well as an extensive collection of handicrafts, many of them the work of Marshall relatives created decades earlier.

During her three-week visit to Dallas in May 1985, Wendy Reves addressed the Art Museum League and met with members of the news media at a press conference staged inside the museum's re-creation of La Pausa. She resumed meetings with George Charlton, Irvin Levy and Harry Parker, whom she referred to as her three favorite "musketeers." Most importantly, she signed a deed of gift on May 23rd formally completing the transfer of the Wendy and Emery Reves Collection to the Dallas Museum of Art. In addition, she was honored at a reception and dinner hosted by the museum's new trustee officers, Chairman Ed Cox and President Vince Carrozza. At the dinner Mayor Starke Taylor welcomed her return to Texas and expressed his appreciation for her monumental gift on behalf of the City. Wendy Reves responded by describing the Dallas Museum as "a beautiful sanctuary of art," and an appropriate home for a reborn Villa La Pausa.

*   *   *

75

On her visit to Dallas in May 1985, Wendy's first opportunity to see the museum's re-creation of La Pausa, she was given a tour of the building by her three favorite "musketeers": (l. to r.) former museum President Irvin Levy, Director Harry Parker, and former trustee Chairman George V. Charlton.

Photo by Nan Coulter

Wendy Reves and Harry Parker at a press conference inside the La Pausa re-creation on May 7, 1985, announcing the gift of the Wendy and Emery Reves Collection to the Dallas Museum of Art.

The new Decorative Arts Wing featuring a re-creation of the Villa La Pausa and the Wendy and Emery Reves Collection opened in November 1985.

Acknowledgements

76 The idea of writing "the Reves' story" first occurred to me at a museum staff retreat in the summer of 1982. At that time I heard Harry Parker describe meetings which he, George Charlton and Irvin Levy had held with a Mrs. Emery Reves of France during the preceding half-year. The meetings concerned a "possible gift" of a large private collection of paintings and decorative arts … if the Dallas Museum of Art agreed to re-create her villa, La Pausa. The Riviera villa, we learned, was renowned for its beauty, its past owners, its present art collection, and the many famous personalities who had stayed there as houseguests, including Winston Churchill, whose *War Memoirs* Emery Reves had helped publish. As Harry Parker described what he knew about Wendy Reves, a celebrated New York fashion model in the 1940s, and Emery Reves, a distinguished publisher and author who twice escaped from Nazi arrest, room photographs of the Villa La Pausa were circulated and we saw the Reves Collection for the first time in its original setting. Everyone present was struck by the quality of the art and the extensive variety of the collections. I was impressed with the naturally dramatic elements of the donors' lives.

In trying to tell the story of Wendy and Emery Reves and the evolution of The Arts Limited Collection in a re-created villa in Dallas, I have relied upon the good will and advice, active assistance and voluntary help of many individuals whom I wish to recognize. Because it was his confidence which led me to undertake this challenge, I thank Harry for the opportunity to discover much about myself. George Charlton and Irvin Levy were instrumental in providing me with a firsthand account of their involvement in the museum's acquisition of the gift. From Martin Gilbert, Churchill's official biographer, I learned of the esteem with which Churchill regarded Emery Reves' friendship and judgment. Georg Solti, Reves' first cousin, described his recollections of the family's Hungarian background. Valerie Fellner, widow of William Fellner, graciously entertained my persistent questions about her husband's and Reves' student days together in Zurich and in later life. To Marc Streitz, I am deeply indebted for sharing with us rare photographs of the French villa his father designed, many of them here published for the first time.

For various reasons, many of them personal, I wish to thank the following for their assistance on this project: Ann Souder, Vicki Vinson, the wonderful Marinovich family of Roquebrune, France, Mrs. Inez Hatley Hughes of Marshall, Texas, Mrs. Raymond Ford of Hallsville, Texas, Becky McKinney-Reese, Annette Schlagenhauff, George Bowles, Dick Clampitt and Amy Schaffner.

There is no substitute for a good editor, and I feel exceptionally fortunate that a visit by Allen Rozelle of Geneva to Dallas coincided with the final preparation of the manuscript. I am equally grateful to Gail Chancey and Melanie Bassett Wright, who served as a reliable sounding board for ideas, labored to copyedit the text, programmed the word processor, and humored me throughout the project.

A special note of thanks is due to Becky Wade, whose sensitivity to art and the quality expected in a museum publication is evident in this book for all to admire.

A donors' biography, of course, would not have been possible without the enthusiastic cooperation of Wendy Reves, who spent hours recording information about her life and that of Emery's, answering my endless questions, and providing documentary and photographic materials without which the biographical essay would lack credibility. I hope that I have conveyed in some small measure the remarkable lifetime achievements she and Emery Reves accomplished in their respective careers and the glorious life they shared together in the Villa La Pausa.

Lastly, I wish to thank my family but especially my wife Kathleen, whose patient understanding allowed me the time to complete this challenge and without whose encouraging support it would not have been possible.

RVR

PAINTINGS, SCULPTURE & DRAWINGS

Cézanne, Still Life, *1900-06, detail*

Introduction

The true glory of the Reves Collection is its superb concentration of Impressionist and Post-Impressionist French art. Comprising a total of almost 70 paintings, drawings and sculptures, these holdings boast major examples by virtually all the leading artists of the period. Corot, Courbet, Daumier, Renoir, Monet, Manet, Degas, Pissarro, Sisley, Toulouse-Lautrec, Rodin, van Gogh, Gauguin, Cézanne, Seurat, Bonnard, Vuillard, Redon, Vlaminck — these and others are all represented in strength, often by more than one work, sometimes by as many as four or five. That the collection is not better known is attributable to Emery and Wendy Reves' sense of privacy. Their many visitors to La Pausa, experiencing the works installed throughout the villa's lovely interiors, inevitably carried away a rich impression of what the Reves had accomplished during their more than thirty years of collecting. No exhibitions of the collection as a whole, or even large segments of it, were ever permitted, however, and although many of the works are familiar from reproduction in various books, articles and exhibition catalogues, they are generally identified in those sources only as "private collection." Exposure of the Reves Collection in its new quarters at the Dallas Museum of Art and through the present handbook and, eventually, through more thorough catalogue raisonnés, will therefore come as a special surprise and joy to public and professionals alike. It also will win due recognition for the connoisseurship of the two individuals who assembled the extensive art collections.

Taken as a whole, the collection represents an encapsulated history of Impressionism and Post-Impressionism, with the distinct educational advantage of presenting several major artists at different stages of their stylistic development. From precursors of Impressionism such as Corot and Courbet to artists who bridge chronologically and stylistically into the 20th century such as Vuillard, Bonnard, and Vlaminck, a full panoply of the visual riches and artistic invention of late 19th century French art is found in all its diversity and ambition. By any measure it was one of the most profoundly creative periods in the history of western art. In the achievements of the Impressionist generation, a newly inspired reorientation of subject matter away from traditional themes toward the realities of modern life was consummated, and a striving for optical veracity going back to the Renaissance reached a peak of development. Not just an abandonment to the senses as sometimes claimed, the movement forged a union between pictorial intelligence (seen in innovative composition, complex technical measures, and important thematic underlays) and a joyful celebration of visual experience as stimulated by light in all its myriad interactions with nature's changing forms. Sensual pleasure is honored, but so also are directness and honesty of observation, painterly craft, and the organizing powers necessary to transform visual sensation into lastingly fresh analogues of experience.

In the sophisticated realism that the Impressionists engendered, however, were planted seeds of revolt. Artists such as Gauguin, van Gogh and Cézanne all came strongly under its sway but eventually reacted against it, realizing it could be developed no further and seeking instead their own personally expressive modes that drew as much from internal and imaginative sources as from external stimuli. The result was a diversity of styles replacing the greater hegemony of Impressionism, each with its own characteristics. Van Gogh's emotional releases, Gauguin's journeys into mysticism and exoticism, Cézanne's conceptual reorderings of nature, Seurat's quasi-scientific examination of the structure of color: these and other tendencies from late in the century, grouped loosely and somewhat misleadingly under the title Post-Impressionism, introduced lastingly important changes in visual thought. For all their diversity, they are linked by an impulse away from naturalism toward abstraction, an impulse which reached its full fruition in the art of the 20th century.

In tracing the manifestation of these developments through the Reves Collection, we encounter many works that are not necessarily grand in scale or impact. Indeed, one of the hallmarks of the collection is its inherent proclivity for works that operate on a quiet, subtle level, works that are gratifying to live with but also make a solid statement about the creative personality of the artist. Corot's *Portrait of Mme. Sennegon*, for example, is not one of his best known paintings, but it captivates us by its exquisite refinements of handling. An early still life by Cézanne entitled *The Water Can* is small and somewhat dark, but reveals upon study the strength of this artist's formalizing vision, while Monet's *Pont Neuf*, unusual in its sketchiness and grey palette, provides an interesting insight into the range of Impressionist climatological observation. Even the van Gogh *Sheaves of Wheat* speaks in a restrained voice. Its pale colors are atypical among late van Goghs, but this very quality of pale, cool harmony accounts for much of its distinctive poetry. It might further be ventured that the Reves' appreciation for understatement lies also behind the truly exceptional quality and depth of the collection's works on paper. Drawings by Manet, Cézanne, Pissarro, van Gogh, Renoir, Toulouse-Lautrec, Courbet, and several others constitute a veritable treasure of late-19th century graphics. Intimate by definition, these works require close study and an eye for linear and tonal nuance, but repay such attention with a moving range of visual, emotional, and documentary information. Indeed, if any one segment of the collection were to be singled out as most important within its general field, it might well be the works on paper.

By pointing out the quieter, more intimate elements of the collection, the impression should not be left that these works are not balanced by numerous examples of a more forceful and dynamic nature. Anyone who knows anything about the Reves would realize that they would also be drawn, at least occasionally, to sheer strength of statement. Gauguin's *Farm at Le Pouldu*, for example, despite its Impressionist leanings, is an essay on synthetic color abstraction. The late Degas *Bathers* demonstrates the monumentality and expressive freedom this artist achieved toward the end of his life. Cézanne's *Still Life with Apples on a Sideboard* is a marvel of chromatic richness, and the Vlaminck *Bougival* is among the most powerful paintings he ever produced. These works stand out through scale and impact and add another dimension to the collection as a whole.

Just as any collecting partnership inevitably divides into certain areas of individual enthusiasm and expertise, so it can be said that Emery Reves was the member of this team most consistently involved in the growth and refinement of their holdings in paintings and drawings. And the record speaks clearly of his astuteness as an acquirer. By World War II he had already assembled and lost to Nazi confiscation an important group of German Expressionist works. Soon after the war he resumed his collecting efforts, switching, however, to the Impressionist field. Among early purchases were the Gauguin *Farm at Le Pouldu* and Degas *Bathers*, acquired from the estate of Ambroise Vollard, the large Vuillard entitled *The Tent*, Renoir's *Duck Pond*, and the Sisley landscape from St. Mammès, all of which are still mainstays of the collection. Before long, Reves was well known to all the major dealers in Impressionist art as a man of discerning taste backed by solid business acumen. Alexandre Rosenberg has

given us in correspondence the following portrait: "I have known Emery Reves during his collecting years, and he was not a man easy to forget, but definitely difficult to describe. Colorful, expansive, congenial, a little bombastic on occasion, he enjoyed life extremely and art very sincerely. His open manners did not hide completely his sharp mind and cunning, and he was a well-known master in public relations. Altogether a generous personality, enthusiastic with a dose of a becoming vanity about his collection. He made a point of setting his standard high, and I think he often succeeded."

Guided over the years by an eye for quality as well as a quest for historical breadth, Emery Reves added to the collection by purchase but also refined it by trade or sale when a particular holding did not, in the long run, live up to his personal standards. Two lesser-quality Pissarros, for example, gave way in the process of assembling an exemplary group of three oils by this artist. For range, works by Morisot, Jongkind, and Monticelli helped round out the historical picture of the Impressionist period, and certain significant sub-themes were pursued, resulting, for example, in a wonderful series of still lifes and a group of works in pastel that rank among the very finest in the collection. A similar historical attentiveness is reflected in the groupings of paintings and drawings from different periods of a particular artist's career. Renoir, Manet, Degas, Cézanne, and Pissarro, to name the most important examples, are all seen through a variety of works manifesting different stylistic and thematic concerns.

Although assembled primarily for enjoyment and enhancement of personal surroundings, the Reves Collection expresses in its range and quality an uncommon intelligence behind its formulation. It is a pleasure to be able to introduce this remarkable group of paintings, drawings, and sculptures to a broader audience through the present publication. Restrictions of space, unfortunately, limit our selection to only 34 works, which are all illustrated in color and accompanied by brief essays. An eventual catalogue raisonné, however, will present the collection in its entirety, along with the documentation that was impossible to include in the present format.

Steven A. Nash
Deputy Director/Chief Curator
Dallas Museum of Art

Emery and Wendy Reves

82

Camille Corot (French, 1796-1875)
Madame Sennegon, *1841*
oil on canvas, 18¼ x 15 inches (46.3 x 38 cm)
signed lower right: "C. Corot/1841"
and dated lower left: "1841"

Although figure paintings of a classical and romantic variety represent a large and important share of Corot's *oeuvre,* he made relatively few portraits. His work in this genre was limited to relatives and close friends, and seems motivated much more by sentiments of intimacy and amicability than any desire for display or social documentation. The works of this nature he undertook are modest in size, generally simple in composition, and most importantly, tender in feeling.

A particularly important sub-group of portraits centers on the family of Corot's sister, Annette-Octavie Sennegon (1793-1874) and her husband, Laurent-Denis Sennegon. All seven of their children were painted by Corot, starting in 1831 with the eldest daughter, Laure. The dates of some of these works are conjectural, but most seem to have been done during the 30s, including the elegant and famous painting of the fourth daughter, Louise Claire. In 1841 and 42, Corot painted the mother (the picture now in the Reves Collection) and the father, respectively.

In its clear and simplified massing of the figure against a dark background, Corot's study of Mme. Sennegon clearly reveals his interest in the portrait lineage of Ingres and Renaissance Italy. It is a work, however, of utmost delicacy and subtlety, in which the soft tonal effects deriving from Corot's landscape style override the hard linearity of these earlier sources. Everything about the portrait speaks of discretion. Through Mme. Sennegon's sharp features and rather awkward clasping of hands, we gain the impression of a somewhat homely and ungainly individual who nevertheless is depicted with loving gentleness. The fine modelling of her features matches in feeling the extreme subtlety of tonal variations in the grey background and grey and violet dress and also the refinement with which she is positioned against a composition of finely differentiated stripes in the wall behind. In so delicate a balance of elements, small details become crucial, such as the coordination of rose and salmon tints in the scarf, bonnet, and facial highlights, echoed by the color of the date and signature at lower left and lower right. In another delicate touch, the round pin at her neckline forms a small visual rivet at the very center of the composition.

Judging from technical evidence, it is possible that the signature on this work may have been added by Corot sometime well after execution of the painting (but before his friend and cataloguer Alfred Robaut saw it and made a drawing of it during Corot's lifetime). The date of 1841, however, judging from the proximity with the dated portrait of Monsieur Sennegon, is convincing.

Jean-Baptiste Carpeaux (French, 1827-1875)
Ugolino and His Sons, *c. 1860*
plaster stained reddish brown, 20¾ x 13¾ x 10¾ inches
(52.7 x 35 x 27.3 cm)
not signed or dated

Despite the fact that his career was marked by controversy and financial hardship, Carpeaux dominated French sculpture during the middle of the 19th century between the generation of Francois Rude and that of Auguste Rodin. His fame, and in some instances his notoriety, were based primarily on major public commissions such as his sculptures for the Fontaine de l'Observatoire, decorations for the Pavillon de Flore at the Louvre, and the hotly debated monumental group called *The Dance* for the facade of the new Paris Opera. He also established, however, an active business in smaller decorative sculptures and portraiture. In all these fields, his work stands out for its sensuously naturalistic surfaces, the pulse of life the artist was able to capture in his forms, and moreover, his infusion of new possibilities into sculptural expression. These qualities made him one of the few sculptors of his century that Rodin found admirable.

The sculpture that launched Carpeaux on his career, and that still stands as one of his finest achievements, is the *Ugolino and His Sons.* Completed in Italy in 1861 following Carpeaux's term as a *pensionnaire* at the French Academy in Rome, it was sent to Paris and given a special exhibition at the Ecole des Beaux-Arts, where it aroused considerable controversy and moved its author into the critical limelight. This fervor of

reaction was due partly to the subject (based on Dante's story of Count Ugolino who, while imprisoned for treason, survived by devouring his own sons), and partly to the risks Carpeaux took in his dramatic, undecorous expression, crowded composition, and strained Michelangesque treatment of anatomy, the latter reflecting an enthusiasm he developed during his Italian sojourn.

Conceived as early as 1857, this work passed through an extended period of gestation encompassing numerous drawings and several clay maquettes, the earliest of which was the basis for the plaster cast in the Reves Collection. While the final sculpture was immaculately and painstakingly finished, this study has all the immediacy and roughness of an oil sketch. It records a stage of development when only three rather than the eventual four dying sons are huddled around the tyrannical father. The influence of Michelangelo's *Moses* and the antique *Laocoön* is clear, while Carpeaux's energetic modelling with clay pellets shows an emotional intensity rare in French sculpture of the period.

It is not known how many casts, plaster and bronze alike, were made of this particular model, but as one of the most popular Carpeaux sculptures, it passed through a long history of reproduction. Several different families of casts have been identified, distinguished by mold marks and degrees of detail. Most of these apparently derive from a plaster cast that Carpeaux left at the Villa Medici in Rome, quarters for the French Academy.

Gustave Courbet (French, 1819-1877)
Still Life with Apples, Pear, and Pomegranates
1871 or 72
oil on canvas, 10¾ x 16¼ inches (27.3 x 41.2 cm)
signed lower right: "G.C. / Ste Pélagie."

Courbet's robust realism, with its penchant for the beauties of texture, color and other material realities of life, found a natural outlet of expression in still life painting. Early in his career, still lifes are found as parts of larger compositions. By the 1860s, however, they had begun to appear as subjects in and of themselves. Flower paintings, studies of fruit, closeups of fish or animals that also serve as a type of still life: all show the same thick buildup of paint, rich color, and strong chiaroscuro that give Courbet's work in this genre so distinctive a materiality. It is possible that he was encouraged in this field by such artists as Manet and Monet, whom he previously had influenced and who remained respectful of his talents and leadership.

This small still life of apples, a pear, and pomegranates spilling from a basket is signed at the lower right and inscribed "Ste Pélagie," the name of the prison where Courbet was incarcerated from September 22 to December 30, 1871, for his supposed role in the destruction of the Vendôme Column during the preceding reign of the Commune. From September 1870, Courbet had served as chairman of an Arts Commission charged with the protection of works of art during the Franco-Prussian War, and under the Commune he was appointed chairman of an Artists' Federation, from which position he agitated for the destruction of the Column as a symbol of imperialism. His role in the actual demolition is ambiguous, but he nevertheless was tried, convicted and sentenced to six months' imprisonment at Saint-Pélagie in the rue du Puits de l'Ermite in Paris. There he was visited by friends and his sister who brought him flowers and fruit, hoping to inspire him to paint. On November 2 he was given brushes and palette with paints and commenced an important series of still lifes. Due to a health problem, however, Courbet was released on parole on December 30 to a clinic at Neuilly. There he continued his still life paintings, sometimes adding the inscription "Ste. Pélagie" as advertisement of the hardship and cruelty he had undergone. For this reason, it is generally difficult to determine if the works so inscribed were actually done in prison or at Neuilly.

Honoré Daumier (French, 1808-1879)
Study of an Actor, *date unknown*
pen and wash on paper, 9¾ x 6⅝ inches (24.8 x 16.8 cm)
not signed or dated

In a brief note on this sketch in his important study of Daumier drawings, K.E. Maison summarized its status and appeal: "A late and most powerful pen drawing, made without any preparation in black chalk or charcoal. The same unusual technique, with large areas of black wash treatment, was used for the Study of a Laughing Man, at Cambridge." One of the greatest draughtsmen of all time, Daumier was able to achieve the most telling and bold effects with a minimum of means. As Maison points out, no preparatory underdrawing exists on the sheet. With a flurry of loose, woven pen strokes, Daumier sketched the essential contours of his gesticulating figure, regularly running off into space with trails of autonomous linear energy, creating suggestions of movement or flickering light. Then, along the shadowed undersurfaces, he added a heavy black wash with fast but confident strokes of the brush. In contrast to the dense shadows, the highlighted side of the body takes on a quality of brilliant lumination, conveying the strength of stage footlights.

In this rapid rendering, Daumier has captured the energy and expression of his unknown actor at a poignant moment, and has even managed an impression of the fuller theatrical surroundings.

In his love of the theater as a source of subjects, Daumier anticipated both Degas and Toulouse-Lautrec. Most often, however, his work focuses on individual actors scrutinized through revealing poses or expressions, rather than ensembles or full views of the stage. It was not the panoply of theater that caught his attention so much as the isolated participants, with their assumed identities (masking their true personalities) and exaggerated sense of self. In these roles Daumier found lessons of human nature, of which he was always a keen student and recorder.

Edouard Manet (French, 1823-1883)
The Spanish Singer, *1861 (?)*
watercolor on paper, 11 x 8¾ inches (28 x 22.2 cm)
signed lower left: "Manet"

The impact of Spanish art and culture permeated Manet's development from the late 1850s through the 60s, as he absorbed the influence of such masters as Velasquez and Goya and worked with subjects projecting a romantic vision of Spanish traditions in tune with a general current of hispanomania sweeping France at the time. One of his most popular essays in this vein was the *Spanish Singer* (or *Guitarrero),* a large painting completed in 1860 and exhibited at the Salon of 1861 (now in the Metropolitan Museum of Art). Although he did not actually travel to Spain until 1865, Manet earlier had arranged sittings in Paris with various Spanish dancers and singers. Some writers have speculated that it is either the well known singer and composer Jérome Bôsch, or the Andalusian guitarist Huerta, who appears in the *Spanish Singer.* The melanged costume of the figure in the painting, however, and the fact that he holds the guitar in a lefthanded, rather awkward fashion, seem to preclude a professional Spanish musician as the model.

The Reves watercolor, which belonged successively to Manet's two friends and supporters, Antonin Proust and Jean-Baptiste Faure, corresponds quite closely with the painting, but its exact origins remain unclear. It may have been executed as a detailed preparatory study for the painting. However, since Manet frequently made watercolor repetitions of his paintings as an intermediary step between the canvas and an etched version of the same subject, the present picture may also have followed the painting and led to Manet's etching of the *Spanish Singer* from 1861-62 (etching and watercolor are of comparable size). A tracing that is known from an early source but now lost might have been made from the watercolor as a further aid toward the etching, although alternatively it could also have been based on a photograph. Presenting yet another possibility, Adolphe Tabarant *(Manet et ses oeuvres,* Paris, 1947) reports that Antonin Proust asked Manet many times for a replica in watercolor of the *Spanish Singer,* which the artist finally provided in 1864.

Interesting in its own right for its strong graphic effects, the watercolor captures on a much smaller scale the combination of realism and sonority that marks the painting. Manet's handling is descriptive yet bold, with a brusque stroking of contours and broad patches of shadow complementing the warm highlights for drama and a convincing sense of three-dimensional space.

Edouard Manet (French, 1823-1883)
Brioche with Pears, *1876*
oil on canvas, 18⅛ x 22 inches (46 x 55.9 cm)
signed lower right: "Manet"

Within the general revival of still life painting in mid-19th century France, for which Chardin was so powerful an influence, Manet emerged by far as the most brilliant practitioner. Either autonomously or as segments of larger compositions, still lifes were a steady concern for Manet starting in the early 1860s, and indeed, his work in this genre earned a popularity and critical approbation that eluded his early, more challenging figure pictures. Given his talent for *la peinture pure,* still life themes elicited full expression of his bold technique, sumptuous manipulation of paint, and sensitivity for light, texture and color.

His *Brioche with Pears* is generally thought to have been painted in 1876, but is closely related to another still life with brioche from six years earlier, now in the David Rockefeller Collection. A comparison of the two pictures is instructive for the stylistic development of his art during this interval. Whereas the earlier version is larger in size and contains more individual objects, it is also more spartanly composed. The brioche, fruit, and flower, and the cloth on which they sit form a monumental diamond in the center of the painting against a dark and neutral background.

Strong highlighting reinforces the geometry of structure. In contrast with this balanced formality, the Reves *Brioche* seems far more relaxed and intimate, with a casual arrangement of objects (which nevertheless joins with the wallpaper pattern to form an upward triangle around the brioche and flower in the center) and an allover animation of highlights and design which help to produce a lighter mood. The flickering touch Manet imparted throughout and the beautiful play of close tonal variations around a grey-blue scale differ from the earlier work's concrete modelling and stark contrasts of value. In general, this work reflects the influence of Impressionism on Manet during the 70s and a move toward more high-keyed effects.

The influence of Chardin must also have been active here in more than a general way. Manet had used brioches in paintings prior to the Rockefeller still life, but never with a flower piercing its crown as found in that composition and the later Reves variant. This unusual motif, however, is seen in a beautiful small still life by Chardin entitled *La Brioche,* donated to the Louvre by the well known collector Dr. Louis La Caze in 1869. Manet painted the Rockefeller *Brioche* just one year later and may well have known the Chardin. The particular meaning of this motif, if indeed it had a significance other than a purely decorative one, has not been traced. Certainly so rich an invitation to the senses (sight, smell, taste, and touch) would have appealed to Manet, if not allegorically then simply as an evocative and joyful experience.

Edouard Manet (French, 1823-1883)
Vase of White Lilacs and Roses, *1883*
oil on canvas, 22 x 18⅛ inches (55.9 x 46 cm)
signed lower right: "Manet"

From 1879 Manet was plagued with a disease of the legs that eventually rendered him an invalid and resulted in his death. Hydrotherapy treatments did little to arrest the course of his affliction, but Manet's spirits never flagged, and in his last years he amused himself with painting small oils, watercolors and pastels, visiting with friends, and writing illustrated letters. Often his still lifes depict flowers which admirers brought to his studio to cheer him.

Vase of White Lilacs and Roses is known to have been Manet's second to last painting before his death on April 30, 1883. Bouquets of springtime lilacs and roses appear in other pictures, as does also the same tall and narrow crystal vase. What sets this painting apart, however, is the unique cross-like structure formed by the vase and two horizontal sprays of lilacs that extend to the edges of the canvas, making for a centralized and symmetrical composition. Given Manet's impending death, one wonders if it is valid to interpret in this composition a religious connotation, conceivably taken even further by the positioning of the three roses at the center of the cross as a symbol of the Trinity.

In any case, the presentation is far from morbid or austere. Indeed, the painting's sparkling color and freshness of handling attest to the delight Manet continued to derive from the world around him even in his illness.

Claude Monet (French, 1840-1926)
The Pont Neuf, *1872*
oil on canvas, 20¹⁵/₁₆ x 28½ inches (53.1 x 72.4 cm)
signed lower right: "Cl. M."

Within the scope of Impressionist subject matter, the city of Paris played a crucial role, offering a wealth of themes for artists attuned to the vitality of modern life and the rapidly changing urban environment. In contrast to the earlier topographical tradition of city *vedute,* with its stress on stability and history, the Impressionists highlighted dynamism, the new and the momentary. They delighted in the visual excitement of crowded boulevards, the spectacle of café society, shifting climatic effects played against architectural backgrounds, and the changes being wrought by industrialization and growth. Characteristic of this new sensibility is Monet's subtle and moody *Pont Neuf,* generally dated to 1872.

Spanning the Seine from the quai du Louvre on the Right Bank to the quai des Grands Augustins, and crossing the tip of the Isle de la Cité with its equestrian statue of Henri IV and the Vert Galant, the Pont Neuf has been a busy thoroughfare and a frequent motif for artists since its completion in the 17th century. Indeed, Monet's close friend Renoir had painted a view of the bridge from precisely the same angle earlier that year (National Gallery of Art, Washington, D.C.). Absorbed by the movement of pedestrians and traffic across the bridge and the colorful vista of summer attire and sunlight, Renoir set up his easel in the second floor window of a café overlooking the bridge and had his brother Edmond engage passers-by in conversation so he could sketch them more accurately. Surrounding architecture is recorded with the same enthusiasm and eye for specifics.

Monet's approach is quite different from that of Renoir. While working apparently from the same position, and thereby adopting the same high but close-in perspective, Monet's aim was that of brusque summarization rather than detailed description. The time of year is later, probably in the autumn, and the brilliant clarity of Renoir's view is replaced by the chilled, moist atmosphere of a rainy day, filtering visual sensation into a harmony of bold shapes and muted color. No less "accurate" than Renoir's depiction, Monet's *Pont Neuf* presents only the essentials of form. With a few deft strokes, Monet was able to capture the silhouettes of pedestrians and horsedrawn carriages as they hurry across the bridge, their reflections casting faint patterns along the damp pavement. A closely matched range of greys, dull blues, tans, and violets conveys the soft, slightly iridescent quality of the afternoon light. Under the bridge pass tugboats, the smoke from their stacks rising in great clouds that add another ingredient to Monet's survey of aqueous effects. This is not a sketch, but a finished essay, and reflects very clearly Monet's confidence of style and personality.

Alfred Sisley (French, 1839-1899)
Road Along the Water at Saint-Mammès, *c. 1879-80*
oil on canvas, 29 x 21 3.8 inches (73.7 x 54.3 cm)
signed lower right: "Sisley."

While the cradle of Impressionism lies west of Paris in the valley of the Seine, Sisley chose to settle southeast of the city in an area more generally associated with the Barbizon school. Starting in 1879-80 he lived successively in Veneux-Nadon, Moret, and Saint-Mammès, close to the Seine, the Fontainebleau forest, and the Loing canal. From this area he later made only occasional excursions. Raymond Cogniat has described his routine: "Within a radius of three or four miles, in Veneux-les-Sablons, then in Champagne and Thomery, Sisley was untiring in the study of the changing seasons and of light, often coming back to the same places, never weary of looking at nature and without displaying any desire to cease this contemplation. Perhaps one reason for this repetition of experience, it might even be called his 'constancy,' was the fact that, unlike his friends, he had not had the good fortune to make a reputation for himself. He continued to live on the thin edge of destitution, frequently obliged to borrow modest sums of money to help him through his difficult stretches …." [*Sisley,* Naefels, 1978, p. 65.]

As this passage suggests, Sisley made numerous paintings of the peaceful landscape in his new environs, including several with almost exactly the same view as the Reves picture. What makes this painting unusual, though, and one of the boldest conceptions in Sisley's *oeuvre,* is the abrupt and symmetrically vertical division of the composition, and the accompanying play between positive and negative space. The deep vista, light tones, and relatively loose brushwork on the left contrast directly with the densely-filled space, darker colors of foliage, and shorter, jabbing brushstrokes on the right. Within this firm, vertical structure vibrate Sisley's highkeyed notations of the effects of summer sunlight. In the sky, fleecy traces of white are woven into the mesh of brushstrokes to suggest high, thin summer clouds. The light that filters through the poplars falls in dappled patches with a distinctly purplish tint, conveying the chroma that is present even in dense shadows.

Although this painting is not dated, it is known to have been sold to Sisley's dealer Durand-Ruel on July 28, 1881. Some scholars have ascribed it to this same year, but early photographic documentation that accompanied the picture when purchased by Emery Reves from Durand-Ruel in 1949 or 50 is annotated with the date 1879. Since both the Seine and the Loing canal flow through Saint-Mammès, the particular road and stretch of water depicted have not been identified. Bridges and viaducts similar to the one in the painting cross both the river and the canal.

Pierre-Auguste Renoir (French, 1841-1919)
The Stolen Kiss (Jules Le Coeur and Clémence Tréhot)
watercolor over pencil on paper, 9¹⁵/₁₆ x 6¹⁵/₁₆ inches
(25.3 x 17.7 cm)
signed lower right: "A. Renoir"

In the summers when the close-knit circle of young "Impressionists" generally parted ways, leaving Paris for the more pleasant, neighboring countryside, Renoir often headed in the direction of Marlotte, southeast of Paris near Fontainebleau, where his friend Jules Le Coeur had bought an estate in 1865. Poor as he was at this time, having left the Ecole des Beaux-Arts two years earlier, Renoir was graciously accepted into the more bourgeois surroundings of his architect-turned-painter friend Le Coeur and his family. During the blossoming of this friendship which lasted well into the 1870s (it is not known under what circumstances Renoir met Le Coeur), Renoir established himself as a painter of figures, producing portraits mostly of his friends and their family members and accepting occasional portrait commissions. This phase of Renoir's career is articulated most succinctly by the well-known and sensitively executed series of portraits of Lise Tréhot, two of which comprise the mainstay of the Reves' collection of early Renoirs. Lise Tréhot, Renoir's soon-to-be mistress, was probably introduced to him by Jules Le Coeur who was, at this time, engaged in a liaison with Lise's sister Clémence.

Douglas Cooper's research into Renoir's early career and his relations with the Le Coeur family has been instrumental in identifying the couple depicted in this small, quickly executed watercolor known as *The Stolen Kiss*. [*The Burlington Magazine,* CI, no. 678/9 (September-October 1959), p. 325.] Although facial features are not clearly defined, we know that the subjects are Jules Le Coeur and his companion Clémence Tréhot, captured in a private moment during a summer stroll. As the man attempts to steal a kiss from the girl, she is taken by surprise, her gait still directed forward as is the rush of her skirts. The lush tonalities of velvety blues create a warm and confined ambiance, adding to the sense of intimate pleasure, a mood Renoir would have been inclined to appreciate in his own retreats with his new love Lise.

Renoir often set down a quick pencil sketch over which he laid his washes. It was a medium he greatly enjoyed for its spontaneous yet coloristically rich results. In the present case, the more opaque background forming an arch over the figures adds depth and stability to the composition. This is the first of Renoir's works depicting young lovers, a theme which he developed more fully in the 1880s in paintings of dancing couples (one of the works in this series, now in the Boston Museum of Fine Arts, is a nearly identical mirror-image of the couple in the Reves' watercolor). The Reves' picture is believed to have been owned by Clémence Tréhot until shortly before her death in 1926.

102

Pierre-Auguste Renoir (French, 1841-1919)
Lise Sewing, *1866*
oil on canvas, 22 x 18 inches (55.9 x 45.7 cm)
signed lower left: "A. Renoir"

The two paintings of Lise Tréhot by Renoir in the Reves Collection bracket an important chapter in the artist's personal and professional life. Although it is not known exactly when or how Renoir struck up a friendship with Lise (it seems most likely that they met through Renoir's friend Jules Le Coeur, whose lover, Clémence Tréhot, was Lise's elder sister), by 1866 she was modelling for him and for the next six years remained his favorite model as well as probably his mistress. *Lise Sewing,* a tender and luministically subtle portrait done under the dual influence of Courbet and Corot, signals the beginning of this relationship, while its companion in the Reves Collection, the *Lise in a White Shawl,* marks its final year. Until these two outstanding examples of Renoir's early development were purchased by the Reves in 1958, they remained virtually unknown outside of Lise's family, through which they descended.

At the time of the first portrait, Lise was 18 and Renoir 25. From this beginning, she can be identified in at least twelve more of his paintings, each time in a different guise. None are more intimate, however, than his first portrait of her, which is invested with a special personal feeling even though it draws upon a common theme treated by other Impressionist artists — the quiet and unselfconscious domestic routine of a woman sewing. The subdued, almost sfumato lighting adds to the sense of quietude. Even the bold stripes of the dress, a garment pattern that reappears in other early Renoir paintings as well as contemporaneous works by Monet, are kept somewhat muted, so as not to overpower the lovely modelling of the face and the focused attention on the poised needle which, like the gold ring, red earring and red hair band, stands out as a bright accent in an otherwise cool palette of greys and blues. The paint itself is applied fairly thinly and smoothly except in the blue cloth Lise is sewing, where the strokes have a lush thickness. The background is especially fluid, with a loose, abstract scumbling of greys and browns that stops just short of the edges of the canvas. Light reworkings are apparent in several areas, and indeed, Renoir signed the picture twice, a very faint first signature appearing 1½ inches below the second.

Pierre-Auguste Renoir (French, 1841-1919)
Lise in a White Shawl, *1872*
oil on canvas, 22 x 18 inches (55.9 x 45.7)
not signed or dated

The association between Renoir and his model Lise Tréhot ended in 1872 when she married Georges Brière de l'Isle, thereafter devoting herself to domestic life. In that year she posed for two last pictures, *The Harem (Parisian Women Dressed as Algerians)* and *Lise in a White Shawl*. Douglas Cooper has written perceptively about the latter: "Our last vision of Lise is, therefore, the loving but slightly melancholy portrait belonging to Mr. Reves in which she is shown with a white lace shawl draped over her black hair. Clearly this portrait must have been painted contemporaneously with *Parisiennes habillées en Algériennes* [dated 1872], and Renoir gave it to Lise, perhaps as a wedding present. Here we come closer to Lise than in any other work, for Renoir has set out simply to extol her attraction and her charm. It forms a perfect pendant to *Lise Sewing* of six years earlier, while yet being very different from it in style and in its winning look." [*The Burlington Magazine,* CI, no. 674 (May 1959), p. 171.]

The exotic flavor of this portrait reveals Renoir's admiration of Delacroix, stated even more forthrightly in *Parisian Women Dressed as Algerians* of the same year. The light, roseate and blue flesh tints derive also from this master and, together with the flickering brushwork in the shawl and hand, show tendencies that were increasingly important in Renoir's mature style. The unabashed affection for feminine charm, tempered here perhaps with a hint of distance or loss, is also a hallmark in the artist's later work.

Pierre-Auguste Renoir (French, 1841-1919)
The Duck Pond, *1873*
oil on canvas, 19¾ x 24 inches (50.2 x 61 cm)
signed lower left: "Renoir"

During the late 1860s, Monet and Renoir constantly worked *en plein air,* attacking the problem of how to capture through vivid brushwork and divided colors the immediacy and vibrancy of sun-struck landscapes. Through their mutual interests, a close friendship and working relationship developed, as John Rewald has described: "From the weeks they spent together at *La Grenouillère* [where they painted similar views of this popular riverside restaurant in 1869] dates a real work-companionship between the two. Whether they studied the same flowers in the same vase or whether they put up easels in front of the same motif, Renoir and Monet, during the years ahead, were to paint more frequently the same subjects than any other members of their group. And in this communion they were to develop a style of expression which at times also brought them closer to each other than to the rest." [*The History of Impressionism,* New York, 1978, pp. 230-32.]

A good example of this close relationship is found in their paintings done near Argenteuil in 1873 of a house on a duck pond. Looking across the pond to a wooden embankment and fence and a house hidden behind trees, their compositions are virtually the same, differing only in details such as the placement of ducks and the inclusion in Renoir's of a boat with two men polling. Both artists had adopted Pissarro's technique of covering the surface with tiny, discrete flecks of paint, and had begun to break down each area into its many constituent hues in order to preserve the shimmer of reflected light and the freshness and intricacy of local color. No contours are sharply drawn; no forms are completely distinct. Rather, the scene is grasped as a unified field of rich optical sensations. By positioning themselves with the house directly *en face,* they set up a vertical, flattened composition in which the various components (water, embankment, house, roof, and sky) form geometric bands as a foil for the allover vibrancy of surface. Thus, underlying structure is preserved.

Renoir tended toward the use of brighter colors and a slightly lighter touch than Monet, and in this comparison, his colors strike a distinctly high-keyed note. Bright oranges and jewel-like blues dominate, all intensified through juxtaposition and complementary colors. Although it is often noted that Renoir and Monet worked side-by-side on this motif, it seems to have escaped attention that Renoir actually produced two canvases, the other version now belonging to a private collector in Dallas.

Berthe Morisot (French, 1841-1895)
The Port of Nice, *winter 1881-82*
oil on canvas, 15 x 18¼ inches (38 x 46.4 cm)
signed lower left: "B. Morisot"

Although less studied and perhaps less appreciated than the other French Impressionists, Berthe Morisot nevertheless made a distinctive and refined contribution to the movement. A protégé first of Corot and then of Manet (who later became her brother-in-law), she absorbed stylistic influence from both but added a delicacy of technique and mood that was all her own. In *Port of Nice,* a picture belonging to a series of studies made at Nice during the winter of 1881-82, one sees the splintery weave of brushstrokes and the light, rather pastel colors that characterize much of her work. Subjects involving water of course had been a primary theme for the Impressionists since the movement's inception, offering a laboratory for the study of reflections, bright light, and shifting, impermanent states of nature. Here, Morisot has framed her view so that the ships and buildings along the shore are pushed into the upper half of the field. This is a compositional device that not only shows the influence of Japanese prints and stresses a sense of unstructured spontaneity, but one that also gives predominance to the picture's true subject — the water itself and its play of movement, reflection, and broken colors.

The Reves' study relates closely to a slightly larger painting of boats in the harbor at Nice that Morisot exhibited at the seventh Exposition des Artistes Indépendants (i.e. the seventh Impressionist exhibition) in March 1882. She had gone to Nice late in 1881 to spend the winter and, despite a lengthy excursion to Italy and the subsequent illness of her daughter, managed to do a considerable amount of painting. Although the Reves' picture is generally dated 1882, it seems more prudent to ascribe it generally to the southern sojourn of late 1881-early 1882.

Camille Pissarro (French, 1830-1903)
The Place du Théâtre-Français, Foggy Day, *1897*
oil on canvas, 21⅜ x 26 inches (54.3 x 66 cm)
signed lower left: "C. Pissarro — 97"

Although Pissarro throughout most of his career was primarily a painter of rural life, in his last years he reached a summit of achievement in a long series of cityscapes done from high vantage points looking down into the busy squares and grand avenues of modern Paris. Executed in hotel rooms from which he carefully observed his subjects under changing seasonal effects and times of day, these vistas have a grandeur that bespeaks the love and excitement he felt toward this beautiful city. The possible influence of Japanese prints or contemporary photographs has been noted, but what sets Pissarro's work apart is his attentiveness to nuances of light and atmosphere and his ability to capture the movement, vitality and immediacy of the experience. Geometries of street, architecture, trees and linear perspective provide a firm compositional structure, but this solidity is then softened by the myriad details and optical impulses that fill his canvases so dynamically. He worked on these pictures in concentrated campaigns and exhibited many of them together, emphasizing their collective, serial harmony.

In Paris as transformed in the later 19th century by Baron Haussmann, the Place du Théâtre-Français, located near the Louvre and Palais Royal, was one of the city's primary hubs, and the Avenue de l'Opéra was one of its grandest boulevards, terminating in the monumental facade and dome of the Opéra. Starting in December 1897, Pissarro took a room at a hotel on the south side of the Place du Théâtre-Français with a window looking across the intersection directly at the Opéra. On December 15 he wrote to his son Lucien: "… I found a room in the Grand Hotel du Louvre with a superb view of the Avenue de l'Opéra and the corner of the Place du Palais Royal! It is very beautiful to paint! Perhaps it is not aesthetic, but I am delighted to be able to paint these Paris streets that people have come

to call ugly, but which are so silvery, so luminous and vital. They are so different from the boulevards. This is completely modern!" On December 22 he left Paris for the country and did not return to the Hotel du Louvre until January 5. Before leaving, however, he had executed a first group of paintings from his hotel window, among which was the Reves' *Place du Théâtre-Français, Foggy Day.* This might very well be the precise picture that Pissarro had in mind when he wrote on December 15 of views "so silvery, so luminous and vital," for it is a study of the glowing transformation of the city by silvery fog, one of the most delicate effects in his whole series of urban vistas. As in other paintings from the same vantage point under sunnier conditions, we look across the square and up the Avenue de l'Opéra, but now the deep view is completely obscured by a soft sheen of fog that seems to be illuminated by the glow of rosy sunlight from behind. Architecture and street are dissolved into an almost abstract flatness of fragile purples, silvers, blues and pale greens. Although the canvas daringly approaches a monochromatic uniformity, as had earlier paintings of foggy scenes by Monet and Pissarro both, it is actually composed of a complex range of color variations.

For some reason, Pissarro seems not to have included this particular picture among the 12 paintings of the same theme exhibited together in a large room at Durand-Ruel's in June 1898. Of these works he wrote to Lucien: "My *Avenues* are so clear that they would not suffer alongside the paintings of Puvis."

Camille Pissarro (French, 1830-1903)
Self-Portrait, *c. 1898*
oil on canvas, 20⅞ x 12 inches (53 x 30.5 cm)
stamped signature lower right: "C.P."

Only four painted self-portraits by Pissarro are known, one from 1873 in the Musée d'Orsay, the Reves painting and a similar picture that are thought to date from about 1898, and one from 1903 in the Tate Gallery. The Reves picture and its companion, which depicts Pissarro with a similar expression and wearing the same smock and beret but in a bust-length format, have traditionally been dated 1900. John Rewald, however, has noted a reference in a letter from Lucien Pissarro to his father from early 1899 mentioning a self-portrait with spectacles, and from this evidence deduced a date for the pair of c. 1898. These works differ from the other two self-portraits in their less formal, less stern presentation. While those pictures convey the patriarchal, almost biblical impression that Pissarro

made on most people, these have a warmer and more spontaneous quality, even exhibiting a certain amount of self-directed wit. Pissarro looks out at us as a weary veteran, his eyes rather tired and his eyebrows raised quixotically. The floppy beret adds a whimsical note. This is not a distant and austere savant but a perceptive, grandfatherly professional.

The Reves self-portrait is the only one in which Pissarro shows himself in ¾ length. He has integrated himself into the architecture of the composition by placing his body directly in line with the vertical axis of the window frame. The horizontally held palette, which has been moved downward several inches, echoes the horizontals of the window and upper and lower edges of the canvas. Pissarro's handling in the outer areas of design is particularly bold and free, helping to funnel attention inward to the face, ringed by dark hat and smock.

This picture apparently was given or left to Lucien Pissarro and remained in his family for many years.

113

Edgar Degas (French, 1834-1917)
Aria After the Ballet, *1879*
pastel over peinture à l'essence on paper,
23½ x 29½ inches (59.7 x 75 cm) (irregular)
signed lower right: "Degas"

In the ballet and opera, Degas found a source of subject matter perfectly suited to the refined elegance and artifice that lie at the heart of his art. As enclosed universes where the imaginary becomes real, they offered enchantment, feminine charm, the transporting power of music, dance and beautiful sets, and artistic discipline at its height. Degas responded with a lengthy series of paintings and drawings which, in their technical and compositional sophistication, stand among the finest achievements of the 19th century. *Aria After the Ballet* (or *Grand air, après un ballet)* exemplifies many of the best traits of the series.

Utilizing a favorite compositional device, Degas places the viewer in the orchestra pit looking up at the stage. The voluted necks of two cellos thrust up into the stage space, forming dominant elements of design that are answered in their diagonal inclination by the gesture of the singer and the contour of the slopes above her. They also force a rapid jump in scale and perspective back to the figures and the sets beyond, a landscape decor of trees, mountains and sky. This off-balance viewpoint and spatial compression, together with the cropping of figures and instruments, freezes a seemingly momentary and spontaneous (but actually quite calculated) composition, given further liveliness by the fugitive effects of lighting and coloration. Particularly striking here is the strong upward illumination cast by the footlights, which throws the singer and dancers into strong relief and helps model their gestures so poignantly.

Degas exhibited this work in the fourth Impressionist exhibition of 1879 simply as *Grand air, après un ballet,* indicating its subject as the singing of the principal aria at the close of one of the ballet segments commonly included in operas of the period. It has been more specifically identified by various authors, however, as representing a scene from Meyerbeer's *L'Africaine,* an opera that Degas knew well and mentioned in his letters. At this time, no firm evidence for such an identification is known, other than the general correlation between Meyerbeer's exotic theme and Degas' rather exotic sets. Unfortunately, the actual sets used in the opera were destroyed by fire in 1895.

The technique, or techniques applied in this work are also interesting, in that they reveal Degas' experimental attitude and the freedom with which he combined media. What appears to be a plate mark surrounds the entire image, which would accord with his common practice of drawing or painting over a monotype, except that no monotypes by Degas of this large a scale are known. The background, including mountains, trees and sky, are painted in "peinture à l'essence," or oils mixed thinly with turpentine, while the foreground (figures and necks of the cellos) are pastel. The pastel seems to be applied, however, over a painted ground, indicating that apparently the whole composition was done first in "peinture à l'essence."

Edgar Degas (French, 1834-1917)
The Bathers, *c. 1890-95*
pastel and charcoal on tracing paper glued to grey board,
42¹⁵/₁₆ x 43¾ inches (109 x 111 cm)
stamped signature lower left: "Degas"

Sometimes entitled *Women at their Toilet* or *Woman Combing her Hair,* this large pastel by Degas focuses on the theme so common in his later work of women in the private act of ablution or grooming, but moves it out-of-doors. At the left of the composition is a large tree trunk and beyond that, the silhouette of a faintly defined cow. The drawing can therefore be more accurately identified as a depiction of women bathers on the banks of a pond or stream, a relatively rare subject for Degas compared to his interior bathing scenes. A much earlier, compositionally different version of the same theme from c. 1875-76 is housed in the Phillips Collection, Washington, D.C., while several late variations center around the Reves pastel and an equally monumental composition of the same dimensions now in the Art Institute of Chicago. These last works may have been done in a series, as Degas sought a personal resolution to the challenging pictorial problem of grandly structuring large-scale bathers into an outdoor setting, a crucial motif in late 19th century French art that had been treated with particular authority by Renoir and Cézanne.

As a procedural shortcut in composing such multi-figured scenes, Degas regularly copied or traced figures from his own earlier works, varying their arrangement and spatial relationships to produce new compositions. He would then have the flimsy tracing paper glued to a support for greater strength before going back to amplify or rework the design. Several drawings are known which show figures from the Reves' *Bathers* either individually or grouped. By mining his own work rather than relying on studies from nature, Degas came to think more and more abstractly about his figural motifs and their formal relationships in terms of line, plane, volume and space. The process of tracing also helps explain the rather odd conjunctions and overlappings that are sometimes encountered.

Another aspect of this drawing that typifies Degas' late work is the exceptionally bold manipulation of the pastel medium. Indeed, lines are often drawn so freely, and color applied in so painterly a fashion, that areas of anatomy or landscape evolve into nearly abstract, non-allusive pattern. His inventive stretching of the medium was constant: areas are rubbed and scraped, layers of color are freely superimposed, strokes are steadily varied in direction, length and width, while some of the color seems to be painted on or embedded with fixative in transparent veils. In the hands of this great master, pastel was transformed from a polite and decorous medium into one of powerful expression. His work in this vein provided one of his most meaningful legacies for twentieth century art.

118

Georges Seurat (French, 1859-1891)
Grassy Riverbank, *1882*
oil on canvas, 12¾ x 16 inches (32.5 x 40.7 cm)
not signed or dated

The studies leading up to Seurat's great masterpiece *Sunday Afternoon on the Island of the Grande Jatte* (1884-86) constitute a review of this artist's crucial stylistic evolution during the first half of the 1880s. Early preparatory works exhibit the lush, loosely woven brushwork and bright but earthy colors he derived from Impressionism, while later, more finished studies show the methodically stippled brushmarks, highly organized forms, and more scientific application of color characteristic of Neo-Impressionism. *Grassy Riverbank* from the Reves Collection can be dated with confidence to 1882, two years before work began on the *Grande Jatte,* but it nevertheless may have played a role in the development of that later picture, as originally recognized by Daniel Catton Rich in his book *Seurat and the Evolution of "La Grande Jatte"* (Chicago, 1935). The topographical composition matches closely that of certain early studies for the *Grande Jatte,* with a diagonal riverbank that comprises more than a third of the picture overlapping a triangular slice of water, beyond which is seen a thin band of green landscape. Across the top, leaves from overarching trees frame the distant river perspective. In the *Grande Jatte,* of course, Seurat populated the foreground with an array of Parisians enjoying a Sunday outing. It is interesting, however, that already in this early sketch one finds a progression of trees somewhat similar to the pattern in the final picture, where there is also an echo of the thin trunk found here to the left of center. Of further note is the stylized S-shape trunk

of one of the trees at the right, which is reincarnated in several later studies. Although reversed in composition, it may be that the oil sketch known as *The Seine seen from the Grande Jatte* [c. 1884, Henri Dorra and John Rewald, *Seurat,* Paris, 1959, no. 107] forms an intermediary between *Grassy Riverbank* and subsequent stages of development.

Whatever its role in other compositional schemes, this picture stands on its own as a fresh and vividly worked outdoor sketch. Fully typical of Seurat's style of c. 1882 are the combed and cross-hatched brushmarks that pull several tones together for luminosity and visual excitement. Here, the broad treatment of greens in the foreground contrasts with the smoother horizontal stroking in the glistening water and the delicately tinted blue and pink sky. An element that cannot be adequately revealed by any reproduction is the use of purple and blue highlights in the tree trunks and foliage to give shadows greater liveliness. In the severed trunk along the left edge we see a device that Seurat was fond of using, either with a figure or tree, as a kind of spatial anchor or proscenium. Croppings and simplifications of this sort typify his efforts to render the structural order underlying natural appearance.

Paul Gauguin (French, 1848-1903)
Portrait Vase of Mme. Schuffenecker, *c. 1889*
glazed stoneware, 9½ x 6⅝ x 7 inches
(24.2 x 16.9 x 17.8 cm)
not signed or dated

Gauguin's three-dimensional work in sculpture and ceramics gave him another field in which to explore the ideas of decorative form and mystical or symbolic subject matter which also preoccupied his better known development as a painter. As early as 1877 he was studying marble and possibly wood carving with the academic sculptor Bouillot, and he would continue to make sculpture throughout his life. His involvement with ceramics, which he took up as a means of supplementing his income, was more limited in duration, dating mostly between 1886, when he started working with the important ceramic artist Ernest Chaplet, and his departure from France for Tahiti in 1891. A small number of ceramic works derive from 1893-95 during the interval between Gauguin's two Pacific sojourns. The total extent of his work in this medium, which he thought of as ceramic sculpture rather than functional pottery, is not known but is estimated to run to well over a hundred examples, of which only about 60 still survive.

The vase in the Reves Collection is generally identified as a portrait of Mme. Emile Schuffenecker, wife of Gauguin's good friend and fellow artist, and has been dated both 1889 and 1890-91. Indeed, the features of the woman match the thin, elongated face with prominent cheekbones and almond eyes found in other portraits of Mme. Schuffenecker by Gauguin, and the vase is thought originally to have belonged to her

husband. Gauguin stayed in Schuffenecker's studio during the winter of 1890-91, and it was possibly during this period of close intimacy that he modelled this work. His rejected advances toward Mme. Schuffenecker during the same winter, however, resulted in a rupture between the two friends in 1891. Alternatively, it is also possible that this vase is the one found, in modified form, paired with a self-portrait vase in the painting *Still Life with a Head-Shaped Vase* of 1889, which would provide a firm terminus date for its production.

The form of the vase incorporates a theme of metamorphosis, with bust-length portrait on one side and a conventional, hour-glass vase shape on the other. On this back side a disembodied hand rests at the top. Through its fingers runs a spotted scarf that encircles the head but, over the forehead, ends in the pointed profile of a snake. On close inspection one also sees that the floral decoration on the protruding form at the rear includes a long, winding serpent in a tree. This rather startling symbol, which expands upon the sinewy lines of the rest of the composition, must refer to the temptation that Gauguin himself was experiencing all too realistically and to which he eventually succumbed.

It is clear that Gauguin had a natural sensitivity for the potentials of the pottery medium. His ceramics, inspired in part by Japanese and pre-Columbian pottery, and partly by current trends in European art ceramics, go far beyond their sources in freedom of imagery and projection into personal, moving expression. His beautiful, painterly glazes, though dependent at first on the technical knowledge of Chaplet, are more adventuresome than those of any contemporary artist.

Paul Gauguin (French, 1848-1903)
Farm at Le Pouldu (*or* The Blue Roof), *1890*
oil on canvas, 28 x 35½ inches (71 x 90.3 cm)
signed and dated, lower right: "P Gauguin 90"

Gauguin, like both Cézanne and van Gogh, passed through a period of Impressionist-inspired development, only to react against Impressionism's veracity in favor of a style more emotional and personally expressive. Gauguin's approach, labelled alternately Synthetism and Cloissonism, involved an abstraction of formal elements, including flattened, simplified color areas linked rhythmically by serpentine contours and a nonrealistic, symbolic use of color, in support of themes charged with religious or mythical meaning. Of decisive importance was a period he spent mostly in Brittany from 1886 to 1891, living and working in close contact with the Breton people and their ancient customs, a source for Gauguin of deep spiritual inspiration.

Farm at Le Pouldu, also known as *The Blue Roof,* is a famous composition from the Breton period depicting a farm compound at the hamlet of Kerzellec close to Le Pouldu. Gauguin had spent his first sojourns in Brittany at Pont-Aven, living at the boarding house of Mother Gloanec in the company of numerous other artists. In October 1889, however, he left Pont-Aven, which had become more and more invaded by tourists, and moved with Paul Sérusier and his pupil Meyer de Haan, to Le Pouldu, where he lived at the inn of Marie Henry. Though impecunious, Gauguin found here a supportive atmosphere and rugged, primitive landscape that competed in his consciousness with romantic yearnings for the South Seas. At about the turn of the year, both he and Meyer de Haan, apparently working side by side, painted the nearby farm compound (which is still standing today in somewhat modified form). Although De Haan's canvas, now in the Rijksmuseum Kröller-Müller at Otterlo, is dated 1889 and Gauguin's is inscribed 1890, the close similarity of viewpoint and composition, including the detail of a woman at the well, indicates that they worked simultaneously, and some writers have suggested that

Gauguin was using the occasion to instruct De Haan and may even have corrected his canvas. The same farm, viewed from the other side, is seen in two other closely related paintings by Gauguin and De Haan, respectively entitled, *The Fields, Landscape at Le Pouldu* and *Landscape, Le Pouldu.*

Gauguin's achievement in *Farm at Le Pouldu* has been aptly described by Robert Goldwater:

> In this picture the programmatic aspects of "synthetism" have receded without disappearing. The bright colors, the enclosed forms, the clearly divided areas are still present. But they are now mixed, as it were, with the Impressionism Gauguin had, during the two years before, so sharply rejected .... He has permitted himself to see the variations of hue and texture on the stone walls, had adapted his brush stroke to the surface, rocks or grass, thatch or bushes, he is rendering; has allowed the sky to blur the distant trees into a fuzzy, light-eaten form. [*Paul Gauguin,* New York, n.d., p. 96]

This sensitivity to naturalism operates within an overall compositional structure which, in its interlocking of rectangular planes and clarity of defined space, may owe something to the example of Cézanne. The Impressionist element is undeniable, but the exaggerations we see here in the green of the foreground, the blue of the long horizontal roof, and the red of the tree in the courtyard, reveal Gauguin's underlying commitment to the use of color according to the demands of emotion and design rather than the dictates of nature.

124

Vincent van Gogh (Dutch, 1853-1890)
Café Terrace at Night, *September 1888*
reed pen and ink over pencil on paper, 24⅝ x 18 ¾ inches
(65 x 47.5 cm) (irregular)
not signed or dated

Among the everyday sites that van Gogh recorded in paintings and drawings during the year he spent in the southern city of Arles (February 1888-May 1889), two of the most famous are cafés. His well known *Night Café* pictures the interior of the Café de la Gare, and his painting and reed pen drawing of *The Café Terrace at Night* show the outside of the Grand Café du Forum. About the latter, van Gogh wrote to his sister on September 9, 1888: "In point of fact I was interrupted these days by my toiling on a new picture representing the outside of a night café … An enormous yellow lantern sheds its light on the terrace, the house front and the sidewalks, and even casts a certain brightness on the pavement of the street, which takes a pinkish violet tone. The gable-topped fronts of the houses in a street stretching away under a blue sky spangled with stars are dark blue or violet and there is a green tree. Here you have a night picture without any black in it … It amuses me enormously to paint the night right on the spot." This painting (now in the Rijksmuseum Kröller-Müller, Otterlo) was possibly influenced by an earlier picture of a café at night by Louis Anquetin and also by a similar composition in a Japanese print by Hiroshige.

It is remarkable not only for its dramatic use of perspective and night lighting, but also for its introduction of the motif of a starry sky, so crucial in subsequent works.

Opinion divides as to whether the ink drawing of the same scene followed or preceded the painting. Its rather poised and studied quality, however, does not have the look of an on-the-spot sketch, and moreover, van Gogh stressed in his letter that he was working on his painting directly from the motif. The few changes between the painting and drawing are not conclusive as to precedence.

It was apparently at Arles when van Gogh began to use an oriental reed pen for his drawings, as further testimony of his love of oriental graphics. He generally employed several pens with a range of tips for different textures and widths of line. Working rapidly, he filled his sheet to the edges with a bold, abundant pattern of forceful strokes, creating tensions of space, rhythm, and contrasting graphic signs which nevertheless are brilliantly resolved into a unified whole. With only pen and ink, he was able to create compositions of great richness and "color." Here, for example, an inventive variety of strokes and notations serves to convey the different tones and textures of buildings, pavement and sky, while the contrast of relatively blank spaces around the terrace with densely worked surrounding areas subtly invokes bright artificial illumination. In van Gogh's allover balancing of design and accent, even relatively minor details such as the paving stones in the foreground take on an independent life.

Vincent van Gogh (Dutch, 1853-1890)
Sheaves of Wheat, *July 1890*
oil on canvas, 19⅞ x 39¾ inches (50.5 x 101 cm)
not signed or dated

After spending a year in the asylum at Saint-Rémy, van Gogh returned in May 1890 to the North of France, this time to the village of Auvers-sur-Oise, a short journey northwest of Paris. He and his brother, Theo, who was still working as an art dealer in Paris, hoped that the closer family contact and the quiet surroundings of the Oise farming region would have a salutary effect on Vincent's health, and through the collector and amateur artist, Dr. Gachet, they arranged for lodgings. During the following, final months of Vincent's life, absorption into rural living helped rekindle an objective spirit in his art as he sought to assimilate his new environment. He remained subject to moods of despair, however, and his painting, as always, directly reflects these vicissitudes.

Sheaves of Wheat is one of the gentlest, most trouble-free of the late works, though its unusually pale colors possibly subsume a comment on the artist's own inner state. The long, rolling contours of the landscape around Auvers may have inspired van Gogh's use of a new 20 x 40 inch format for many of his canvases, as he capitalized on the potential stability and quietude of a dominant horizontal. Here, however, one is given only a rudimentary indication of perspective, the surface being filled with an almost abstract pattern of long, undulating brushmarks flowing in intermixed currents and eddies. Instead of the violent rhythms in many of the paintings done at Saint-Rémy, the pace of strokes in *Sheaves of Wheat* is more relaxed and orderly, more caressing of the shapes described, whether a shadow on the ground, an expanse of field, or a tassel-headed bundle of wheat. The overall paleness of blue, green and brown, sparked here and there with a stronger red or blue, adds to the effect of a flattened decorative tapestry or mosaic. One senses that van Gogh greatly enjoyed painting these irregular, somewhat comical bundles, each with a slightly different posture and stance and each endowed with a bit of friendly human personality. Empathy for his subjects was a strong characteristic of the realism in van Gogh's art, and one sees it even here in his lighthearted treatment of inanimate objects. He must have felt a special attraction for this subject, having treated similar motifs on several earlier occasions.

Many of the late paintings can be accurately dated from references in van Gogh's letters. Although this picture has not been associated with any of these passages, his description of another, related work (letter no. 643, June 17, 1890) illuminates his intentions and interests: "I am trying to make studies of wheat, like this (I just can't seem to draw it), nothing but blue-green stalks, long leaves like ribbons, green and pink in the reflection, ears turning light yellow, bordered with the soft pink of the dusty bloom — a pink bindweed down below twisted around a stem. Against such a very lively yet restful background, I would like to paint portraits." One writer has speculated that the Reves painting of harvested and bundled grain is one of the very last that van Gogh produced (Jan Hulsker, *The Complete Van Gogh: Paintings, Drawings, Sketches,* New York, 1980, p. 480).

Paul Cézanne (French, 1839-1906)
The Water Can, *c. 1879-80*
oil on canvas, 10½ x 13¾ inches (26.7 x 34.9 cm)
not signed or dated

The group of three paintings (including a masterful watercolor) by Cézanne in the Reves Collection provides an overview of this artist's mature development and his revolutionary approach to pictorial structure. In these three works, all different in scale, date and mode, one finds a forceful expression of the stylistic ideas that left so profound a legacy for 20th century art.

The earliest is a small still life entitled *The Water Can,* named for the tall metal vessel at its center. Its date is not precisely known and has been the subject of considerable discussion. Some historians have conjectured that the patterned wallpaper appearing here and in several closely related works can be localized to a house or an apartment which Cézanne occupied in the years 1879-80 and 1881-82 respectively. Others point to the thin, fluid application of paint and varied brushwork, which contrast with the thick, patterned strokes characteristic of Cézanne's Impressionist phase of the 1870s, as evidence of a later date around 1884-85. In correspondence, Theodore Reff has pointed out, however, that so severely simple, almost archaic a composition seems unlikely during the mid-80s, when Cézanne had progressed to a new complexity of structure, and that the thin surface could be a result of the picture having been less thoroughly worked than other still lifes of c. 1879-80.

It is this quality of freshness and directness, both in the handling and the straightforward placement of objects, that lends the picture much of its charm. Nevertheless, the stamp of a disciplined, organizing mind is clearly in evidence through studied relationships of shape, color and weight which work through the painting in a series of progressions and measured cadences. Within the central diagonal running from the wallpaper at upper left downward and outward to the crumpled napkin at the right are a wealth of connecting themes: the echo of floral patterns on the wall and bowl, for example; the dialogue of circles and ovals existing between the orange and the shapes and mouths of the various vessels; the conscious contrasts of texture and reflectivity; the linked chain of dark shadows which takes on an almost autonomous life, but also helps to give a solidity which balances the tendency toward flattened space. To help enliven the neutrality of tabletop and rear wall, the brushwork becomes particularly active and thin in these areas, while a somber play of blues, greys and browns revolves around the brighter tints of the orange at the center. Even in so small a picture, all elements participate in an integrated architecture of design that foretells the increasing formalism evolving in Cézanne's development.

Paul Cézanne (French, 1839-1906)
House in the Country near Aix, *c. 1885-87*
oil on canvas, 25⅝ x 32⅜ inches (65 x 82.2 cm)
not signed or dated

House in the Country near Aix dates from several years after *The Water Can* and shows the constructive method of Cézanne's middle years now directed at landscape painting in a style Meyer Schapiro has aptly characterized as "an original poetic harmony of the artificial and the natural." [Schapiro, *Paul Cézanne,* New York, 1952, p. 70.] The motif is familiar and unassuming: a small, blocky masonry house with red tile roof, typical of the provencal countryside, with stands of trees on either side and a rough clearing in front. It is a type of building that appealed to Cézanne for its solidity and clean lines and that appears frequently in his work as a constructive device and/or foil for nature. Here it seems mute, without human presence or history. And there is nothing the least bit dramatic or even very picturesque about the scene in general. Yet, Cézanne is able to create his own *visual* drama through his decisive manipulations of the natural motif.

Unlike many landscapes in which he used a high perspective for a grand, panoramic view, the vantage point here is low and close-in, so that the forms loom large and powerful. The house is particularly dominant, sitting squarely in the center of conjoined compositional masses and mediating between the loose, foliate shapes and warm colors of the trees to either side and the barer, cooler expanses of foreground and sky. These shapes fit together in a calculated set of diagonals, overlappings, and stabilizing verticals and horizontals. The inclined lower silhouette of the tree at the left pulls one into the picture space and initiates a diagonal recession past the house and into the trees at the right. The eye then returns leftward along the nearly flat diagonal formed by the tops of the trees and roof. Anchoring the center of the picture are the architectural verticals and horizontals, which have a natural analogue in the stripped trunk of the bare tree left of the door. This small tree, a crucial ingredient, is indicative of Cézanne's subtlety of design. Its bareness matches the one bare tree on the skyline and reinforces the sense of arid southern landscape. Its trunk, highlighted against the shadows behind it, starts upward in a necessary vertical but then forks out, the left branch echoing the diagonal contours of the rocks at the lower left, the sides of the roof, and the foreground mounds, all establishing a counterdirectional from the lower right to upper left.

The balancing of warm and cool tones is another structural element that also helps convey the brilliant intensity of summer light and atmosphere. Couplings of rose and blue, green and yellow, green and blue, and rose and yellow work together throughout, animated by Cézanne's constantly nuanced and varied inflections of the brush. Although the patterns of brushmarks stand out boldly, the paint is actually laid on with a delicacy that contrasts with the overall power of presentation. In this technique is already felt the tendency toward thin, watercolor-like stains of paint that marks the later, final period of Cézanne's development.

Paul Cézanne (French, 1839-1906)
Still Life with Apples on a Sideboard, *1900-06*
watercolor on paper, 19⅛ x 24⅞ inches (48.5 x 63.2 cm)
not signed or dated

This magnificent late watercolor by Cézanne achieves both monumentality and an almost explosive expressiveness. Familiar objects from the artist's still life repertoire are gathered on a rectangular wooden kitchen table. With the tabletop tipped downward toward us and other forms adjusted in profile for the collapsed perspective of flattened space, we look directly into his poised grouping from the height of the bowl of apples. The top of the wine bottle and side and bottom of the table are cut off by the picture frame, adding to the sense of spatial compression. The arrangement is basically pyramidal and, despite the overlapping of flattened forms, Cézanne's assertive drawing and light/dark modelling preserve a sense of three-dimensionality. Yet, his brilliant colors, the remarkably free and impulsive brushwork resulting even in undisguised drips and splatters, the exploitation of uncovered patches of white paper, and the superimposed washes of varying transparency animate every inch of the composition, opening up all elements to a sense of breathing and pulsating life, and mitigating all traces of the static and permanent. In this close harmony of movement and stability, shapes tend to move in and out of focus, from pure energy and light to something more tangible. The viewer becomes absorbed into the space of the painting and Cézanne's process of translating perceived reality into spatial notations of line and color. From here to the further advances of Cubism seems a short step. Never strictly intellectual, Cézanne's late work is marked by an emotional identification of the artist's creative power with the creative forces of nature in general. It has been pointed out that the table in this painting, with its scalloped apron, appears in several late works and is still found in the artist's studio as it exists today at Lauvres. It must be differentiated, however, from a similar table with bowed legs which can be found in his earlier paintings and drawings.

While the exact date of the Reves watercolor is problematic, due to the lack of evidence for an internal chronology of Cézanne's late work, it can be placed in the years 1900-06 during his great culminating phase.

Henri de Toulouse-Lautrec (French, 1864-1901)
The Last Respects, *1887*
ink and gouache on paper, 25¾ x 19⅜ inches
(65.5 x 49.2 cm)
signed lower right with anagram: "HTreclau"

Lautrec made this touching and dignified drawing, entitled *The Last Respects* or *Le dernier salut,* as an illustration for a song published by his friend Aristide Bruant in the little journal *Le Mirliton* in March 1887. Several studies and variations exist, but this is the definitive composition. In the foreground a workman stands erectly, his cap in his hands, his head inclined dolorously toward a funeral cortege in the background. Shown in dark silhouette, a horse-drawn hearse accompanied by several mourners on foot proceeds slowly up a curving road. In a masterful economy of line and spatial indications, Lautrec presents the bare essentials of form and pulls attention up through the sparse design of the lower quadrant to the converging diagonals and overlapping motifs toward the top. The thin, tremulous outlining of the man contrasts with the bolder black and white treatment of the background, and the daring conjunction of his profile and the distant silhouettes not only creates an

immediate spatial leap but also tends to intensify the communication of his feelings. A light underdrawing is visible throughout in blue pencil and reveals a number of pentimenti.

Among his many haunts in Montmartre, one of Lautrec's favorite was Bruant's *Le Mirliton* cabaret. He went there frequently to observe the motley crowds drawn by Bruant's boisterous personality. Always full of energy and mischief, this songwriter-turned-cabaret-proprietor gained his reputation for the insulting behavior and comments with which he "greeted" his patrons at the door or from the stage. He combined this strangely popular routine with his own colorful songs, works that enjoyed considerable celebrity for their stark realism and, in focusing on themes of destitution, shared a language of poignancy and perceptive characterization with the drawings of Lautrec. In connection with his cabaret, Bruant published the magazine of the same name at irregular intervals, and 77 numbers appeared in all, between October 1885 and December 1892. Often he printed the lyrics to his songs, and on five occasions, Lautrec supplied the illustrations. *Le dernier salut* remained in Bruant's personal possession until the sale of his collection in 1905.

Henri de Toulouse-Lautrec (French, 1864-1901)
Femmes de Maison, *c. 1893-95*
pastel on emery cloth, 24 x 19⅝ inches (61 x 49.9 cm)
signed lower right: "H T Lautrec"

Like Degas and Manet before him, Toulouse-Lautrec turned his back on time-honored thematic conventions to record with audacious objectivity the harsh, unvarnished facts of everyday life in modern Paris. Lautrec's social realism, however, went further than his predecessors in unveiling a colorful but often unsavory and decadent world of brothels, dance halls, lower-class cafés and social rejects. It was a world in which Lautrec himself lived and thus could report with the intimate knowledge of an insider. With his incisive draughtsmanship and his genius for capturing personality through a salient expression or gesture, he populated his canvases and drawings with a cast of characters who seem as fresh and affecting today as ever.

One of his favorite subjects was prostitutes in their daily milieu, and in 1892 he launched a long series of paintings and drawings of brothels in which he strove for absolute authenticity of detail and mood. Prostitutes are shown in moments of relaxation and boredom, dressing, awaiting customers, preparing for health inspectors, or sharing amicable or amorous embraces. Similar themes are found in the Japanese prints which

Lautrec loved and collected and also in small, private works by such artists as Guys and Degas, but only Lautrec unflinchingly invested this iconography with a new monumentality and simultaneously coaxed from his subjects a sense of dignity and universal humanity.

In the pastel *Femmes de Maison,* preserved in a stunningly vivid state, we see two prostitutes from the rear, one clothed in a long pink dressing gown and the other nude except for an indication of stockings rolled up over her knees. The slight incline of the figure at the left suggests that they are talking as they lean over a dresser or rummage in a drawer. At the right is a bed with a brilliant blue cover or robe draped over it. The eye naturally starts at the left of the composition with the outermost figure and streams back into space diagonally to the right, following the richness of color and stroking, but the true fulcrum and focus of the picture is the central nude, her back rendered with a combination of naturalism and sculpturesque beauty. Whereas the handling in surrounding areas is loose and energetic, here the modelling is more tightly knit, Lautrec tracing the curves of anatomy and the contrasts of highlighting and shadow with an extensive range of tints. It is interesting to note, for example, that some reflections on her back pick up the blue highlights from the right, while others echo the pinks from the left. To insure a solid bite from the pastel stick, Lautrec used emery cloth as his ground, an unusual technique that comes from the 18th century *pastellistes.*

No firm documentation for the dating of this work is known. It is generally placed between 1893 and 1895, and is traditionally thought to have been shown in Lautrec's uncatalogued exhibition at Maurice Joyant's gallery in 1896.

Auguste Rodin (French, 1840-1917)
The Poet and the Contemplative Life, *1896*
Marble, 72 x 21¾ x 23 inches (183 x 55.3 x 58.5 cm)
signed on base on right side: "A. Rodin"

Although Rodin's reputation today rests primarily on his modelled work in clay, plaster and bronze, this great artist also displayed a natural talent for direct carving, and his many marbles, a source of esteem during his lifetime, have recently received heightened critical attention. While the tactile manipulation of materials involved in modelling tended to promote Rodin's dramatic and exclamatory treatment of anatomy, carving in stone encouraged different expressive proclivities. The subtleties of surface he was able to achieve in finely grained marble as well as the translucency and sense of atmosphere became vehicles for softer, often more poetic, sometimes sentimentalized or decorative interpretations. In the actual execution of the marbles, his studio *praticiens* played a major role, working from plaster models under the master's careful supervision. He himself, however, generally added the finishing touches.

The Poet and the Contemplative Life, also known as the *Dream of Life* and even *The Seasons,* dates from Rodin's full maturity, when his international reputation was reaching its zenith. It was commissioned in 1894 by his faithful patron and supporter Maurice Fenaille, who had purchased other works including a group of figures to surround his swimming pool and later would publish a deluxe study of Rodin's drawings. Soon after its completion in 1896, *The Poet and the Contemplative Life* was exhibited at the annual Salon of 1897 and later in the Rodin exhibition held on the Place de l'Alma in 1900. Reaction to the sculpture can be judged from Léon Maillard's statement in a book on Rodin published in 1899 that "Maurice Fenaille … commissioned from Rodin a work of the highest fantasy, which commanded general admiration." A plaster version, without the head at the top, is housed in the Musée Rodin in Paris (102 cm high).

In its complex form and iconography, this work embodies themes mingled in other of Rodin's major sculptures. While the idea of a decorated column as a monument is analogous to the spiralling *Tower of Labor,* the upward flow of figures calls to mind the swirling masses in the *Gates of Hell,* the elaborate base in the *Monument to Claude Lorrain,* or the complex *Apotheosis of Victor Hugo.* Here, the figures move serenely among various attributes: two of them are drowsily reading, a male and female with wings (symbolic of love?) seem to float upward on clouds, a satyr-like figure near the top reaches down into a long garland of fruit and leaves, while at the lower back we find an ensemble of musical instruments, fruit and decorative masks relating perhaps to the seasons. Surmounting the column, on a decorated capital, sits a brooding, melancholic head with downcast face, reminiscent of the 1886 marble entitled *Thought* which Rodin based on the sensitive features of his then mistress and assistant, Camille Claudel. Placed at the apex of the composition, as if meditating on what falls below, this disembodied head seems to personify the spiritual powers of the poet in the 19th century sense of inspired, transcendent imagination. It commands the other aspects of life, including the arts, knowledge, love and natural cycles and fecundity, as they decoratively animate the column. As a whole, the sculpture stands as another chapter in Rodin's continuing celebration of poetic/artistic genius.

Maurice Vlaminck (French, 1876-1958)
Bougival, *c. 1905*
oil on canvas, 32½ x 39⅝ inches (82.5 x 100.7 cm)
signed lower left: "Vlaminck"

The height of Vlaminck's artistic creativity came during the brief but feverishly productive years of his Fauve period, about 1904-07. Of all the Fauve painters, he was the most impetuous, the most exuberant in his reinterpretation of nature as a vision of clashing colors and form. Early influences included van Gogh and the Neo-Impressionists, but he soon outdistanced all predecessors in his emotional use of raw color, blunt and aggressive brushwork, and abrupt juxtapositions. As he put it, "My ardor led me to risk everything and hold back nothing, in defiance of all the conventions of the painter's craft ...." In another revealing statement, he could almost have been describing the painting entitled *Bougival:* "I used to go to work right out in the sunshine; the sky was blue, the wheatfields seemed to be stirring and trembling in the torrid heat, with hues of yellow covering the whole scale of chromes; they quivered as if they were about to go up in flames. Vermilion alone could render the brilliant red of the roof tiles on the hillside across the river. The orange of the soil, the raw, harsh colors of walls and grass, the ultramarine and cobalt of the sky, harmonized to extravagance at a sensual, musical pitch. Only the colors on my canvas, orchestrated to the limit of their power and resonance, could render the color emotions of that landscape."

Bougival is one of the most powerful of all Vlaminck's works. In 1900 he had taken a studio with André Derain, fellow pioneer of Fauvism, in the village of Chatou located in the valley of the Seine west of Paris, an area made famous by the Impressionists. Bougival lies nearby on the opposite bank of the river and farther south. In Vlaminck's painting we are situated high on one of the hills bordering the Seine, looking across to the next hillside and the river in the distance, which makes a sharp bend near the horizon. The compositional format is one used in other of his large landscapes, with a diagonal plane along the bottom establishing the foreground, which overlaps another, larger diagonal plane for the middleground, topped by a narrow band of sky. In this restless play of angles, the only true verticals and horizontals are found in the architecture anchoring the compositional center. Vlaminck's system of colors has a planar structure also, with brilliant red confined to the foreground, trees and rooftops, a spatially recessive palette of dark greens and mustard yellows in the middleground, and a still more recessive mixture of light blues, greens, yellows and pinks in the river and sky. Counteracting this progression is the general vehemence of brushwork, although even here, the stroking tends to assume different, consistent patterns in each major area. Clearly, an instinct for order underlies the emotional pitch of Vlaminck's style, an attribute of the classical French tradition absorbed via Cézanne.

Edouard Vuillard (French, 1868-1940)
The Tent, *1908*
distemper on paper mounted on canvas
29½ x 44¼ inches (75 x 112.5 cm)
signed lower right: "E Vuillard"

We know from Vuillard's personal journal that he painted *The Tent* in July 1908 at the villa Ker Panurge at Penchâteau in southern Brittany, where he spent the summer with the Joseph Hessels, who had rented the villa, and other close friends. On July 16, Vuillard travelled by train from Paris to the neighboring town of Le Poulignen with Alfred Athis Natanson and his wife and daughters. On the 28th, the Bonnards arrived as well as Vuillard's mother. A journal entry for July 29 records a painting of "la tente," which most likely is this picture, though it might conceivably refer to another painting of the same subject now in a private Swiss collection. Several major works evolved from Vuillard's summer sojourns around this period in Normandy and Brittany, and reflect a sociable routine of leisurely pleasures and distractions. In this case, we look into a striped tent set up in the garden of the villa for protection from the sun, with three figures huddled together in conversation. A fourth figure stands on the more distant terrace at the left. Photographs taken of the villa and gardens by Vuillard show that the tent was placed near the garden wall overlooking the beach at Penchâteau.

In general, Vuillard's work from this period evidences the new infusion of light and space, the brighter palette, and the fluid naturalism of draughtsmanship that mark his stylistic development from about 1900, as he moved away from the intimacy and dense patterning of his Nabi period. *The Tent,* however, stands out for its bravura execution. Perhaps inspired by the bold perspective of the striped overhead awning rushing back into space, Vuillard summarized the scene with broad, dashing strokes of color which establish an allover calligraphic animation. Against the brown of the support that he allows to show through in many areas, his highlights of yellow, blue, red and green convey a sense of strong direct sunlight, despite the picture's general brownish cast. Through these bright chords of color and the sketchiness of technique, a feeling of on-the-spot immediacy is preserved, even though we know that Vuillard was working in this case, as he often did, from drawings (two small pencil sketches for *The Tent* are included in the Reves Collection).

Photographs by Vuillard and Alfred Athis Natanson help to identify the figures in the picture. Seated to the left, with a yellow sun hat, is Lucie Hessel. To her left, with his bushy beard, is Tristan Bernard. On the right is almost certainly Marcelle Aron, later Bernard's wife. The male figure in the distance is probably Joseph Hessel. Hessel was a prominent art dealer in Paris whose wife shared a particularly affectionate liaison with Vuillard for many years. Bernard was a well known novelist and playwright associated with the Revue Blanche group.

Like many of Vuillard's later works, *The Tent* is painted on distemper or *à la colle,* a technique he mastered as a decorator of theater sets during his early career and eventually favored for the beautiful matte tones it produced. It involves mixing dry pigments with glue and painting them into a ground which is also sometimes prepared with glue. After its completion in the summer of 1908, the painting had an interesting history. It was acquired in September 1908 by the Bernheim-Jeune Gallery and exhibited there in November. In 1919, however, Vuillard took it back in exchange for another work, and at his death in 1940 it formed part of the "atelier collection." (For documentation on this painting we are indebted to Antoine Salomon and Juliet Bareau, currently compiling a complete catalogue of Vuillard's work.)

Odilon Redon (French, 1840-1916)
Flowers in a Black Vase, *c. 1909-10*
pastel on paper, 34⅜ x 27 inches (87.3 x 68.5 cm)
signed lower right: "Odlon (sic) Redon"

The full mystery and magic of Redon's art are present in this large and beautiful pastel. It is free of the overt symbolism that gives much of his work so haunting an impact, and seems to evince a more purely decorative intention. Yet the intoxicating richness of its color, the glowing luminosity Redon was able to achieve through the pastel medium, and the spatial ambiguities of the composition, all give this work an ethereal, dream-like quality that raises it well beyond the realm of naturalism.

Pastel, black crayon, and charcoal were particularly congenial mediums for Redon, since they permitted the tonal depth and soft lighting he valued so highly. In his earlier development he worked mostly in black and white, producing densely shaded drawings he called his "noirs," but about 1895 he took up pastels more regularly and through them discovered a new world of color. At first the artist favored meditative figure studies and mystical themes, but after 1900 Redon concentrated more and more on bouquets of flowers. Because of his thorough absorption in his subjects and attention to detail, it is often possible to identify particular floral species. One also finds a repetition of certain vases, such as the black one seen here. The descriptive impulse, however, often gave way to flights of imagination, as Redon freely worked his compositions into a profusion of color and forms often floating in what approaches an abstract space. Linear definition is almost completely lost, and pure colors laid side by side, whether in pastel or oil, produce a special luministic intensity. In works such as the Reves pastel, where the patterning is so expansive and free, the sense of a personal, interior vision is particularly strong. Redon's flowers, his "fragile and scented beings," are transformed into spiritual statements that had a recognized topicality within Symbolist circles and added greatly to his reputation toward the end of his life.

Pierre Bonnard (French, 1867-1947)
Vase of Flowers, *c. 1935*
oil on canvas, 37 x 17½ inches (94 x 44.5 cm)
signed lower right: "Bonnard"

Already beginning to emerge in Bonnard's work during the first decade of the century was a dramatic shift away from the intimacy of scale and mood, the *Japonisme,* and the warm but restrained colors of his Nabi period. Spurred on by the break-throughs of Fauvism and Cubism but headed decidedly in its own direction, Bonnard's late work seems to describe a modern Golden Age. Personal, psychologically weighty themes are sometimes present, but the chromatic intensity of his colors, the shimmer of his thinly painted, almost iridescent surfaces, and the pleasantness of his subject matter make for a general feeling of well-being. Although his work is often thought of as a late manifestation of Impressionism, it has a distinctly modern edge. Bonnard commonly painted from memory or drawings rather than directly from the motif, thus allowing his free interpretations and associations to guide the colors and forms. The subjective mood that results is just as characteristic as his distortions of drawing and space and his love of richly patterned composition.

Still life painting played a central role in this late development. For pleasure and diversion from large-scale, ambitious figure and landscape paintings, Bonnard regularly made smaller pictures of flowers or fruit or tabletop settings. At times, these more "domestic" exercises also served as experimentations in color or structure. Almost always, they show him at his most intimate and direct. In *Vase of Flowers,* a typically lush bouquet sits in a vase well known from other still life paintings, except that here its handle is broken. Visible in areas through the thin skeins of paint is a loose underdrawing in pencil. Throughout, Bonnard's brushwork has a scurrying rhythm as it moves through and around the leaves and flowers, rarely slowing for a larger, smoother form. The space itself seems to be activated in bursts of of brilliant light and color. It was partly by allowing the white of the canvas to reflect through the subject that Bonnard achieved so glowing an effect.

Because of the stylistic consistency of Bonnard's late work and his habit of not inscribing his canvases, individual paintings are often difficult to date precisely. It is known, however, that the present picture was acquired in 1935 directly from the artist by his dealer, Bernheim-Jeune and Co., as part of a group of "recent works." It therefore is thought to date from shortly before that time.

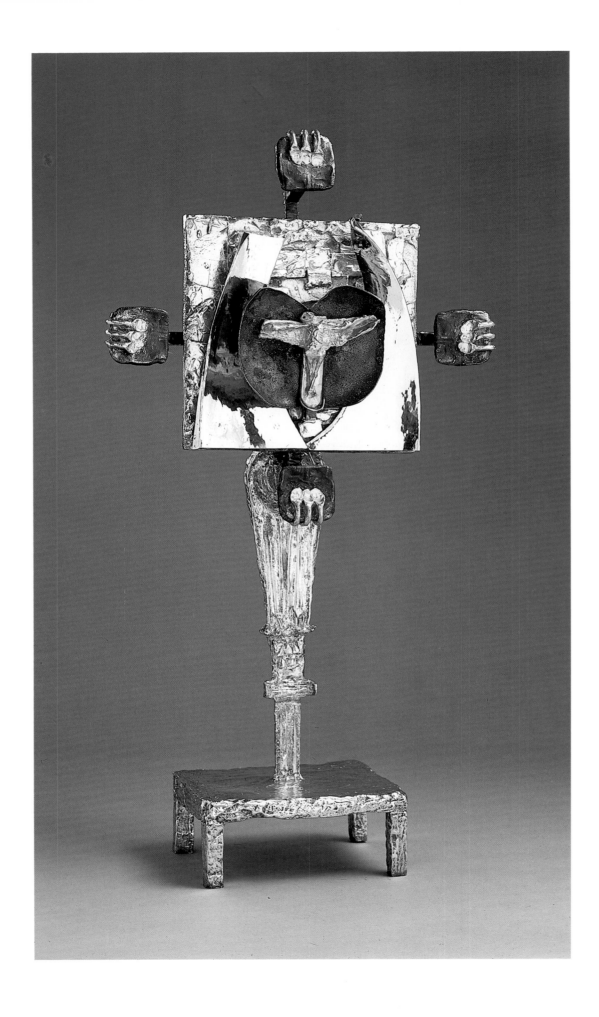

Graham Sutherland (English, 1903-1980)
The Cross of Ely, *1964*
gold and silver, 43½ x 22 x 12 inches
(110.5 x 56 x 30.5 cm)
not signed or dated

Sutherland's work during the 30s and early 40s was dominated by expressionistic abstractions from nature, so that when commissioned in 1944 by the vicar of St. Matthew's Cathedral in Northampton for a painting of the *Crucifixion* to accompany Henry Moore's *Madonna and Child,* the project came as a special challenge. It represented his first life-size figure painting and introduced a series of religious subjects leading eventually to the *Ely Cross.*

This work, his most ambitious sculpture, also came as a commission. With an enlightened belief that good modern art could harmonize with the Romanesque and Gothic splendor of their cathedral, authorities at Ely ordered as a collaboration between Sutherland and the architect-goldsmith Louis Osman a gold and silver cross for the nave altar. Work was completed in May 1964 for the enthronement of the new Bishop of Ely.

The cross stands 43½ inches high and weighs 77 pounds. Complexly formed from 45 separate parts, it consists of a square central plaque, supported vertically from a high stand, which is surrounded on all sides by four pads with gold finger-like additions representing the hands or power of God. At the center is a small crucifix set against a heart suggesting love, devotion and eternal life. The silver forms were cast by the Morris Singer Foundry in London and several of them (the "hands" and heart) were then enamelled in black niello. The gold crucifix was cast by Johnson Matthey of Hatton Garden. The overall design is attributed to Osman, while Sutherland contributed the crucifix with heart and the gold fingers.

With its precious metals, highly polished surfaces, and rough modelling, the cross gleams in even dim ambient light. Indeed, it was this reflectivity (together perhaps with the cross's highly modern character) which caused church leaders to reject it in 1965 after its initial installation. The Dean of Ely was quoted as saying that "because of the way its surface is broken up it becomes almost invisible in its position on the high altar …." Donations made to the church to pay for it were returned, and the cross was transferred to the Worshipful Company of Goldsmiths in London, which also helped to fund it. It was purchased from this group by the Reves, who had seen it on exhibition prior to installation at Ely and had been deeply moved by its power. Five years later, Sutherland, a close friend of theirs, presented to them the wax model for the crucifix. The central section of the sculpture, including the crucifix and heart, was cast in silver in an edition of nine by the Marlborough Gallery in 1964.

Acknowledgments

150   A considerable amount of new research, lies behind the descriptions contained herein, and we would like to extend our special thanks to the numerous individuals who freely provided information for their completion. First and foremost, a debt of gratitude is due to Annette Schlagenhauff, McDermott Curatorial Intern at the Dallas Museum of Art, who worked long and hard on the documentation. Our mutual efforts were greatly aided by the generous assistance of the following scholars, archivists and museum professionals: Caroline Godfroy, Hélène Pinet, Alexandre Rosenberg, Juliet Bareau, Antonie Salomon, Delphine Montalant, Alain Clairet, Gloria Groom, Rick Brettell, Sandy Easterbrook, Shelley Fletcher, Michael Goodison, George Shackleford, Daniel Rosenfeld, Denise Gazier, Rosalyn Frankel Jamison, Jean Sutherland Boggs, Johannes van der Wolk, Albert E. Elsen, Anne Roquebert and Theodore Reff. Staff members at numerous museums and galleries kindly answered questions for us, and we would like especially to acknowledge: Galerie Rosengart, Lucerne; Valley House Gallery, Dallas; Galerie Nathan, Zürich; Wildenstein and Co., New York; M. Knoedler and Co., New York; Tooth Paintings, London; Alex Reid and Lefevre, Ltd., London; Hirschl and Adler Gallery, New York; Barnes Foundation, Merion; Arts Council of Great Britain; Museum of Modern Art, New York; The Metropolitan Museum of Art, New York. We are further indebted to the library staffs of the Dallas Museum of Art and the Kimbell Art Museum, to conservators Jacqueline Gilliam, JoAnn Griffin, Carol Smiley, and Perry Huston and Associates, and to Vicki Vinson and Monika Sigmar.

SAN

DECORATIVE ARTS

Cabinet on Stand, *Europe 17th century, detail*

Introduction

When Harry Parker first told me about the treasures of Villa La Pausa I was excited to think that Dallas would at last have a diverse collection of decorative arts. Until now, the only decorative art on display to residents of and visitors to this area has been the distinguished Hoblitzelle collection of English silver. Although the Wendy and Emery Reves collection has some excellent examples of English silver, it also encompasses European furniture and other woodwork, ironwork, textiles, and Chinese export porcelain — aspects of collector interest scarcely represented in the Southwest. Visitors to the Reves Collection will experience a variety of impressions: the austere elegance of a Spanish Renaissance carpet, the Baroque exuberance of a carved and gilded mirror frame, the intricacy of a marquetried cabinet, the enamelled brilliance of a coat-of-arms on a Chinese plate sent to Europe two hundred and fifty years ago. It is through these reflections of history and connoisseurship that we gain a deeper appreciation of the decorative arts. As we speed towards the twenty-first century, leaving a wake of plastic and paper discards, it becomes more and more necessary for us to pause and savor a past in which the beauty of one's surroundings was the best part of living.

David T. Owsley
New York City

Cupboard in Two Sections
Carved walnut
French c. 1500-1600
h: 83¼" w: 40¼" d: 18⅞"

154   Gothic furniture of the 15th and early 16th century was usually made of oak. Case pieces, morticed and tenoned like the panelled wall, often appeared to be extensions of it. Chief among several popular designs was the linen-fold pattern, used for wall boarding, on the backs of settles, high back armchairs, and the sides of chests and cupboards. Chests served as closets. Stools and benches were the most common forms of seat furniture.

During the 16th century, walnut gradually replaced oak for finer furniture, since it was less apt to splinter and could be carved more easily. It also looked better, taking a rich polish like a patinaed bronze. Architectural in form, Renaissance furniture relied on relief ornamentation contained within a rectangular outline. Many pieces of furniture could be disassembled; chairs folded up for easy transport by cart to the owner's second or third estate. There he would reside for several weeks, collecting rents, before moving to another property.

In furnishing their Riviera villa, Emery and Wendy Reves shunned the vogue for 18th century French decoration. Instead, they mostly collected late Renaissance and Baroque pieces made in the Mediterranean area and the Low Countries. The tables, with their rich surface patinas, provided surfaces not only for dining but also for the display of their large collection of porcelain, metalwork, small sculpture, glass, and silver. Outstanding among the furniture collection are a rare late 16th century carved walnut cupboard, two exceptionally fine late 17th century marquetried cabinets on stands, and a group of inlaid small cabinets and boxes. Another interesting aspect of the collection is the group of early Victorian black lacquer and papier maché furnishings which Mrs. Reves assembled before it became fashionable.

France was introduced to the Italian Renaissance Mannerist style with the construction of the Palace at Fontainebleau under the patronage of King Francis I. The influence of the Italian and French architects and decorators at Fontainebleau on their French counterparts was profound and continued into the early 17th century. One of the French designers was Jacques Androuet Ducerceau whose design for a chimneypiece, published in 1561, contains three standing male figures which probably inspired those on the upper section of this cupboard. His designs for silver ornamentation, published in 1576, include a grotesque mask flanked by two scrolls which may be the source for this pediment's central motif. The strapwork, husk, and palmette designs of the front and sides of this interesting cupboard are also in the Mannerist style which the cabinetmaker probably learned from an engraving.

Cupboard in Two Sections
Carved walnut
French c. 1600-20
h: 71" w: 53½" d: 22½"

156   The device of narrowing and recessing the upper section of a two-section cabinet was adopted from 16th century Italian furniture; the result is a less massive, more graceful design. In this cupboard, the relief-carved allegorical panels of Spring and Summer above are smaller than those of Autumn and Winter in the lower section; this reduction in scale adds grace to the proportions. This early 17th century Mannerist style is broader and more pictorial than that of the late 16th century cupboard with its strapwork panels and large scale three-dimensional figures. Here the male and female half-figures have palmetted heads similar to those in a design for a buffet by Jacques Androuet Ducerceau. His engravings for silver decoration may have inspired the foliated male masks on the lower drawer fronts.

Stand
Carved wood painted and gilded
Italian 17th century
h: 48"

158   In the 17th century, Baroque palaces and great houses had huge rooms and halls which demanded freestanding, three-dimensional objects for decoration and to support candelabra, sculpture, and ceramics. This stand is carved in high relief with grotesque feline masks, pierced leafage, and authoritative Baroque C-scrolls above paw feet.

Reclining Armchair
Walnut frame, needlepoint covering, and iron
Dutch c. 1650-75

While sitting in this chair the occupant or his attendant
could adjust his position by means of a bolt protruding
from the arms which engages a ratchet on the back-
posts. Leg rests pull out from the mouths of the lions'
head arm terminals. The back of this chair as well as
the arm supports, arms and seat have been recovered
in early 18th century needlepoint.

Cabinet on Stand
Wood with ivory and wood marquetry
gilt metal, mirror
Probably Antwerp or Paris, second half 17th century
h: 68½" w: 49½" d: 17"

One of the grandest examples of cabinetwork in the Reves Collection is this rare architectural form collector's cabinet. The front and sides are entirely covered with ivory panels marquetried with shaded woods and tinted ivory in a variety of floral designs probably based on Flemish, German, or French engravings. The marquetry colors are green and shades of brown against an ivory field. Each panel is outlined with ebony and with wider borders and pilasters sprinkled with mother of pearl bits on a black ground, a technique probably derived from 17th century Japanese Namban wares.

The upper section, the center with a gilt metal classical female figure, has vertical drawers on each side of a two-tiered architectural door front which opens to reveal a stage-like interior with tortoise-shell-covered steps, a pair of marbleized colonettes, and floral marquetry drawers. The stage is panelled with mirrors and has a central tortoise-shell niche which formerly contained a statuette. The floor of the stage is of pink marbleized ivory panels outlined with ebony in a Baroque pattern. The cabinet rests on a matching six-legged stand.

Cabinet on Stand
Continental Europe 17th century
Wood, tortoise shell, wood and ivory marquetry,
mirror, gilt metal
h: 67⅝" w: 56¾" d: 20½"

162   This marvelous collector's cabinet is a simple architectonic block sumptuously ornamented with red-tinted tortoise-shell, ivory, and wood marquetry, and mounted with gilt metal. The two niched, central doors, which once housed gilt bronze statuettes, are ordered by three classical pilasters, which, because of their ivory stringing, appear to be fluted. They have high quality gilt metal capitals and applied pierced mounts. The insides of the doors are inlaid with Moorish star forms, perhaps a Spanish influence. The stage-like interior is inset with marbleized colonettes supporting a balustrade before a painted garden scene dominated by an imposing peacock. The floor, inlaid with diminishing geometric shapes, is evidence of the continuing interest in Renaissance perspective. The drawers surrounding the central doors are finely marquetried with tinted and untinted ivory and shaded woods in imitation of Florentine hardstone inlays known as *pietra dure*.

Armchair (One of a pair)
Walnut and caning
English c. 1690
h: 53½"

164 Flemish-influenced Baroque chairs like this were popular during the reigns of Charles II, James II, and William and Mary. Their crests and front stretchers often contained elaborate scrolls, flowerage, and even cherubs holding cyphers or coats-of-arms. Towards the end of the 17th century this style of chair became less elaborate and lighter in feeling. Here the back splat is caned and flanked by scrolls. The caned square seat would originally have had a cushion. The turned rear legs and back posts are block and ball and baluster. Ball feet were introduced with the accession of William III in 1689. The scrolled crest is flanked by knop-finialed blocks which are carved in relief with flowers similar to those on the handholds of the scrolling, crisply edged *Pembroke* arms.

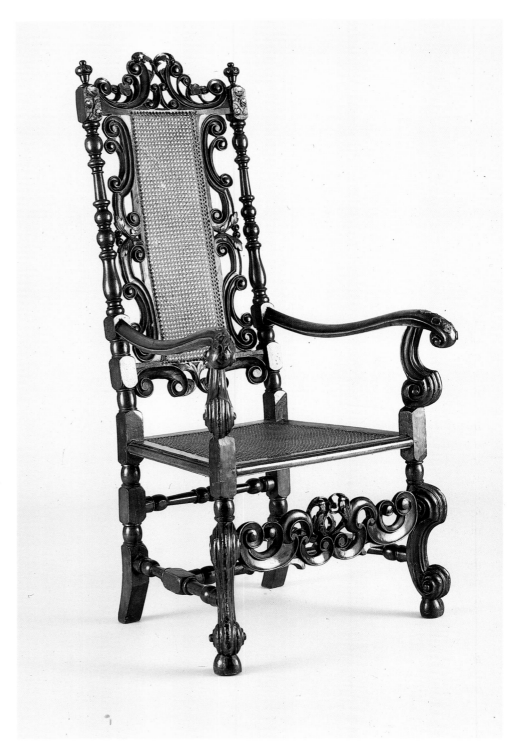

Small Cabinet

Nut or fruitwood inlaid with
other woods, shell, and ivory
German dated 1611
h: 12¾" w: 16" d: 9⅞"

During the Renaissance many-drawered small chests
and cabinets were popular storage places for personal
objects, curiosities, and valuables. Often these were
created less for storage than as works of art in themselves. Marquetry had become a fine art and was used
in wall paneling as well as in case and seat furniture.

This two-door cabinet is fitted with seven drawers
inlaid with human, bird, vine and leaf designs of
mother-of-pearl and ivory shaded with inked engravings. These designs were probably copied from late
16th century engravers. The cruciform quartering on
top of the cabinet and on the door panels, and the
female saint holding a cross remind today's viewer that
not only was the 17th century an age of rich interior
decoration, but an intensely religious one as well. The
three initials on top probably stand for the first and last
names of a man and his wife, suggest that this cabinet
may have been a wedding present.

Small Cabinet (Contador)

Ebonized wood and brass
Portugal 17th century
h: 18⅛" w: 21½" d: 12⁷⁄₁₆"

The simple rectangular form of this three-drawer cabinet is covered with applied wavy moldings and panels,
pierced brass drawer plaques, corner mounts, carrying
handles, and backplates. The fronts of the three horizontal drawers are each compartmented into three,
thus multiplying and enriching the design as faceting
does on a gemstone.

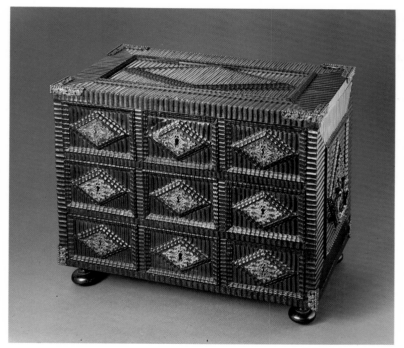

Small Cabinet with Handles
Walnut with ivory and iron
Spanish early 17th century
h: 12¼" w: 17⅛" d: 11½"

166   Of typical architectural *vargueño* form, this small cabinet originally would have rested on an arcaded trestle stand or on another cabinet instead of having feet. Vargueños often have fall-fronts which double as writing surfaces and prevent the drawers from falling out when carried. In this one, the iron drawer studs act as drawer pulls and are reminiscent of the larger studs used on 15th century Spanish doors. Pierced iron mounts decorate the borders and are used as backplates for the iron handles on each side. The molded wood and ivory decoration is architectural rather than anthropomorphic, for Spanish decorative arts continued to be influenced by the Islamic aversion to human and animal representation even after the Moors were expelled in 1492.

Small Chest with Barrel Lid
Wood, ivory, and gilt metal
Continental Europe 17th century
h: 13⅝" w: 18¾" d: 11¾"

The shape of this chest is simple, but it is lent sophistication by its fine geometric panels of brown and black wood compartmented by ivory fillets. The ends of the lid are inlaid with a fan design, their ivory centers engraved as shells. The bail handles are squared to conform to the shape of their panels. This chest would probably have stood on its own frame, or on a cabinet or table. It may have been used to store documents. The style of the gilt lockplate suggests that this handsome chest was probably made in Spain.

Hinged Box
Wood inlaid with shell, brass, pewter, silver
Netherlandish c. 1700
h: 5¾" w: 14⁵⁄₁₆" d: 9⅜"

The technique of inlaying metals and shell into wood
was practiced by German and Netherlandish gun stock
makers in the 17th and early 18th century. This remarkable box has a guilloche pattern border and circular dot patterns of pewter, overall scrolling vine and
dot patterns of brass, and engraved silver key es-
cutcheon, and tinted shell engraved with parrots and
flowers. The amusing engraved coat-of-arms of the
Willoughby family is in mid-18th century Rococo style,
and the four corner ovals engraved with the mono-
gram of a member of that family who owned the box,
are in the neo-classic taste of the later 18th century.
This box was apparently updated for new owners.

Chair with Tufted Slip Seat
Lacquered wood, papier maché, mother-of-pearl
English c. 1830-45
h: 2' 10½" w: 1' 7⅜" d: 1' 10"

Lidded Box with Chinoiserie Design
Black lacquered wood inlaid with tinted shell
European c. 1830-50
h: 2¹/₁₆" w: 11³/₁₆" d: 10¼"

168 On the front of this chair, wafer-thin pearl shell has been glued to the surface and clear lacquered. The legs and seat rail are wood, the crest is papier maché. The Reves' bedroom is furnished with many fine examples of papier maché furniture and small decorative objects. Papier maché is a mixture of pulped paper and glue or paste pliant enough to be molded and which is surprisingly strong when hardened.

Variations of this formula have been used in the decorative arts at least since the 1640's when branches for lighting fixtures were made from it. In 1672 the scientist Robert Boyle recommended papier maché for decorating picture frames and other *movables*. Frederick the Great built a factory in 1765 in Berlin for making papier maché. In the early 19th century, the firm of Jennens and Bettridge of Birmingham, England, made some of the finest papier maché delicately inlaid with mother-of-pearl.

Chinoiserie was Europe's idea of Indian and oriental decoration. It was fanciful rather than being based on actual drawings by the few artists who visited the East. The vogue for Chinoiserie began in the late 17th century and lasted fitfully for about 150 years. In the 18th century Chinoiserie scenes were published by artists such as Jean Pillement in Paris and Paul Decker in Nuremberg. They were adapted by weavers, printers, embroiderers, silversmiths, and pottery and procelain decorators. At home, ladies *japanned* boxes, trays, and pieces of furniture using a lacquering formula first published in Oxford in 1688 by Stalker and Parker.

The Chinoiserie scene on the lid of this box depicts a lord seated under a canopy on a Rococo *chaise lounge* smoking a long opium pipe, flanked by attendants who wear their hair in a queue, and one of whom has scrolled-toe slippers. The box is fitted with five smaller boxes, the tops of which are inlaid with mother-of-pearl floral sprays.

Bed Headboard
Painted and shelled lacquered wood within metal posts
English or French 1835-45
h: 4' 9¾" w: 4' 7⅝"

The Victorian taste for drama is evidenced by the use of a black lacquered background against which is set a profusion of multi-colored shelled and painted flowers and gilt Gothic revival patterned borders. The lavender, pink and blue glinting mother-of-pearl inlays further accentuate the naturalistically painted roses, daisies, morning glories and other flowers. At the top, the dripping gold-looped clusters of wisteria create a lux-uriant fantasy anticipating the later taste for rooms with a single theme such as James McNeill Whistler's *Peacock Room,* now in the Freer Gallery, and Levy Dhurmer's *Wisteria Room,* recently purchased by the Metropolitan Museum.

Mirror Frame
Carved wood gessoed and gilt
French c. 1660-80
h: 46½" w: 39"

170 The history of the mobile picture frame begins in the 16th and 17th centuries with the emergence of easel painting. Mirrors have a much longer history. The Egyptians, Greeks, Etruscans, and Romans used polished bronze to admire their reflections. In 625 A.D. Pope Boniface IV gave a silver mirror to the Queen of Northumbria. In the middle ages polished metal or glass backed with thin sheets of metal was used. In 17th century palaces and houses of the rich, mirrors were sometimes set into wainscoting, window openings, or ceilings, though by the turn of the century they were mostly free-hanging. Venetian glass makers were the first to develop glass mirrors commercially; they backed the glass with a mixture of tin and mercury. Louis XIV's minister, Colbert, owned a Venetian glass mirror almost 4' by 2'. Framed in silver, it was appraised at more than double the value of a painting by Raphael. Although they serve different artistic purposes, picture frames and mirror frames usually consist of the same three elements:

   a) blind frame: a structural base of local wood usually of poor quality.
   b) profile: the forward surface of a trim piece which curves backwards or forwards.
   c) decoration: consisting of carved, inlaid, applied or tooled wood, stucco, mother-of-pearl, tortoise shell, ivory, or metal.

In large workshops there was a division of labor: joiners prepared the structure, carvers created the moldings and ornaments, and gilders finished the assembled product. Long treated merely as a convenient means to display paintings, picture frames have recently been recognized by some museums as independent works of art and have been exhibited as such.

The French word for crown prince is *dauphin*. It also means dolphin, a favorite motif in French art whenever the throne boasted a crown prince. In this large frame, acanthus and grape leaves, clusters of grapes, a wicker basket, and nude youths playing with dolphins are finely carved motifs. Louis XIV's eldest son was born in 1661; perhaps the dolphins allude to him.

Picture Frame
Wood with tortoise shell and gilt metal
Flemish or Spanish 1650-75
h: 30⅛" w: 28⅛"

Extensive use of tortoise shell decoration on frames, boxes, and cabinets was one result of the world-wide sea trade of Spain and the Spanish Netherlands (Flanders). Here a sumptuous effect is achieved simply by contrasting the buffed tortoise shell hearts and sausage shapes with the rippled, ebonized wood moldings. Frame makers often used colored papers or metallic foil behind the shell or tinted it, as here, to enrich its color.

Mirror Frame
Ebonized wood marquetried with wood, ivory, shell
French or Flemish c. 1685
h: 22" w: 20"

Dutch and Flemish still-life painting reached a high point in the 17th century and influenced designers of marquetry panels for case and seat furniture, mirror and picture frames in England and France as well as at home. In this frame the ebonized outer borders contrast with the finely executed inner border consisting of green tinted ivory, mother-of-pearl, and dark and light-shaded wood marquetry in uninterrupted flower designs which include two perched birds.

Crested Mirror Frame
Carved wood gessoed and gilt
Italian or Flemish c. 1690
h: 56" w: 37½"

172   Baroque exuberance abounds in the massing of leaves
and flowers carved in high relief on this large frame.
Cherubs hold a shield intended for a coat-of-arms. A
border of flowers interrupted by blank areas, rather
than continuous flowerage, indicates a late 17th
century date.

Picture Frame
Carved wood gessoed and gilt
French c. 1740
h: 19¼" w: 18" d: 3⅜"

Authoritative late Baroque basal scrolls combine with
Rococo leafed and bossed shells, frilled C-scrolls, leaf-
ribbed S-scrolls and flowers in a particularly rich setting for a small Louis XV oil painting.

Picture Frame
Carved wood gessoed and gilt
French c. 1735-50
h: 36½" w: 29¼" d: 2¾"

This frame is finely carved with typical Louis XV period
motifs of scrolls, shells, and frilled swags of naturalistic
flowers.

Iron and Bronze

Iron from meteors was known to earliest man. It was worshipped in Mesopotamia and formed into precious beads in Egypt as early as 4000 B.C. It was smelted from ore at least by 3500 B.C. The Phoenicians paid tribute to the pharaohs in iron. Greeks and Romans valued iron for its strength but preferred bronze for art. They used iron clamps to fasten stone building blocks laid without cement, and indoors to reinforce couches and tripods. Roman legionnaires wielded iron swords in battle. Medieval blacksmithing reached its artistic height from the 11th to the 13th century. On their anvils smiths heated and reheated the ore to white or red heat, their repeated hammer blows giving it great strength and ductility, forming it into artistic, often fantastic shapes. Sometimes they struck the hot iron into dies the way hot wax is pressed into seals; the 13th century West door mounts at Notre Dame Cathedral in Paris were fashioned in this manner, although the architectural use of iron probably originated in England.

In the 14th century smiths began to work in cold iron in order to reproduce stone tracery in metal. Only in the early stages was heat used. Using vise and saw, chisel and drill, the smith became like a woodworker, shaping the iron, bolting and riveting it together without heat, or tenoning and morticing as in joinery. Door knockers, handles, and locks were made in this way. The 15th and 16th centuries became the age of the locksmith and the armorer. In the 16th century, when fireplaces were moved from the center of the room to the wall, firebacks and andirons were made of cast iron. Iron canons, cheaper than bronze, were first cast in England in 1544. Grave slabs were sometimes made of cast iron. The 17th and 18th centuries saw a taste for wrought iron balconies, stair rails, fan lights, and imposing gates. During the first half of the 19th century cast iron gates and balustrades superseded wrought iron.

Iron became industrialized around 1860, and its artistry declined. With the increased mechanization of the 20th century and the advent of disposable plastics, there is now a renewed appreciation for handcrafted objects, and antique ironwork is one of the most satisfying areas of interest.

Lockplate
Iron with applied iron
German c. 1500
h: 13¾" w: 17¾"

The medieval and Renaissance period produced locks of beautiful case design, but the artists paid less attention to convenience and security than we do today. This imposing lockplate probably adorned a large wood chest. The upper tracery, central ribbon decoration, and lower ogee scrolls are characteristic of late Gothic style. There are zoomorphic heads in the right and left borders. The splayed shape is most often found in Germany. Small decorative pieces of cold iron have been chiseled out and attached to its sheet iron backing.

Lockplate and Hasp with Relief Decoration
Gilt bronze
North Italian c. 1560
h: 8⅞" w: 6⅞"

176   Since antiquity the Italians have preferred marble and bronze to iron. History has preserved ancient Roman bronze keys, but their more corrosive iron locks have disintegrated. This beautiful lockplate, enriched with Renaissance motifs in relief, relates more to sculpture and jewelry than to blacksmithing. It appears first to have been cast, then the details sharpened with a chisel before gilding. Possibly intended to secure a cabinet door or chest, it has acquired a mellow patina from much handling.

On the hasp is a relief of an oval coat-of-arms under a standing female figure who holds an overflowing shell on her head. The plate is relieved with military trophies and C-scroll cartouches, one of which contains the keyhole, and with two scarf-draped seated female figures whose poses ultimately derive from Michaelangelo's *Dawn*. The right and left borders contain ewers, grotesque masks, and shields. The four corners were once held in place by nails with gilt fleur-de-lis heads.

Knockers and Backplate
Iron
French, probably Bordeaux, c. 1720-40
h: 15" w: 12½"

The buckle-form handle consists of two confronted C-scrolls and a turned ball strike. The *a jour* cutout scrolled backplate is a fine example of late French baroque design which is authoritative, yet elegant and airy.

Messenger Box
Wood overlaid with cut-out iron
French c. 1500
h: 4½" w: 4¾" d: 6½"

Sometimes called *girdle boxes,* these small strongboxes were used by couriers to carry important documents or money. This wood box is reinforced with iron strips and a tracery of pierced iron. Note the formidable lock and the rings used to attach the box to the messenger's belt.

178

Small Domed Coffer with Bail Handle
Etched iron
German, possibly Nuremberg, 17th century
h: 3½" w: 4¾" d: 3¹/₁₆"

These miniature strongboxes held coins and jewels,
and were easy to carry on journeys. In this one a hasp
hides the keyhole. The designs of heraldic single birds
within borders of leafed scrolling vines are copied
from engravings of the period. Nuremberg was a
center for this type of etched ironwork.

Six Keys
Chiseled iron
European 17th - 18th century
lengths: 5¹/₈" to 7"

Since the Renaissance, keys as well as locks have often
been regarded as works of art. The French architect
Jacques Androuet Ducereau, who died c. 1585, was the
first to publish designs for keys. The art of the locksmith reached its height in France during the first half
of the 17th century under King Louis XIII who, in his
teens enjoyed working at the smith's forge and bench.
These keys were probably chiseled from cold iron.

English and Other European Silver and Glass

In 1660, after a decade of somber Puritanical rule, the English welcomed the return to monarchy under King Charles II with an outpouring of joy and new wealth and thirty years of extravagant Baroque style. This was reflected in a change of silver design from simple forms and plain surfaces to more exuberant, ampler shapes, and elaborate cast and engraved repoussé ornamentation inspired by continental Eurpoean prototypes. Extravagance at court was evidenced by the use of silver for vases, chandeliers, andirons, wall sconces, mirror frames, toilet sets, and even, as at Versailles, sheeting for furniture. Cupboards and sideboards of the wealthy were heaped with large silver tankards, plates, bowls, and cups. But with the exile of James II in 1686 came the sober Dutch Protestant influence of William III. Economic belt-tightening as well as a shortage of silver resulted in a taste for plain, smaller scale silver objects. Often architectural in form they frequently lacked any ornamentation other than molding, knops, and the glimmer of light reflecting on their facets. This simple style persevered through the reign of Queen Anne (1702-14) and into that of George I (1714-27).

The special beauty of the silver objects made during the early years of the 18th century is partly due to the high content of silver in the metal used. During the silver shortage of the late 1690's, unscrupulous persons took to clipping slices from silver coins, which were of the 925/1000 purity, and selling them to silversmiths. To discourage coin clipping, Parliament decreed in 1697 that the standard for silver objects be raised from 925 to at least 950 parts pure silver in 1000. This was the Britannia standard. The law remained in effect until 1719 when the silver supply from the Americas was plentiful and England prospered. Britannia standard silver has a subtle softness and warmth which combines beautifully with the simple elegance of Queen Anne design. Later, during the reign of George II, English taste in silver changed again. It was affected by the richness and elaborateness of the French Rococo, partly due to the continuing contacts between London's Huguenot silversmiths, such as the great Paul de Lamerie, and their continental cousins.

The Reves Collection contains several examples of English silver made during the William III, Queen Anne, George I, and George II periods, as well as a fine Danish tankard which is in the Baroque taste.

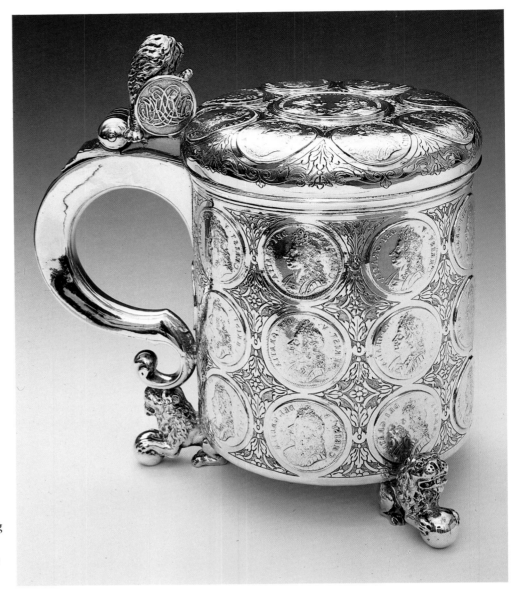

Lidded Tankard Inset with Silver Coins and a Medal
Copenhagen 1728
Maker: Carsten Lauridsen
h: 8½"

180 Although the practice of embedding coins and medals in ornamental objects was more common in Germany and Scandinavia than in England, this Danish tankard contains many of the design elements of the English Baroque style of 1660-90 which persisted on the European continent after it lost favor in England. The fullness of the cylindrical body, broad double scroll of the handle, heraldic and sculptural quality of the feet and thumbpiece, are elements often found in English Baroque silver. The thumbpiece lion holds a shield with the royal cypher, and three lions holding spheres support the tankard. The sides are inset with three horizontal rows of silver krone struck between 1693 and 1696 which display the bust of King Christian V wearing the Order of the Elephant. The lid encases a large medal of Christian facing Queen Charlotte Amalie. The reverse of the medal appears on the underside of the lid and depicts the heads of five royal children. The medal was designed by Anton Meybusch and was cast in 1695 to celebrate the king's April 15th birthday.

Pair of Silver Candlesticks
Britannia Standard silver
London 1702
Maker: John Bache
h: 8½" w: 4⅞"

Silver objects of the late 17th and early 18th century were often architectural in form. Despite their thin gauge these candlesticks appear substantial because of the stepped moldings and gadroons of their octagonal bases which support stop-fluted columns with octagonal flanged fixed nozzles. The chased tooling used in this decoration strengthened the walls as well as ornamented them. The shield-shaped cartouches appear to have been once engraved. Under the footrim of one of the sticks are engraved the initials I P under P, doubtless the first and last initials of a husband and wife. The candlesticks may have been a wedding or anniversary gift.

Three Casters
Britannia Standard silver
London 1719
Maker: Thomas Tearle
h: 6½" and 5¾"

This set of octagonal baluster-form casters is a perfect example of Queen Anne design: simple, elegant, and decorative. Eight plain panels descend from octagonal knobs to form covers which recall the paneled domes of baroque churches such as St. Paul's in London; they are pierced with tiers of scrolling flowers and plumes. Three of the eight plain panels of the sides are engraved with a contemporary coat-of-arms. The flanges at the rims of the lids and the moldings about the waists both divide and unite the composition, enticing the viewer's eyes around the casters. The molded octagonal feet echo these horizontals and provide sturdy bases as well. The Britannia standard silver gives a special richness to these beautiful casters. The largest was probably used for sugar, the smaller two for pepper; salt was usually served in open trenchers.

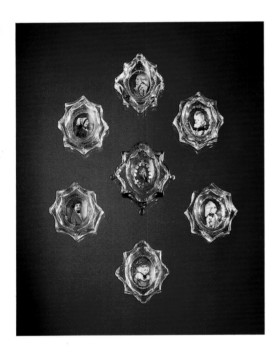

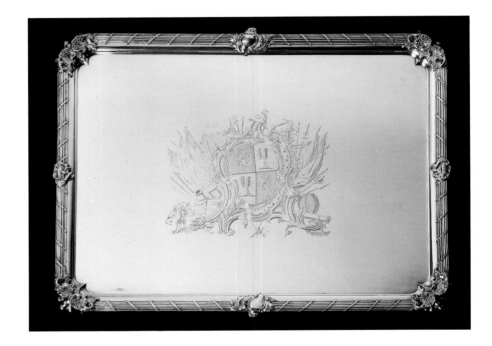

Seven Salt Cellars and One Silver Holder
Reverse painted cut lead glass (Verre Eglomisé)
Austria or Bohemia c. 1775-90
Cellar h: 1¹⁄₈" l: 3" w: 2¹⁄₂"

This group of octafoil-shaped cut glass salt cellars is painted on the underside with portrait busts of ladies and gentlemen in late 18th century dress, who may have been actual personages or else illustrations from a play or novel. Two of the salt cellars retain their original silver holders (one shown) with cutout sides and paw-and-ball feet. Because salt corrodes silver, glass liners were often used with silver holders. Reverse painting on glass, sealed with varnish or with another is *eglomisé,* from an 18th century Parisian artisan, Jean-Baptiste Glomy (d. 1786), who used it on picture frame mounts.

Footed Tray
London 1747
Maker: probably John Le Sage
l: 23³⁄₁₆" w: 17³⁄₁₆"

Raised on four claw-and-ball feet, this large rectangular tray is impressive for its size and the fine quality of its engraved arms and Rococo cartouche flanked by banners, spears, cannons, and other military paraphernalia. The ribs of the cast rim are faciated with ribbons and its shaped corners and centers are shelled, providing a lovely frame for the shining expanse of plain, polished silver and intricate Rococo engraving.

Table Setting
Silver, glass and porcelain on wood table
European 17th and 18th centuries

Festive luncheons and dinners on their 17th century
banquet table set with period porcelain, silver and
glass were frequent occasions at Villa La Pausa. Here
we can see the rare gilt and enamel-decorated
cabbage-top Chinese export porcelain soup tureen
flanked by two of the Reves' four English mid-18th
century candleabra, flatware, plates, salt trenchers and
pepper casters. All the stemware was handblown in
England during the first half of the 18th century.

The silver cigar holder in the left foreground was
reserved for Sir Winston Churchill, a frequent guest.

Chinese Export Porcelain

184 Carried by the sailing ships of great 16th century world explorers, Chinese blue and white porcelain appeared in Europe a few pieces at a time and was viewed as a curiosity. Sometimes it was mounted in gilt silver and placed in curio cabinets next to other rarities such as nautilus shells, branch coral, ostrich eggs, and carved coconuts.

With the greatly expanded Far Eastern trade of the Portuguese, Spanish, Dutch, and English during the 17th century, underglaze blue decorated porcelain arrived in European ports by the tens of thousands of pieces, and became tableware and interior decoration for the rich and an increasingly well-to-do middle class which preferred it to more breakable pottery. Its designs were copied in tin-glazed earthenware at Dutch, English, and French potteries in the late 17th and early 18th centuries. Sometimes these pottery copies, slightly altered, as well as painted wood models, hand-colored drawings, pewter and silver objects, were sent to China to be copied in the lighter, sometimes translucent, chip-resistant porcelain. Europe did not learn how to make porcelain until 1708 and it remained an expensive luxury during the succeeding decades. Sophisticated Europeans became bored with blue and white ware and despite higher prices demanded porcelain decorated with the more colorful overglaze enamel combinations known as famille verte, famille noire, and famille jaune, which were being developed at the great kiln site at Jingdezhen (Ching-tê Chên) in Jiangzi (Kiansi) Province under the patronage of the art and trade conscious Qing (Ch'ing) Dynasty Emperor Kangxi (K'ang-Hsi; reigned 1662-1722). During the reign of his son, Yongzheng (Yung Chen; 1723-35), the palette of the porcelain painter was greatly expanded by the introduction of a red derived from gold which could be mixed with an opaque white to create various shades of pink. During the reign of Qianlong (Ch'ien Lung; 1735-95), the whole range of enamel colors was fully developed and designs were introduced which remain popular today.

Trading vessels usually carried *supercargoes,* commercial agents in charge of buying and selling or bartering merchandise. They, as well as the captain and officers, were allowed a small percentage of the value of the entire cargo as private concessions. They often handled commissions for friends or business associates at home, and in this way much of the special order enamel-decorated Chinese porcelain, in particular armorial dinner services, came to Europe during the 18th century. By the 1740's much of the porcelain made at Jingdezhen (Ching-te Chen) was decorated in Canton so that it would be ready by the time the ships set sail for home.

Baluster Vase

Porcelain with overglaze famille verte enamels
Chinese c. 1700
h: 28⅜"

This important baluster vase is well painted, beautifully proportioned, and colored with famille verte *wucai* (five color) enamels: translucent green, eggplant purple, yellow, iron-red, and black. The decorative scheme is planned to entice the viewer's eyes around the vase by the placement of the rectangular white background scenes which do not line up in a vertical axis. These scenes are surrounded by and contrasted with a framework of border panels painted with a light green seeded ground scattered with orange-red and purplish lotuses and soaring butterflies in black, white, yellow, aubergine, and orange-red. One is never quite sure whether the scenes are two-dimensional plaques placed in front of the seeded borders, or are to be considered as windows through which the objects or animals are viewed in the distance. This ambiguity acts as a lively counterpoint to the vase's calm purity of form.

The animals in the waist panels are the mythical flying unicorn, or qilin (kylin), and on the opposite side a tiger gazing at a phoenix. The Buddhist *Hundred Antiques,* or *bogu* (po ku), appear in between the panels. The upper and lower panels have landscapes with peonies, rockwork, grasses, and other natural elements. On the shoulder are four secular symbols within lotiform reserves which represent the *Four Gentlemanly Pursuits:* music, chess, learning, and painting. Foot and lip borders have lotuses reserved on an iron-red ground. There is an underglaze blue double-ring mark on the underside which often appears in Kangxi (K'ang Hsi) period porcelain.

Charger Depicting Archery Contest
Verso of Charger
Porcelain with famille verte overglaze enamels
Chinese c. 1700-20
di: 24¹/₁₆"

186 This large plate is a superb example of the full range of Kangxi (K'ang Hsi) period famille verte *wucai* enamel decoration. The iron-red, blue, yellow, eggplant purple, and predominant translucent green are carefully yet freely applied. The scene depicts an equestrian archery contest in the presence of the Imperial Manchu court. The faces of the courtiers and archers and the manes, tails, and legs of the horses are particularly well drawn. The rim is enamelled with alternating panels of chrysanthemums and brocade patterns. The underside is enamelled with scrolls supporting lotuses and with the eight Buddhist symbols. Inside the top rim is an underglaze blue double ring mark enclosing an unidentified two-character mark within a double square.

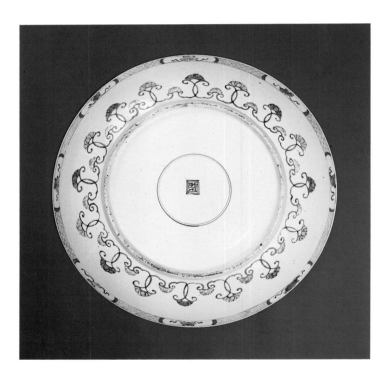

Octagonal Plate
Porcelain with overglaze famille verte enamels
Chinese c. 1725-30
w: 17¾"

188   This octagonal plate is one of three of the same pattern
in the Reves Collection. It is a well painted con-
tinuation of the late K'ang Hsi famille verte palette of
translucent green, iron-red, and purple. The ridged
border derives from a European silver dish, though the
octagonal shape originated with Japanese porcelain.
There are two long-tailed birds in the central scene
amidst impossibly large flowers, a railing, a tree, and
four iron-red long-tailed birds in the seeded green
border alternating with groups of iron-red peonies.
Plates such as these were probably meant for display
rather than use.

Five Vase Garniture
Famille Noire overglaze enamelled porcelain
Chinese, Kangxi (K'ang Hsi period) 1662-1722
hs: 12½" to 16"

Possibly first seen on temple altars by 16th or 17th
century European visitors to China, garnitures of vases
became popular items of interior decoration in Europe
during the later 17th century continuing through the
19th century. They were used in Holland and elsewhere
ranked on mantelpieces, on overdoor cornices and
cabinet tops as well as on tables and shelves. Sets of
three, five or seven were common, the potiche form
usually being central and flanked by beakers or otherwise alternating the shapes depending on their
combinations.

The rich black ground is rare and sets off the
eggplant purple plum trees and their yellow-centered
white blossoms as well as the green, purple and yellow
rockwork and peonies. Outlined in iron red in each
potiche are four petal-form reserves with famille verte
enamels of birds, leaves and the branches and
blossoms. The two beaker vases have similar decoration differently arranged. All bear underneath double
rings encircling a single artemisia leaf in underglaze
blue marking which often appears on K'ang Hsi period
porcelain. One of the lids was probably replaced.

Wall Fountain and Cover
Porcelain with famille verte overglaze enamels
Chinese c. 1710-25
h: 16⁵/₁₆"

190 Inspired by European faience models, ribbed wall fountains with matching domed covers and basins underneath were a popular item of everyday use made and decorated by the hundreds at Jingdezhen (Ching-tê Chên). Most of the basins have not survived. This fountain, in famille verte enamels, has naturalistically portrayed fish and crabs in iron-red and purple, probably a derivation of traditional Chinese animal designs. Chinese legend is the inspiration for the confronted fish at the top that have been transformed into dragons. The scallop shell's stripes are similar to those on a pair of Reves kendi-form bottles. A metal spigot protrudes from the mouth of a monster mask that is flanked by a wide trellis-pattern border which has shrimp in the reserves.

Shell-Shaped Ewer and Basin
Porcelain with overglaze enamels and gold
Chinese c. 1720
Ewer h: 12⅛" Basin w: 14⅝"

Probably based on a late 17th century European silver,
pewter, or faience model, this washing set may well
have been made for the Portuguese market. The panelled strapwork designs in blue, red, and gold are
attributable to Jean Berain whose pattern book, published in Paris in 1711, affected a variety of European
decorative arts during the late Baroque period. The
pitcher's double curved handle ends in small scrolls
which echo the larger one. The basin, in the shape of a
scallop shell, has a notched edge which allows it to be
used as a shaving basin and to fit neatly around the
base of the nautilus-shaped pitcher when not in use.

192

Plate with Arms of Namur
Porcelain with overglaze enamels
Chinese c. 1720-25
di: 19"

A series of large famille verte and underglaze blue
plates and other display pieces were commissioned by
the Dutch to be made and decorated at Jingdezhen
(Ching-tê Chên) in four different patterns. Each suite
contains the names of twenty-two or more provinces,
countries, or towns in England, the Netherlands, and
France. This plate displays an early use of rose in the
figures, robes, feathers of the angels' wings, and the
blossoms in the outer border reserves. It is one of the
earliest pieces to incorporate the pink enamel developed by Andreas Cassius of Leyden in the mid-17th
century and imported to China by the Jesuits about
1715. The fish and crustacea in the inner border relate
to those on the Reves Kangxi (K'ang Hsi) famille verte
wall fountain and derive from the same traditional
sources. This pattern, decorated with an architectural
gateway framing the arms, is perhaps the most unusual
and attractive of the four. Namur was part of the Spanish Netherlands in the 16th and most of the 17th
centuries. It was fought over by the English under
William III and the French under Louis XIV during the
late 17th and early 18th centuries. Today Namur is one
of the nine provinces of Belgium.

Bowl, Cover and Stand in Peach Form
Porcelain with famille rose overglaze enamels
Chinese c. 1760
Bowl with cover h: 5⅜" Stand l: 9"

In China the peach is a symbol of longevity. It is
coveted in a society in which old age is extolled, the
elderly cherished, and ancestors venerated. This bowl,
or tureen, as well as its lid and stand are peach-form
and have naturalistic twig and leaf handles. The lid is
relief-molded with peaches. Each piece is finely
painted; the selection of colors is lovely and the asym-
metric design of peonies, chrysanthemums and other
flowers is imaginative.

Pair of Bottles
Porcelain with overglaze famille rose enamels
Chinese c. 1730-35
h: 8½" di: 6½"

Although their unusual shape is probably copied from
Middle Eastern water pipes, or *kendi,* and they are
sometimes described as nursing bottles, these colorful
porcelains may have been bought by Europeans
merely as decorative objects. The newly developed
famille rose enamel palette is used lavishly on the
roll-over lip, shoulders, reserves, and neck. Rose also
appears in the unusual striping of the spouts and
globular sides. Similar striping can be seen on the
shell of the wall fountain (fig. 72), confirming the early
date of these bottles and the probability that they were
intended for the Portuguese market.

Plate: Ladies with Parasol Pattern
Underglaze blue and overglaze enamels
Chinese 1740
di: 13"

194 In 1734 the Dutch East India Company entered into a three year contract with the artist Cornelis Pronk of Amsterdam to supply the company with drawings for porcelain patterns which could be copied in China or Japan. His best known and probably first drawing, *Ladies with Parasol,* is the design source for this plate and several others in the Reves Collection. Pronk's original drawing, preserved at the Rijksmuseum, is more sensitive, elaborate, and refined in color. This plate, probably made and decorated at Jingdezhen (Ching-tê Chên), reduces Pronk's palette to three colors: coral red, blue, and gold. It belongs to a group of similar ware known as *Chinese Imari.* This popular *Ladies with Parasol* pattern appears in both Chinese and Japanese porcelain, and later at the Cozzi porcelain factory in Venice. Because of the high cost of commissioning special orders, the Dutch East India Company's profits declined and they did not renew their contract with Pronk. Apparently his style of Chinoiserie was not different enough from actual everyday oriental designs to warrant Europeans paying its higher price.

A Plate and One of a Pair of Jugs
After A Design by Cornelis Pronk
Porcelain with overglaze enamels
Chinese c. 1738
Plate di: 14⅛" Jug h: 9¾"

The *Arbor* pattern used here is a rarer design by Cornelis Pronk than his *Ladies with Parasol*. It depicts two Sino-European ladies under a yew hedge arbor with four children about and three ducks swimming in the foreground. The palette of the wide chain motif border and topiary arbor is a lush green. Some of the flowers in the cartouches and the roses climbing the arbor towers are rose enamel. The finely painted row of shells or plumes is reminiscent of a few surviving pieces of tea services probably from Pronk's studio that feature large single plumes in translucent purple

enamel. The appearance of the ladies is quite similar to those in the *Parasol* plates, though these are executed with greater finesse. The shape of the border cartouches is most un-Chinese, and the jug form may derive from European prototypes in silver or earthenware. Similar jugs have been found mounted with European silver or pewter hinged lids; these jugs, however, never had lids.

Plate with Silvered Border (one of a pair)
Porcelain with overglaze enamels and silver
Chinese c. 1730-40
di: 8⅞"

This delicate and finely painted plate is one of an
identical pair. Its double border decoration is unusual
and is enriched by a rare use of silvered enamel
(moyin) on the rim, which also has alternating gold
and enamel outlined reserves of blue enamel flowers
and gilt lotuses within a brocaded grisaille rice grain
pattern. Black and gold outline the central cartouche
which has a polychrome enamel scene of a lady playing a lute-like *qin*. She sits in front of a chest of

drawers and is flanked by blue, orange-red, and lavender containers, two of which hold *ju-i* headed
sceptres or ladles.

An early 18th century visitor to Jingdezhen (Ching-
tê Chên), the French Jesuit missionary Father d'En-
trecolle observed Chinese decorators experimenting
with the use of silver on porcelain and reported it in a
letter dated 1722.

Plate with Exotic Fortress City
Porcelain with overglaze enamels
Chinese c. 1740-50
di: 15¼"

The well of this rare plate is decorated with a scene of the approaches to a walled town along the banks of a river. The three, possibly Dutch, burghers standing among the shrubs in the left foreground and the converging lines of the riverbanks project the rest of the scene into the distance. Despite the Renaissance architecture glimpsed at left, the fortified buildings, towers, and domes within the walls are probably fanciful and may be intended to suggest a Near Eastern locale. The four border reserves within feathery cartouches contain familiar European scenes of figures, castles, and riverscapes possibly derived from Meissen harbor scenes popular during the 1720's to 40's, or from German or Dutch copper engravings. The predominantly orange, or iron-red, palette is varied with rose, yellow, and translucent green, and, for the sky and water, a delicate blue.

Set of Five Armorial Vases
Porcelain with overglaze enamels
Chinese 1740-50
h: 11⁵⁄₁₆" to 11⁵⁄₈"

Sets of vases of alternating shapes were a popular European mantelpiece decoration from the late 17th through the 19th century. Each pear or baluster-shape vase in this *garniture de cheminée* is molded with raised panels for enameled armorials or scenes of a bird on a flowering branch. Contrasting with the smooth ground of the painted panels is an overall raised opaque white enamel *(bianco sopra bianco)* grain and flower pattern covering the rest of the vase. The late Baroque style of the mantling about the arms suggests that this set was decorated during the 1740's. The arms are continental and belong to the Odrone family.

Armorial Plate
Porcelain with overglaze enamels and gilding
Chinese c. 1735-40
di: 13⅜"

The wolf's head crest and lozenged arms of the Pigot family are flanked by late Baroque scrolled leaf mantling boldly painted in gold-heightened red and black enamels. In the well there is a gilt spearhead border and a delicate gold-heightened trellis border interrupted by five floral cartouches. The rim has a wide *laub und bandelwerk* grisaille and gold border of elegant Baroque scaling, strapwork, peacocks, and flowers. It is similar to grisaille borders appearing on du Paquier period Vienna porcelain and to border patterns of contemporary printed books. Bottle books and porcelain could have been brought to China by Jesuit missionaries. At the rim's apex is a self-sacrificing mother pelican feeding her young with her own blood known as a *Pelican in her Piety*.

Armorial Plate with Grisaille Border
Porcelain with colored and grisaille overglaze enamels
Chinese c. 1740
di: 14"

This elegant plate was made for the van Herzeele family of Holland whose arms and those of another family can be seen at center. The arms are surmounted by a coronet supported by a white griffin and yellow lion. The ground of the well is beautifully painted with an overall opaque white enamel design of leaf scrolls in a technique known as *bianco sopra bianco*. The well is edged by a gilt spearhead border. The rim is finely painted with a *laub und bandel*.

Pair of Cisterns or Jardinieres (one of a pair)
Porcelain with famille rose enamels
Chinese c. 1730-50
h: 15¼" di: 22¼"

This pair of large bowls was used for the storage of
liquid or as jardinieres for flowering plants or other
small trees. Their main decoration of large scale tree
peonies and other exotic flowers is painted in the
famille rose palette. The borders are of key fret, scroll,
spiral, and blossom. The applied mask handles are
pierced, possibly for cords to tie down a cover or to
serve as carrying handles, which once had metal or
porcelain rings.

Tureen Stand with Carp Design
Porcelain with overglaze enamels
Chinese 1750-60
l: 19⅝" w: 17³⁄₁₆"

The naturalistically painted carp, which seems to approach us three-dimensionally, provides the only color on this shaped tureen stand or platter outside of the gold fishnet and spearhead border and the four floral sprigs. Perhaps inspired by a Portugese Baroque silver or faience prototype, this stand was probably made for the Portugese market. No doubt it went under a fish-shaped molded tureen intended for fish soups and stews. The life-like carp with its rose tail, the vigorous twist of his body, his delicate pectoral fins, the endearing wide-eyed innocence of his whiskered head, is a delightful tour-de-force.

Tureen, Cover, and Stand
Porcelain with overglaze enamels and gold
Chinese c. 1750-60
Tureen h: 7¹/₁₆" w: 11¼" Stand di: 12½"

Two Lidded Teapots with Stands
Porcelain with overglaze enamel and gold
Chinese c. 1750-60
Teapot h: 3½" Stand di: 6½"

Since porcelain could be made and decorated cheaper in China than in Europe, models were sent to China to be copied. This shell-handled tureen was probably copied from a Meissen porcelain prototype which, in turn, relies on an earlier European silver form. The enamel harbor scenes with black and iron-red cartouches are similar to those found on European porcelain. The grisaille landscapes and rose bird-and-flowering-branch scenes within gold cartouches on the rim are stock Chinese designs from the decorator's repertoire. The gold spearhead borders were used extensively during the thirty years between 1740-70, and are probably a simplified version of European Baroque lambrequins developed by Canton decorators for China trade porcelain. They were re-adapted by European decorators for use on European porcelain.

Introduced into Europe during the 17th century, tea drinking was a popular custom by the middle of the 18th century. Tea, spices, silks, and porcelain made up most of the cargoes of the sailing ships of the Dutch, English, Danish, Swedish, and Portugese East India Companies. Wealthy Europeans demanded more varied and colorful tea wares than the familiar blue and white Canton. The Reves Collection has a group of unusual teapots which indicate how China responded to this increasingly sophisticated taste.

The teapot on the left is of traditional Chinese shape with sloping, swelling sides and a domed lid. It has applied porcelain reliefs of plum blossoms, twigs, and chrysanthemums as well as painted borders in iron-red and gold. The lid finial is naturalistically modeled in the form of a leafed twig. The other teapot is the same shape, but has applied leaves, twigs, and squirrels in iron-red, green, and gold.

Footed Dish (Tazza)
Porcelain with overglaze enamels and gold
Chinese 1752-60
h: 3½" di: 11¼"

Armorial Tureen with Cover and Stand
Porcelain with overglaze enamels
Chinese c. 1760
Tureen with lid h: 13" w: 14¾"
Stand l: 17½" w: 14⅛"

202 During the 18th century, Denmark's Asiatic and West Indies trade was extensive as well as highly profitable. Her flag can be seen flying from the three-masted man o' war flanked by open-jawed fish in the lower border of this tazza. At the top of the gold enhanced black penwork border, a regal peacock proudly fans its tail. In the center of the circular dish, colorful figures of the sea gods Neptune and Amphitrite hold scrolled shields bordered by flower-filled cornucopia. The left shield contains a portrait bust of Queen Juliana Marie who married King Frederick V of Denmark in 1752; the right shield displays her cypher. The dish is fluted to suggest a shell. The three squat paw-footed legs with lion masks are tame reminders of the heraldic lions supporting earlier Baroque furniture and smaller objects, such as the Reves' Danish Baroque silver tankard.

This delightful paw-footed, shell-bodied and lidded, claw-handled tureen has very little Chinese about it except its place of manufacture. It was copied directly from a Rococo Hochst faience model designed by Ignaz Hess which probably traces to a European Rococo silver original. The scattered floral sprigs are painted in thick, flat enamels possibly inspired by those on European watchcases; the colors include green, blue, purple, and opaque yellow and a shaded rose. The coronet, lion supporters, rocailles, and arms on the left are those of Van Dam of Flanders; on the right, those of De Moffaert of Limburg. The tasteful additions of turquoise add sophistication to this marvelous, vaguely zoomorphic tureen.

Tureen with Cover and Stand
Porcelain with overglaze enamel decoration
Chinese c. 1766-70
Tureen h: 9⁷⁄₁₆" w: 14³⁄₈" d: 11⁷⁄₁₆"

204 One of a pair in the Reves Collection, this tureen is octagonal and raised on a plain solid foot for insulation. It has hare's head handles colored iron-red as is the leaf, or shell, form finial. There are festoons of thickly painted flowers about the borders, and sprays elsewhere. The arms of Mawbey impaling Pratt are for Sir Joseph Mawbey who married his cousin, Elizabeth Pratt, in 1760. He was created baronet in 1765 and since these arms include a baronet's hand, they must date thereafter.

Soup Tureen with Cover and Stand
Porcelain with famille rose overglaze
enamels and gold
Chinese c. 1780
Lidded tureen h: 13¼" l: 16½"
Stand l: 16"

This tureen is a magnificent example of a Chinese adaptation of a European silver design. Ribbed, leaf-footed, and with cabbage finial, its form is possibly derived from a tureen like the one in the huge French silver service made for Empress Catherine the Great of Russia in 1775 and presented by her to her favorite, Count Orloff.

The scrolled *Indian* plumed mask handles, which trace to the headdresses of oriental and South American princes seen in 17th century European travel engravings, and the delicately painted naturalistic European style strewn flowers, are holdovers from earlier Rococo Meissen porcelain.

The tureen's four-square stance, faciated leaf-and-berry molded border, and the entwined green and gold leaf painted border, are neo-classic elements in later 18th century taste. The sparing use of overglaze enamel colors — rose, green, iron-red, purple — as well as gold, embellish the lovely white porcelain rather than obscuring it as in often overdecorated 19th century porcelain.

Beaker Vase with 'Tobacco Leaf' Pattern
Porcelain with famille rose overglaze enamels
Chinese c. 1780-1800
h: 15¾"

Surely once part of the three or five vase mantelpiece garniture alternating with covered vases, this beaker is decorated in overglaze enamels with the last and most popular Chinese 18th century floral pattern known as *tobacco leaf*. It was probably inspired by fanciful textile designs rather than by precise botanical drawings of a tobacco plant. The large blossom resembles a hibiscus or passion flower.

205

Carpets and Other Textiles

Holbein Carpet
Knotted wool
Anatolian 16th century
l: 20' w: 8' 9"

Piled carpets were probably known in ancient Greece and Rome, though none survive. 5th century Coptic rugs made of a looped pile do, however, exist. In the 7th century, the Arabs swept across North Africa gathering Egyptian and Berber converts to their forces, and in the 8th century, conquered Visigothic Spain brought their rug-making techniques to the West. Though they probably existed long before, rugs woven in Spain are first mentioned in the 12th century and refer to those made in Murcia, a province in southeast Spain. The earliest known depiction of a Spanish carpet in European painting is an armorial star carpet in a fresco in Avignon painted c. 1345.

After the expulsion of all non-Christians from Spain in 1492, many Islamic Moors converted to Christianity and remained. The geometric patterns of their rugs and other decorative arts, sometimes called *Mudejar* or *Hispano-Mauresque,* were discarded by the mid-16th century in favor of the Italian Renaissance style.

Emery Reves collected a notable group of Spanish rugs as well as examples from Portugal, Anatolia, the Caucasus, and India. The Reves' interest in textiles encompasses 17th century European silk woven ecclesiastic vestments incorporating stitchery, wool tapestry fragments, silk brocades, and an outstanding 19th century needlepoint rug.

In the 13th century Marco Polo wrote of the great Seljuk Turkish carpets of Anatolia. This weaving tradition continued even after the decline of the Seljuks and the rise of the Ottomans in the 14th-16th centuries. European scholars, uncertain of the names of the sites of Near and Middle-Eastern carpet manufacture, called them by the names of the artists in whose paintings they appear. Hans Holbein's 1533 double portrait, known as *The Ambassadors,* shows a table covered with a carpet that has large octagonal medallions. This type of carpet is called *Holbein,* as are those with a smaller octagon pattern even though their earliest appearance in Western art is in a 1451 fresco by Piero della Francesca. *Holbeins* appear in more than fifty paintings, mostly Italian, and usually dating from the early 16th century. After 1650 they are absent, for it was then that the arabesque-patterned Ushaks known as *Lotto* carpets became fashionable, their design and color was more stereotyped.

Large and small pattern *Holbein* carpets made in Anatolia were copied in Spain and are distinguished by the single warp Spanish knot with guard stripes in Spanish designs. Both *Lotto* and small pattern *Holbein* rugs have borders whose designs derive from Kufic writing. Spanish borders often have pseudo-Kufic writing facing outwards on three sides so that a person walking around the rug may read it. On Anatolian borders, the writing faces inward so that it may be read by a person seated in the middle of the rug.

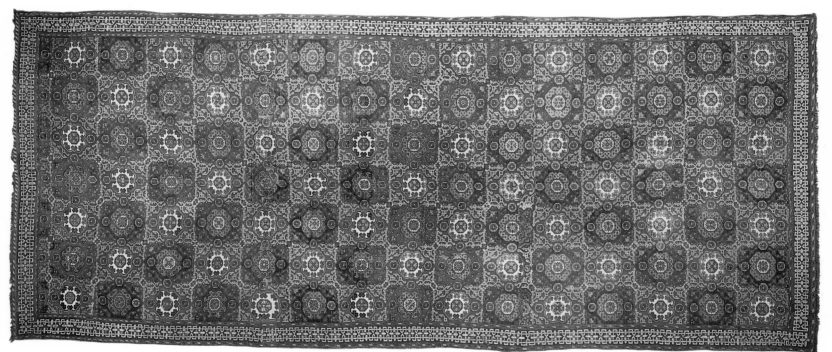

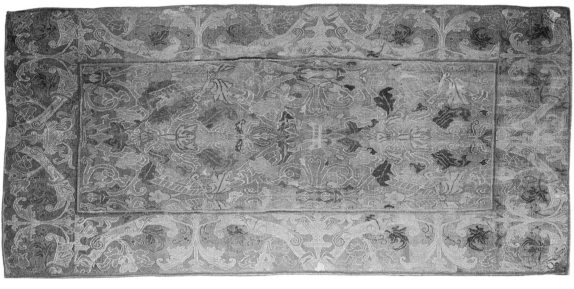

Carpet
Knotted wool
Spanish, Alcaraz c. 1550-1600
l: 10' 5¾" w: 5' 2½"

Alcaraz had long been a famous Moorish rug making center in Murcia when, in 1504, the town presented Queen Isabella with a gift of several rugs. During the 16th century reigns of the Emperor Charles V and King Philip II, Alcaraz rugs are frequently listed in the inventories of royal residences.

    The wide borders of this rug have motifs of flowers by themselves and in holders flanked by scrolled straps. The ordered lush foliage of the central field is inspired more directly by North Italian Renaissance than Islamic style.

Carpet
Knotted wool
Spanish, Alcaraz c. 1550-1600
l: 11' 8½" w: 7' 10"

This very fine salmon, red, yellow, and blue rug has borders with alternating pairs of confronted and addorsed monsters. The large central rectangular field has an overall trellis design with leafed crosses at their intertices and tiny cruciform quatrefoils within the trelliswork reminding us of the then recent Christian unification of Spain. The pattern of this rug is more indebted to the Italian Renaissance than to earlier Moorish geometric designs.

Embroidered Carpet
Wool
Portugal 17th century
l: 9' 8¾" w: 8' 7"

Portuguese embroidered carpets of this period are very rare and have always been in great demand for their charm. In this rug the central medallion is a heraldic royal two-headed eagle with a heart-shaped body surmounted by a stylized plumed crown which has a single three-petal tulip finial. It is surrounded by four quizzical armorial lions *passant* and their some-what bedraggled consorts. Against the violet ground flowers and animals of all kinds — rabbit, deer, bulls, butterflies, and other insects — appear as line drawings in a folk lexicon of plants and animals.

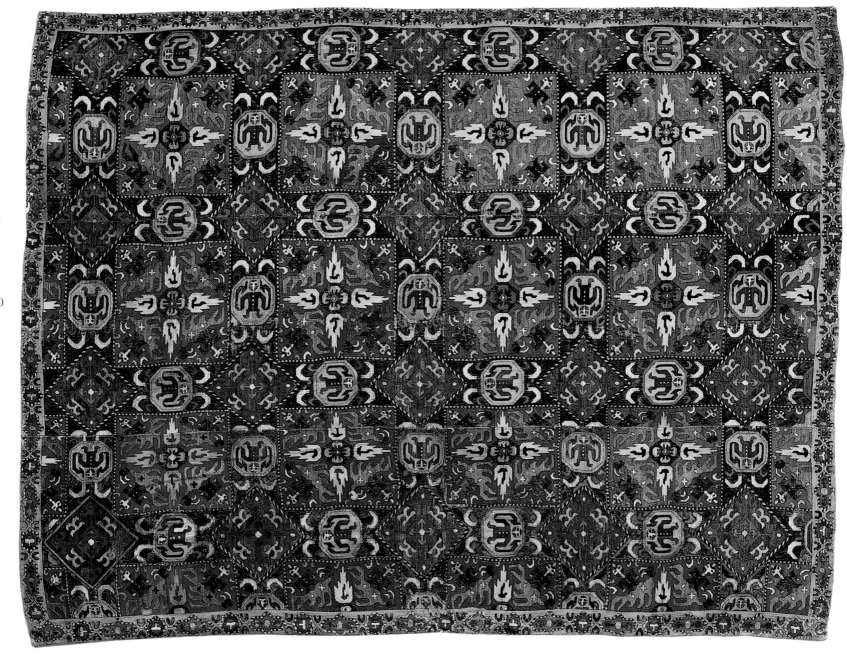

210

Rug or Cover
Embroidered silk on cotton
West Caspian (aka South Caucasus) c. 1700
l: 6' 8¾" w: 5' 4⅛"

Wide borders enclosing squares are interrupted by octagons and lozenges. Single male figures stand within each octagon, their arms transformed into arrowheaded scarfs. Each square has a floral center and a man either on or behind a serrated goat in each corner. The leaf forms sprouting from the octagons and within the lozenges are hooked, a characteristic of these rugs. Few of these delicate and charming West Caspian silks have survived without restoration. This example is pieced.

Stitchery Panel Fragment
Flat stitch silk on linen
Probably Italian or Spanish
l: 84¾" w: 28¾"

This beautiful panel is a continuous colorful feast of
scrolling large-scale flowers and leafage interspersed
with small birds and butterflies. Simplified but similar
motifs are found on the drawer-fronts of the ivory
plaqued cabinet on stand in the Reves Collection (fig.
39). Such patterns were disseminated by engravings
published in Germany, France and the Low Countries.
This design is similar to one by the 16th century
Nuremberg engraver and publisher Virgil Solis
(1514-62), who published over 600 woodcuts and engravings for the use of stuccoists, woodcarvers, met-
alworkers and textile embroiderers and weavers.

Dalmatic (Church Deacon's Robe) (one of two)
Silk damask with appliqué panels and gold
Spanish or Italian 17th century
l: 45¾" w: 59" (across sleeve)

A dalmatic is a wide-sleeved robe worn over the alb
and cassock by a deacon at High Mass. This one is of
red silk damask onto which are sewn cuffs and *clavi*
descending to an apron of appliqué work composed of
light colored silk strapwork, flowers and leafy scrolls
stitched with gold-wrapped threads over a red velvet
ground. The bird with open wings represents the
Holy Spirit.

Brocade Panel

Silk velvet
French or Italian c. 1700-25
l: 87½" w: 22⅛"

Brocades such as these were used as wall coverings, bed and window hangings and for upholstery in the Louis XIV and Régence periods in France. They reflect the influence of the Italian Renaissance as well as the East in the ordering of the large scale flower and leaf pattern, which here includes a European style crown.

214

Bizarre Brocade Panel
Silk
Venice early 18th century
l: 73³⁄₈" w: 22¹⁄₂"

This panel belongs to a group of finely woven silk
brocades called *bizarre* because of their eccentric patterns. They were a specialty of Venetian weavers. The
larger areas of gold wrapped silk threads are balanced
with lovely pink and blue flowers on a natural silk
ground. It is now bordered with silver gallooning.

Back of a Chasuble
Embroidered silk with silver wrapped threads
Spanish 17th or early 18th century
l: 47³⁄₄" w: 30"

Symbol of Christ's love, the chasuble was traditionally
worn by members of the clergy on special occasions.
The shape of this chasuble back with an uncrossed
central applied panel is typical of those worn in Spain
in the 17th and 18th centuries. The front is fiddle
shaped. The central vertical blue velvet panel is applied with vase and plant motifs and has silver
wrapped threads.

Embroidered Rug
Wool
French or English c. 1835-45
l: 9' 2½" w: 7' 9⅞"

The Victorian reaction to the austere forms, limited palette and small designs of the neoclassic taste of the late 18th and early 19th centuries was a profusion of large-scale polychrome forms. These large beautifully shaded cabbage roses, leaves and branches are dramatically set against a black background. Note the pink and white *trompe l'oeil* border which appears to be a three-dimensional ribbon.

Two Panel Textile
Silk brocade with silver
French c. 1835-45
l: 82⅜" w: 41⅝"

The invention of the Jacquard loom revolutionized the textile industry by semi-automating weaving. The blue herringbone pattern figured ground is achieved by the Jacquard punched card process. High quality fabrics such as these which revived the Louis XV and Louis XVI styles were in great demand by the new industrial society. The quantity and variety of silver wrapped silk threads, as well as the taste and subtlety of coloring of the garland of roses, violets, morning glories, leaves and shells, is equal to the high level of 18th century work.

Acknowledgments

218   I should like to thank Harry Parker for letting me participate in this exciting new acquisition and for assigning Vicki Vinson to assist me in compiling the decorative arts section of this catalogue. Her willingness, resourcefulness, and unfailing good humor have made my work possible as well as pleasurable. Other members of the Museum staff who have been especially helpful are: JoAnn Griffin, John Lunsford, Steve Mann, Carol Robbins, and John Wilcox. David Wharton must be commended for the quality and taste of his photographs. Colleagues and friends in New York and London who have increased my knowledge in several areas and to whom I am most grateful are: Allan Chait, Julia Curtis, Clare Le Corbeiller, David Sanctuary Howard, Marion Chait Howe, Letitia Roberts, William Ruprecht, Kevin Tierney, Suzanne G. Valenstein, Wengo Wan, and David Wille. Special thanks to my wonderfully patient secretary, Reily Hendrickson.

DTO

CHRONOLOGY

Chronology

Emery Reves

1904 b. Sept. 16
Bacsfoldvar, Hungary
1914 family moves to Budapest
1924 attends University of Zurich where he meets John von Neumann and William Fellner
1926 receives doctorate in political economy
1927 moves to Berlin and works as company publicist before becoming free-lance journalist
1930 escapes from Berlin and establishes Cooperation Press Service in Paris
1935 signs Winston Churchill as author for articles syndicated by Cooperation Press
1940 escapes to England after the fall of France and is made a British subject
1941 moves to New York City and begins propaganda work on behalf of allied cause
1942 *A Democratic Manifesto* is published
1945 *The Anatomy of Peace* is published
1946 begins work for World Federal Government
1947 purchases foreign language rights to Churchill's *War Memoirs*
1953 buys the Villa La Pausa from Coco Chanel
1955 Churchill visits La Pausa for first time
1979 builds chalet in Glion, Switzerland
1981 d. Sept. 5
Montreux, Switzerland

1914-1918 World War I
1920 League of Nations founded in January
1927 Duke of Westminster buys La Pausa and builds villa for Coco Chanel
1939-1945 World War II
1983 DMA begins construction of decorative arts wing in February
1984 new Dallas Museum of Art opens in January
1984 after obtaining export permits, Director Harry Parker returns to Dallas in April with The Arts Limited Collection

Wendy Russell Reves

1916 b. May 2
Marshall, Texas
1921 parents separate
1928 moves with mother to Haynesville, Louisiana
1930 parents reunite and family moves to San Antonio, Texas
1931 begins modeling
1933 marries Lt. Al Schroeder in Hawaii (later divorced)
1935 moves to Washington, D.C.
1938 moves to New York and establishes modeling career
1940 marries orchestra leader, Paul Baron (later divorced)
1946 first meets Emery Reves
1948 reunites with Emery Reves
1949 leaves for Paris on modeling assignment
1949-1953 travels extensively with Emery Reves in Europe and the United States
1954 remodels the Villa La Pausa
1964 marries Emery Reves in Thonex, Switzerland
1981 begins search for beneficiary of The Arts Limited Collection
1982 receives Dallas Museum officials in January to discuss possible gift
1983 signs Donation Agreement with DMA in May
1985 visits Dallas in May to approve DMA re-creation of La Pausa
1985 returns to Dallas for opening of reborn Villa La Pausa in November

1948

1949

1954

221

1955

1984

1965

1985

Museum Staff 1985

222 **Office of the Director**

Harry S. Parker, III *Director*
Ann Souder *Executive Assistant*
Becky McKinney-Reese *Administrative Assistant*

Curatorial

Steven A. Nash *Deputy Director/Chief Curator*
John Lunsford *Senior Curator*
Carol Robbins *Curator of Textiles*
Sue Graze *Curator of Contemporary Art*
Rick Stewart *Curator of American Art*
Irene Martin *Assistant Chief Curator*
Vicki Vinson *Curatorial Assistant*
Ginger Geyer *Adjunct Advisor/Collection Management*
Katherine Wagner *Administrative Assistant*
Clare Greer *Curatorial Secretary*
Jacqueline Gilliam *Conservator of Paper*
Jo Ann Griffin *Conservator of Objects*
Elizabeth Simon *Curatorial Assistant*
Lee Clockman *Photographer*
Annette Schlagenhauff *Curatorial Intern*

Exhibitions

Barney Delabano *Curator for Exhibitions*
Anna McFarland *Assistant Curator for Exhibitions*
Manuel Mauricio *Head Preparator*
Russell Sublette *Preparator*
Mark Snedegar *Preparator*
Larry Edgemon *Preparator*
Cayse Cheatham *Preparator*
Larry Harmon *Carpenter/Packer*
Jim Touchstone *Assistant Carpenter/Packer*

Registrar

Debra Richards *Registrar*
Steve Mann *Assistant Registrar*
Anne Gendreau *Assistant Registrar*

Education

Anne R. Bromberg *Chairman of Education*
Roberta Mathews *Associate Educator/Gateway Gallery*
Barney Malesky *Associate Educator/Outreach*
Melissa Berry *Special Programs Coordinator*
Stone Savage *Audio Visual Technician*
Joyce Hagan-Brenner *Coordinator, Tour Programs*
Aileen Horan *Education Volunteer Coordinator*
Joseph Baruday *Outreach Assistant*
Mary Mills *Administrator of Visual Resources*
Eileen Coffman *Slide Librarian*

Library

Donna Rhein *Librarian*
Amy Schaffner *Associate Librarian*

Public Affairs

Robert Milbank *Asst. Dir. Public Affairs/Gen. Counsel*
Brad Uecker *Corporate Membership Director*
Ryland Stacy *Associates Membership Director*
Beth Beran *Museum League Coordinator*
Pam Maedgen *Special Events Director*
Jackie Terris *Administrative Assistant*

Membership

Jane Simpson *General Membership Director*
Elizabeth Rucker *Acting Membership Director*
Linda Miller *Asst. Dir. for General Membership*
Pat Franklin *Membership Assistant*
Geri Harris *Membership Assistant*
Elizabeth Bell *Membership Assistant*
Barbara Barron Safely *Membership Secretary*

Administration

Jean Folwell *Director of Finance & Administration*
Karla K. Wigley *Administrative Assistant*
Susie Lamb *Director of Personnel*
Donna Lemmings *Operations Secretary*
Karen Wilkins *Receptionist*
Debra Wittrup *Receptionist*

Comptroller Office

Lee Breeden *Comptroller*
Cathy Jones *Assistant Comptroller*
Patsy Harris *Systems Analyst*
June Browning *Endowment & Restricted Funds*
Winifred Wilson *Operations Analyst*

Publisher's Note

Contrary to what some may think, a publication does not magically appear like Athena springing forth fully grown from the head of Zeus. A book, however modest in size, always represents the combined talents of many individuals. And though they receive recognition in other ways, the cast of people who produce a book, often under demanding circumstances and with remarkable results, deserve our heartfelt thanks.

In this publication, Becky Wade has created a design which enhances the marvelous art the book is intended to honor. Lad Cmajdalka furnished the composition type in record time. The quality of David Wharton's photography illustrates itself. Special photography was performed on different occasions by Nan Coulter, Daniel Barsotti and, most recently, Donovan Reese, who photographed the museum from the LTV Tower on short notice and with arrangements made by Marguerite Steed and Karen Bradley.

We are especially grateful to two individuals, Vicki Vinson and Melanie Bassett Wright, whose combined efforts and organizational skills have been instrumental in the creation of this publication. Also helpful in providing assistance at various stages of the project were Gail Chancey, photographer Lee Clockman, Melissa Berry, Katherine Wagner, Mary Mills, Eileen Coffman, and Fran Crabb of Ed Barnes' office in New York.

Authors Steve Nash and David Owsley contributed the heart of this publication by writing such personally meaningful and scholarly catalogue entries on art works which they themselves selected to represent the rich diversity and quality of the Reves Collection.

Congratulations and thanks are due not least to the Balding + Mansell staff, whose color engravings, quality lithography and manufacturing expertise ultimately created the appearance of this fine art publication. I especially wish to recognize Guy Dawson and Michael Wojtowycz for their respective roles in collaborating with the Dallas Museum on this project, which they produced expeditiously and in such a handsome manner.

RVR

224